What others are saying abou

FAITH-BASED FRAUD

"Who, what, when, where, why, how and so what? Warren Smith is a master of answering the classic questions for news reporting."

–**Russ Pulliam**, Indianapolis Star

"A saying holds that sunlight is the best disinfectant. Warren Smith explains why shining sunlight on churches and ministries in America is important. Mismanagement of resources or dishonesty by ministries is a sin against God and a bad testimony. I appreciate Warren's rigorous work to hold Christian leaders and institutions in America accountable and transparent for high ethics and standards."

–**Paul Glader**, Director of The McCandlish Phillips Journalism Institute, The King's College

"Warren Cole Smith's work at MinistryWatch is important. His new book, Faith Based Fraud, is a guide for helping churches and ministries navigate the future."

–**Phil Cooke, Ph.D.**, Producer, Author of *The Last TV Evangelist*

"Faith Based Fraud provides a welcome reminder of the function and value of assertive investigative reporting. These well-researched and accessibly written stories are informative and cautionary. Faced with challenges to rebuilding Jerusalem's wall, Nehemiah prayed to God and posted guards. Smith's recounting of leadership failures suggests we should constantly be doing the same."

–**Alan R. Freitag, Ph.D.**, Professor of Journalism & Fulbright Scholar, Lt.Col., USAF (Ret.)

"Warren provides a service to the whole Christian community by telling the hard truth about both individual sin and organizational inadequacies."

– **Dr. Marvin Olasky**, Editor in Chief, *WORLD*

FAITH-BASED FRAUD

Learning from the Great Religious Scandals of Our Time

By Warren Cole Smith

FAITH-BASED FRAUD published by:
WILDBLUE PRESS
P.O. Box 102440
Denver, Colorado 80250

ISBN 978-1-952225-56-7 Hardcover
ISBN 978-1-952225-55-0 Trade Paperback
ISBN 978-1-952225-54-3 eBook

Book Cover Design by Heidi Allums

Interior Formatting by Elijah Toten
www.totencreative.com

Dedicated To
Rusty and Carol Leonard

Contents

Introduction

The Case for Accountability

Why did I get into journalism?
Because I had too many friends.
– Anonymous

Be nice.
– My mother

You shall know the truth, and the truth
shall set you free.
– Jesus

In 1993, I took a job that moved me and my family from Georgia, where I had spent most of my life, to North Carolina.

This job was with a "Big Six" accounting firm, and it was a good job. To be honest, I was surprised to get it. I had spent most of my career working for small companies, or as a writer and teacher. So when I landed this job in the up-and-coming sunbelt city of Charlotte—a job with an expense account, a pension plan, and a corner office on the thirty-fourth floor of the Bank of America Corporate Center—I decided this was probably my last, best shot at corporate respectability. My goal, after getting my family settled in our new home, was to keep my head down, not rock the boat, and try to keep the job long enough to prove that my hiring wasn't somebody's idea of a joke.

However, soon after moving to North Carolina, I discovered something about my new home state that disturbed me. North Carolina had an "abortion fund." It was a fund of about $1.5 million that paid for the abortions of about five thousand low-income women a year.

I was surprised, even shocked, to learn of this fund. I considered myself pro-life, but I had not been actively involved in this cultural battle. I knew abortion existed and was in fact common, but I did not know that taxpayer money—my money—paid for these abortions. I can't explain exactly what happened in me, but I awakened to the world around me in ways I had not been awake before.

As strange as it may seem for a guy with a mortgage and a minivan and a job in corporate America to say, that moment radicalized me.

But what to do? I could stop paying taxes, but that hardly seemed the right approach. Jesus told his followers to "render to Caesar the things that are Caesar's," even though he surely knew the Caesar of his day did things as abhorrent as those of the state of North Carolina.

Ultimately, I said to myself, "If Christians just knew about this, they would become outraged, too. What we need is a communication tool—a newsletter or newspaper or magazine—that would educate the Christian community." I now call this the *Field of Dreams* approach to entrepreneurship: "If you build it, they will come."

I had an undergraduate degree in journalism, and a master's degree in English. I had been a reporter and editor. Even those jobs outside of journalism, in marketing and public relations, had involved various forms of publication management. So I thought producing this publication could be my unique contribution to the Christian and pro-life cause. It might not be as direct in nature as those involved in the front lines of these battles as pastors, preachers, or evangelists, but I had even then come to believe in the power of words to change minds and lives. It had happened in my own life.

So in November of 1993, I published an eight-page newsletter: *The Charlotte Christian News*. Ultimately, we expanded, and by 2000, we had become a weekly tabloid newspaper called *The Charlotte World*. By 2003, we had other newspapers around the country.

I built it, and some came. In our short history, we were twice named Christian newspaper of the year by the Evangelical Press Association. Nonetheless, two recessions, an industry-altering shift in technology, and other factors hurt newspapers. *The Charlotte World* published for fifteen years, but ultimately became one of thousands of newspapers that closed its doors in the aftermath of the Tech Bust, 9/11, and the 2008-2009 financial crisis.[1]

But those papers served a powerful purpose in my life. They helped me discover my true vocation, which was journalism informed by a Christian worldview. But I also learned—both during that time, and later with *WORLD*, where I have served in various editorial and leadership roles for more than a decade—that Christians have a distaste for hard-hitting investigative journalism, especially when it concerns their own.

Touch Not God's Anointed

Sometimes this distaste gets wrapped in biblical language. When I wrote a story critical of a ministry leader, I would inevitably get emails from people telling me to "touch not God's anointed." (see Psalm 105:15.) This verse is so often abused and misused by pastors and ministry leaders that I began to call it a "get out of jail free" card. ("Proof-texting"—or taking a Bible verse out of context to make a point—is the expression for this practice.)

Those who are more biblically literate might tell me that the person I've written about deserves criticism. However, they say the proper action is to confront that person face to face, as Matthew 18 instructs, and then follow a biblically-prescribed process of reconciliation and restoration.

I have a high regard for these arguments. Indeed, just so you will have no doubt about my own position, let me be clear on this point: I believe that Scripture is the inerrant word of God and is "profitable for teaching, rebuking, correcting and training in righteousness" (2 Timothy 3:16).

But both a valid interpretation (hermeneutic) and the proper application of Scripture are essential. Those who use these verses to justify the bad behavior of Christian leaders ignore many other, and equally relevant, verses. For example, what about verses (James 3:1, Titus 1:5-9) that clearly hold teachers and pastors to higher standards?

Furthermore, even if you accept the admonition to "touch not God's anointed" as absolute and without exception, by what process do you determine who is "anointed" and who is a rank charlatan? After all, Scripture also warns us "Satan himself masquerades as an angel of light. It is not surprising, then, if his servants masquerade as servants of righteousness" (2 Corinthians 11:14-15).

Then, of course, there are those who may not be servants of Satan, but are imperfect and fallible servants of God. In other words, they're human beings.

We all tend to err, and most of us don't like to put ourselves in situations that expose our errors. That's why the rise of the parachurch organization and the nondenominational church are such significant and troublesome developments in our time. The structure of independent churches tends to insulate senior leadership from transparency and accountability, and I will make the case in this book—as I did in a previous book, *A Lover's Quarrel with the Evangelical Church*—that attempts to avoid transparency and accountability are reasons they have proliferated.[2]

The rise of the nondenominational megachurch has also made it easier for charlatans to shelter themselves from accountability. This statement may not seem obvious. In fact, it may even seem counterintuitive. After all, most pastors of large churches will tell you that they feel they are under a microscope, that they are recognized everywhere they go. But being recognized on television is not the same as living a life characterized by transparency and accountability. Most megachurch pastors *are* celebrities; they *are* recognized everywhere they go. But their very celebrity status tends to insulate them from people who will tell them the truth about themselves.

The legal and financial structures of these churches also tend to stifle efforts of accountability. More and more churches are independent, autonomous. More and more pastors are celebrities. More and more congregations are cults of their pastor's celebrity. This now common phenomenon in the twenty-first century evangelical church damages people, damages congregations, and damages the Gospel message.

The Celebrity-Led Church

Consider, for example, Darrin Patrick. Patrick was a rising star in evangelicalism, especially in Reformed circles. The church he founded as a young man, Journey Church, grew rapidly. Patrick became the vice president of the Acts 29 church-planting network. But he was fired from Journey for what church elders called misconduct, including "inappropriate meetings, conversations, and phone calls with two women" and an abuse of power.[3]

Unlike many in his situation, though, Patrick admitted his faults and got counseling. He went through a restoration process that lasted twenty-six months. That restoration process included face-to-face meetings with many of the people Patrick had wronged. "Another very impactful part of the plan was the privilege to sit in front of dozens of people, honestly regarding how I had hurt them, and being able to apologize specifically for my sin," he said in a 2019 interview. "Though incredibly painful, I'm very grateful that I had the opportunity to do that."

When he returned to ministry, it was not as a senior pastor, but as a teacher and preacher. He was under the authority of a senior pastor.

Patrick talked about losing his church in another interview early in 2020. He talked about being part of a group of young pastors who became celebrities with book deals, speaking gigs, fame, and money but little spiritual maturity.

"It was a recipe for disaster," he said.

Patrick said his early success led to an obsession with keeping up his image rather than his soul. "I was spending a lot of energy creating and sustaining my image," he told podcast host Chris Smith. "It's so subtle. I am trying to influence people for the gospel. You have to have a social media presence, you have to speak at conferences."

Patrick said he eventually became isolated from many of his friends when he was pastoring Journey Church. "I stopped pursuing friendships," he said. "Another way to say that, I stopped being known. And that was the beginning of the end."

I would like to say that this story had a happy ending, but it does not. Despite all the sincere efforts Darrin Patrick made, much emotional and spiritual damage had been done. On May 7, 2020, he died of a self-inflicted gunshot wound.[4]

Here's another example. On the strength of Steven Furtick's speaking skills, enthusiasm, organizational skills, and personal charisma, all of which are significant, Charlotte's Elevation

Church grew from start-up to more than four thousand in regular attendance in just a few years. That growth caught my attention, so I went to see him. In 2008, I interviewed Steven Furtick for an article in *The Charlotte World*.[5]

What I saw was a sincere and gifted young man. He had a small but enthusiastic staff that was doing all it could just to hold on as Elevation Church's growth skyrocketed. Furtick, at the time of my interview with him, was twenty-eight, and most of his staff was within a few years of his age. No deacons. No elders.

"We're a staff-led church," he told me. This structure has become increasingly common in recent years. It was the model used by Mark Driscoll's Mars Hill Church, in Seattle, before its implosion and ultimate dissolution. When I interviewed Furtick, the Mars Hill experience was still in the future, but it was already obvious to me that this structure had many problems, so I asked, "Who signs your staff's paychecks?"

"What do you mean?" he replied.

"I mean, at the end of the day, who has the power to hire and fire these guys?"

"I do," Furtick said.

I paused for a second to let that answer sink in both with him and with me. Then I asked, "So if push comes to shove—and at some point it will—do you think these guys will put their families' well-being at risk to bring you bad news about yourself? Some word of instruction, or correction?"

Furtick's answer was unequivocal. "Absolutely."

I have no doubt that Furtick truly believed what he said. But I also have no doubt that he is walking a very risky high wire. The slightest breeze will upset his delicate balance. Indeed, in the years since my interview with him in 2008, Furtick has seen his share of controversy, including questions about his theology and his lifestyle.[6]

One of my favorite expressions is from baseball great Yogi Berra, known for his Yogi-isms. One of them is: "Predictions are dangerous, especially predictions about the future." With Yogi Berra's advice duly noted, I am nonetheless willing to predict that Furtick and Elevation Church are headed for crisis. I pray it is not the kind of spiritual and emotional crisis that afflicted Darrin Patrick. Though it is now impossible to rule out that possibility for megachurch pastors. They are, after all, still human and have enormous stresses placed on them, perhaps greater stresses than *should* be placed on them. In recent years, we have seen the suicides of several celebrity pastors, including the 2019 suicide of Jarrid Wilson[7], the 2020 murder-suicide of Richard Logan[8], and 2018 suicide of Andrew Stoecklein.[9]

More often, though, the crisis takes the form of a scandal.

These scandals are usually either financial or sexual scandals, brought about by the temptations of money and power that fast-growing megachurches create for those in senior leadership, especially when those temptations come to them at an early age, as they often do. Though we must also admit that the scandals do not happen just to young pastors, such as Mark Driscoll and Darrin Patrick. As we will see repeatedly in the pages that follow, money and power, combined with what is usually a lack of strong accountability structures, make a heady but ultimately toxic cocktail for anyone, including such venerable and celebrated leaders as Ravi Zacharias.

Celebrity-driven churches that manage to avoid scandal find their crisis to be more of an existential one. For all the reasons I will discuss in this book (and for many more I discussed in *A Lover's Quarrel with the Evangelical Church*), they begin to doubt what they are doing. The early excitement and the superficial signs of growth give way to this reality: the discovery that the back door of such churches is open only slightly less wide than the front door.

And even if the church continues to grow, most of the people in the pews become spectators, not leaders. This appears to be the trajectory of Chicagoland's Willow Creek Community Church, which we discuss in Chapter 9.

Churches and leaders who are teachable see these early warning signs, take them seriously, and make adjustments. Usually, these adjustments involve giving up their own power. They do this by nurturing other leaders, so the focus of the church (or ministry) isn't focused on one man. They start new churches. They develop others within their church. They tend their flocks rather than merely entertain them. They, in short, become true pastors.

They include such men as Capitol Hill Baptist Church's Mark Dever, in Washington, DC, who has purposefully planted churches within just a few miles of his current church. He has intentionally kept the size of his church relatively small, in part by encouraging members to attend these nearby church plants—which are completely autonomous and not in any way under his or his church's control.[10]

Tim Keller of Redeemer Presbyterian Church in New York City has the gifts and success—*New York Times* bestselling books, for example—to have become a celebrity. But Keller's notoriety has been a by-product. Indeed, he often shuns the spotlight.[11]

Matt Chandler, pastor of The Village Church in Dallas, had pioneered the multi-site model of church governance: One church, many locations, often with the sermon piped in on a video screen. This is a model that many large evangelical churches have embraced, including Elevation Church, founded by Steven Furtick, and Willow Creek Community Church, founded by Bill Hybels. However, in 2017, Chandler and The Village Church abandoned that model, and the various sites of the former Village Church embarked on a path toward autonomy.[12]

And they are not alone. It would be easy to read this book

and think that evangelical Christian leaders are luxury-seeking, spotlight-hogging narcissists. The vast majority of Christian leaders are not. They serve quietly, faithfully, sacrificially, humbly. But when the money and people are flowing, it is far too tempting just to ride the wave, to convince yourself that all these people and all this money are signs of God's anointing. It is easy, in other words, to forget the example of Jesus, who, when the crowds gathered, often drove them away with hard sayings, tough challenges (Mark 10:21, for example). Or he retreated from them, as he did when he left more than five thousand on the north shore of the Sea of Galilee to minister to one demon-possessed man among the tombs on the south shore (Mark 5).

So even though most of this book's pages are filled with stories about waste, fraud, and abuse—real stories, carefully reported and (I hope) interestingly told—the true message of this book is a spiritual one. That message is this: *The problems I recount in this book are not organizational problems that can be solved with new regulations and procedures. The problems are spiritual and theological ones that merely manifest themselves as organizational problems.* And just because your organization may not yet be manifesting the symptoms, we should all be mindful of the underlying spiritual pathologies.

Polity Matters

All of this takes me back to the story of Steven Furtick and Elevation Church. I want to be clear that I do not mean to "pick on" them or single them out. Indeed, they might not be worth discussing much were it not for the fact that megachurches such as Elevation and Willow Creek and Mars Hill have become a significant—some might even say dominant—characteristic of the religious landscape of the American church and, indeed, of the church worldwide.

A few paragraphs ago I mentioned Seattle's Mars Hill Church. Under the leadership of Mark Driscoll, it became a model for Furtick and others. Driscoll was twenty-six when he founded the church in 1996, and that church, while it claimed Reformed theology, rejected the presbyterian polity—or church governance structure—that also came out of the Reformation, a form of polity that many Reformers believed was essential for maintaining a doctrinally sound and orderly church.[13]

Mars Hill was staff led, a practice Elevation and many other megachurches have embraced. Mars Hill had elders, but they were hardly independent. Well over half of church's elders were on the payroll of the church. This situation created a tremendous financial disincentive to confront the pastor on any spiritual or theological or prudential error.

I use the past tense in describing Mars Hill Church because it is no more. I devote a chapter to this story later in the book, so I won't spend time on it here except to say this: Reality always wins. These flaws in a church's structure, and in the character of its leaders, lead to one of two inevitable conclusions: reformation or destruction. The purpose of this book is to warn Christian leaders away from the path of destruction, and to show them how to continue on the upward path of constant reformation. Former secretary of education William Bennett is fond of saying that the "plural of anecdote is not data." In other words, it is important that we not extrapolate from the experience of one or two bad or questionable situations and say, therefore, that all are bad or questionable. It is especially important to note that—as of this writing, anyway—Steven Furtick has not been involved in any of the illegal or unethical behaviors described in this book. But it is just as important to note that when I first conceived of this book, more than ten years ago, the same could have been said of Mark Driscoll, Darrin Patrick, James MacDonald[14], Jarrid Wilson, Ravi

Zacharias, and many others we will mention in this book. Today, alas, that is not the case.

Still, I note with some sadness that almost every faith-based fraud in this book started out with the best of intentions. If you could have asked the twenty-eight-year-old Jim Bakker or Mark Driscoll or Ted Haggard, another former megachurch pastor and president of the National Association of Evangelicals who was caught in a sex scandal,[15] about the behaviors that ultimately brought down their ministries twenty years later, they would undoubtedly have said more or less what the twenty-eight--year-old Steven Furtick said to me when I interviewed him. They had good intentions, they had adequate guard rails, they had appropriate transparency and accountability. That could never happen to them.

But they did not, and it did.

I want to emphasize, too, that checks and balances, processes that create accountability and transparency, are put in place not solely or even primarily to punish the guilty, but to protect the innocent, and to aid to those who start out faithfully in ministry, to aid them to *finish* as well as they *started*. I pray Steven Furtick never succumbs to the temptations of his position, but if he does, such systems could protect him from falling to these temptations. That is why an implicit question is in every story in this book: Were the rises and falls of the people we discuss in this book incidental or inevitable? Certainly, some ministries and churches get big and powerful without having the kinds of scandals we saw with Jim Bakker, Ted Haggard, Jimmy Swaggart, Mark Driscoll, James MacDonald, Ravi Zacharias, and others. And, as we will read, many smaller ministries and churches have their own problems. But I think it is fair to say that ***where money and power are concentrated, and where accountability and transparency are minimal, fraud and scandal are all but inevitable consequences.***

Supersize Me

So, are pastors such as Steven Furtick headed for a fall? Are their churches headed for a crisis of identity and schism? I hope and pray not. But the examples I have already cited are far from the only ones, as we will see. They are representative of a common phenomenon in the evangelical church. That phenomenon is unique to the late twentieth and early twenty-first centuries. That phenomenon is the megachurch.

Today, in the early- to mid-twenty-first century, every big city in America has some version of Elevation or Mars Hill—that is, an independent, nondenominational megachurch with a celebrity pastor. San Diego has The Rock Church and David Jeremiah's Shadow Mountain Community Church. Tampa has Lifepoint. Until it imploded, Tampa also had Paula and Randy White's Without Walls International Church. In Houston, it's Joel Osteen's Lakewood Church. Chicago has both Harvest Chapel and Willow Creek Community Church—both of which had pastors who resigned in the midst of scandal.

And this phenomenon is not limited to big cities. Conway, Arkansas, with a population of about seventy thousand, is home to New Life Church, which has weekly attendance topping fifteen thousand. Durham, North Carolina, has two churches with more than ten thousand members, Summit Church and World Overcomers Church.

The list goes on and on. Megachurches, those with two thousand or more in weekend attendance, numbered barely a dozen in 1970. By 2020, the number exceeded three thousand. *Outreach Magazine* publishes an annual list of the one hundred largest churches in the country. Being a "megachurch" with two thousand attendees will no longer even come close to getting you on that list. The smallest church on that list in 2019 was Action Church of Orlando, Florida, with 4,328 attendees.

It's also worth noting that less than half the churches that were on that list in 2005, when Mark Driscoll was on the cover of the magazine, made the 2019 list. Some of the churches, such as Mars Hill and Without Walls, had collapsed. Others—such as Eddie Long's New Birth Missionary Baptist Church in Atlanta—had become so wracked in scandal and turmoil that they are today mere shadows of their former selves.

Lord Acton was correct when he said "power tends to corrupt, and absolute power corrupts absolutely." Therefore, scandals in the evangelical church—especially as the church becomes larger and more powerful—should be no surprise, because the megachurch and the large parachurch concentrates power in the hands of the few. The falls of high-profile preachers such as Jimmy Swaggart, Jim Bakker, Ted Haggard, Ravi Zacharias, and Todd Bentley, and the divorces and scandals surrounding Paula White and Benny Hinn, are only a few among many on a long, sad list.

Adding to the trouble is the fact that in 1970, almost all of the megachurches were a part of a denomination that had a clear process of ordination, of church governance, and of church discipline. Today, almost half of the megachurches in the United States are nondenominational churches. Many of them have almost no system for dealing with either doctrinal or behavioral errors. That is why following a process anything like the one prescribed in Matthew 18 is almost impossible in most evangelical churches today.[16] Celebrity preachers often insulate themselves from those who are likely to confront them about personal sin.

A Return to First Principles

So where does all of this leave us today? In the movie *Apollo 13*, astronaut Jim Lovell—in a famous understatement—radioed from space, "Houston, we have a problem."

When we see the faith-based frauds described in these pages, we might borrow that line and say with equal understatement, "Christians, we have a problem." My question is this: What is the nature of that problem? Is the problem merely a few errant televangelists, a few "bad apples" who just need to be plucked from the barrel? Or is the problem more endemic, more generalized, more systemic?

When the extent of the Apollo 13 problem became obvious, Gene Kranz, the flight controller in charge of the mission, told his team of engineers, "Work the problem, people. Let's not make it worse by guessing."[17] And they did. The result was that a huge problem that could have resulted in tragedy became one of NASA's and, indeed, one of America's, finest hours.

So let's spend a few minutes following Gene Kranz's example and work the problem before us. It seems to me that a logical place to start is with the question why. Why do faith-based frauds continue to recur?

If we are truly to work this problem, we must return to first principles. The first principle of all of creation is this: "In the beginning God created the heavens and the earth." The Bible tells us that God's creation was "good," even "very good." Nonetheless, mankind was not satisfied. "Good," even "very good," was not good enough. It wasn't enough for us to serve God joyfully and to have intimate fellowship with God. We wanted to be God. We preferred our definition of "good" and "very good" to God's definition. The consequences of that preference were catastrophic for mankind and for all of creation.

Humans still want to be God. We "will to power," as Nietzsche said. When we do not have power, we typically fall either into cynicism and despair, or we scramble and claw our way toward our definition of power. Sometimes that scramble manifests itself as ruthless ambition, sometimes as a mindless optimism that tells us that we can have—no, we *deserve*—our best life now.

And we will do whatever it takes to achieve that life. That usually involves the quest for money. Sometimes it's sex. But money and sex are usually proxies for the real object of our quest: power. Or—said more precisely—autonomy. Again, we want to be our own god.

Because we humans find the quest for power irresistible, many of us also find the exercise of power exhilarating. However, if we achieve god-like status, no matter how small our kingdoms, we do not possess the wisdom or mercy of God, so when we get this power, we inevitably abuse it.

For this reason, all just societies place limits on the accumulation of too much power—too much autonomy—in the hands of one or a few people. To cite a relevant and accessible example, one of the great innovations of the American founders was the separation of powers among the three branches of government, a separation explicitly written in to our constitution and specifically designed to mitigate the "will to power."

However, this American experiment was not wholly without precedent. Many historians tell us that the American form of government owes much to church structures. Indeed, many of the framers of the American Constitution were also active churchmen. They were only too aware of their own and their fellow citizens' "will to power," their desire to "be as God." They focused much of their energy in the drafting of America's founding documents on preventing that lust for power from being realized.

The Role of Journalism

For this very reason, too, freedom of the press was guaranteed in the First Amendment to the Constitution. Over the years, a free press has come to be called the Fourth Estate, an additional estate, or power, to check the ambitions of the three branches of government. In other words, the first and most vital role of journalism—to speak truth to power—is an idea that springs directly from the Judeo-Christian notion of original sin. The doctrine of original sin teaches us that we seek darkness rather than light, autonomy rather than submission to authority. Journalism, rightly understood and practiced, provides that vital role.

It is therefore tragic and ironic that many Christians have come to disdain journalism, and investigative journalism in particular.

The irony deepens when we realize that the rise of journalism and the rise of Christianity are intertwined. Indeed, we could make the case that the Bible is more a book of journalism than a book of history. The Bible is full of eyewitness accounts. It contains brilliant and vivid reportage. In Genesis 2, God tells Adam to "name" the animals. In Revelation 1, Jesus tells John, "Write . . . what you have seen." These are the instructions you might hear in a newsroom, the instructions of a wise editor to a young reporter. They are also instructions that I know have put the steel in my backbone from time to time, when it was tempted to turn to jelly.

These are instructions that give journalists a true biblical mandate.

Given that, Christians should be at the forefront of investigative journalism. Historically, they have been. The Christian worldview has motivated many committed believers to become journalists, or "public intellectuals," over the centuries. I have made a case elsewhere for the great reformer John Calvin being the first modern journalist.[18] John Milton's epic poem *Paradise Lost* shaped the thinking of perhaps every statesman of America's founding era and every pastor and theologian of the First Great Awakening. The passing of centuries now allows us to see that his *Aeropagitica*, which was the first vigorous and learned defense of a free press, may rival *Paradise Lost* as Milton's greatest contribution to humane letters.

More recently, in 1851, Henry Raymond, a Bible-believing Presbyterian, founded the *New York Times*. The paper immediately became known for its exposure of fraud, corruption, and deceit. The *Times* helped expose, for example, the politically corrupt Tweed Ring that swindled millions of dollars from New York City.

Perhaps the most interesting example of the *Times*' reporting from this era is its coverage of abortion. Christians today think (with ample evidence) that the *Times* is liberal and anti-Christian and certainly pro-abortion. But in the 1870s, the *Times* sent undercover reporters into abortion facilities. They reported what they saw with details that electrified and sometimes horrified their Victorian-era audience. Consider these closing lines from an 1871 report by Augustus St. Clair on New York City's abortionists: "The facts herein set forth are but a fraction of a greater mass that cannot be published with propriety. Certainly enough is here given to arouse the general public sentiment to the necessity of taking some decided and effectual action."[19]

And, indeed, such reporting did "arouse the general public sentiment" so much so that many back-alley abortion facilities were raided and closed.

We might reasonably ask at this point: What happened? How did the *New York Times*—and almost all other media outlets—go from the kind of reporting Augustus St. Clair did in 1871 to the kind of reporting that it and almost all other mainstream media outlets do today?

The complete answer to that question is beyond the scope of this book. Anyone who wants to explore that question in detail should read Marvin Olasky's classic 1988 book, a book I helped revise in 2013, *Prodigal Press: Confronting The Anti-Christian Bias of the American News Media*.

But I will mention that the 1925 Scopes Monkey Trial and the Alger Hiss espionage trials of 1948-50 were defining moments. These major media events put mainstream reporters and editors on one side of a significant cultural issue and Bible-believing and evangelical Christians on the other side of that issue. The rift between media and Christians created by these and other events widened over time. Today we find mainstream media and conservative Christians on opposite sides of a great chasm, so far apart that each side can hear the other only when the voices become loud and shrill.

One of the consequences of these events was a separatist mentality among evangelical Christians and increasing disdain and indifference towards evangelical Christians by the media. In the 1850s, the *New York Times* would print the sermons of leading clergy on its front pages. Today, most major newspapers no longer have a full-time religion reporter, and they quote sermons only when the quotes can be used to show the hypocrisy of the preacher. It is no wonder that a 2016 Gallup survey found that only 32 percent of Americans trusted the media, a record-low number. [18]

But that disdain and the chasm it has created, no matter how justified we Christians feel in contributing to it, comes at a horrific cost. The great works of art in history—such as Dante's *Divine Comedy* and the aforementioned *Paradise Lost* by John Milton—were works of the Christian imagination. Today, Christians have lost their place as culture makers. Today, Christians fight culture wars not realizing that the culture has already been lost. Theologian Robert Webber, who taught for many years at Wheaton College, once said, "The most pressing spiritual question of our time is: Who gets to narrate the world?" The Greek philosopher and musicologist Damon of Thebes said, "Give me the songs of a people, and I care not who writes the laws."

Christians no longer write the songs or tell the stories of our people, and we are finding the Christian worldview has rapidly been written out of the narrative.

The church's neglect of journalism as a profession, a sacred calling, has exacted a massive toll on both the church and civic culture. We no longer "move the needle" in national conversations on important issues. Perhaps more importantly, the agenda for important cultural conversations is set by those who make no room for a Christian worldview.

The lack of a wise and vigorous journalism enlivened by a Christian worldview not only impoverishes the culture, but also weakens the church. Christians have forgotten that, as E. Stanley Jones said, "My critics are the unpaid watchmen of my soul." That is true, too, of wise critics of the church. A tree can continue to grow even as its roots succumb to disease. So, too, can a church. But in the case of both the tree and the church, when the disease finally takes its toll, the bigger it is, the harder it falls. How much better it is to treat a disease before it comes fatal.

So, to say it plainly***: investigative journalism is vital to the maintenance of liberty and justice.*** And liberty and justice are not just American ideals or Western ideals or Enlightenment ideals. They were first, and remain, biblical ideals.

Another important way anemic Christian journalism weakens the church is this: when we Christians do not tend to our own housecleaning, the resulting public scandals taint us all. This may not be fair, but it is nonetheless true. Scandalous behavior that goes unchecked, that has been allowed to fester because of our silence, reflects on us all.

As I said at the beginning of this introduction, I live in Charlotte, North Carolina. A suburb of Charlotte is Fort Mill, South Carolina, which was the home of Jim and Tammy Bakker's PTL Network until its implosion in 1988. The *Charlotte Observer* won a Pulitzer Prize for the almost nine hundred stories they published about the PTL Network over a three-year period. But by the time the *Observer* started seriously covering the Bakkers, the organization was already sick unto death. So all the *Observer* was able to do was expose the disease. Its coverage offered no hope, no cure, no redemptive or restorative path forward.

By contrast, what would have happened if a Christian journalist, years earlier, had asked questions—not just about sex and money, but about theology and practice? Indeed, Joel Belz told me that shortly after he founded *WORLD*, he started getting letters and phone calls from people asking him to check into the affairs of the PTL Network. "But we were so small then," he said. "Fighting for survival. We simply couldn't look into what was going on there. I will always wonder how things might have been different if we could have."

How might the Bakkers have responded? Would they, or those around them, have taken early, corrective actions? Would they have built in systems of accountability that would have provided early warnings of and helpful therapy for Jim Bakker's increasingly erratic behavior? The sad truth is that we'll never know.

All we do know is that for many Americans, Jim and Tammy Faye Bakker were the most prominent evangelicals in America. To many Americans and to the world, they were the face of the American evangelical church. That scandal and others like it, many of which are documented in this book, tarnished not only those who were directly caught up in the scandal, but also those who knew better but chose not to speak up.

It is no wonder that Americans have lost confidence in the church.

And that loss of confidence in the church, this loss of credibility, could not have come at a worse time. Vital political and economic issues have always had moral components, but that is even more the case today. From abortion to marriage to sexuality to science, we have never had a more urgent need for a credible Christian perspective. And there is no time since we have been tracking such numbers that the Christian perspective has been held in such low esteem.

This crisis in credibility has real consequences, not just for the culture, but for the mission of the church as well. More Americans than ever have simply given up on religion. They refuse or now lack the theological discernment to distinguish between evangelical leaders with a true biblical worldview and those who are rank charlatans. To distinguish Jim Bakker from Jim Dobson, Tim Keller from Kenneth Copeland, Joel Osteen from Rick Warren. Americans are more likely to lump them all in the same pot and reject them all or choose their favorite based more on style than substance.

Then, like the cynical and doomed Mercutio in Shakespeare's *Romeo and Juliet*, who was mortally wounded in the conflict between the Capulets and the Montagues, so too does a cynical and secular world declare "a plague on both your houses."

The Promise and Failings of Journalism

This failure of the general public to differentiate evangelicals by theology and practice is at least in part a failure of journalism to tell the stories of Christian leaders in fair and faithful ways.

The purpose of this book is to tell some of these stories. But I hope to tell these stories in particular ways. I want us to see that where transparency and accountability are present, organizations and the individuals who make those organizations tend to thrive. And where secrecy and autonomy prevail, spiritual and financial disease tend to follow.

I will be the first to admit that stories with morals are too often preachy and off-putting. So this kind of storytelling is always a risky enterprise. However, I will do my best to avoid clunky sermonizing. My goal was to pick the right stories to tell, and let the stories speak for themselves. Nonetheless, at the end of each chapter, I do step back from the story and attempt to extract a theme, and the last chapter of the book not only summarizes these lessons but even hazards a few recommendations. I hope, however, that by the time we get to those recommendations, the journey we have been on together will make these recommendations seem, if not obvious, at least sensible.

A Personal Note About Television Preachers and Healing

Much of what follows is highly critical of television preachers and so-called faith healers in particular. For that reason, I want to be plain about a few things.

First, I believe that the sovereign God of the universe absolutely has the power to heal and to perform other miracles.

Secondly, I want to be clear that we are all sinners. When seen from the moon, the highest peaks on Earth are indistinguishable from the deepest valleys. So it is when we look at the righteousness of man from God's perspective. The best of us fall far short of God's righteousness. So my criticisms of people in these pages are not exercises in self-righteousness. I am not saying, "They're bad and we're good."

What I aim to communicate is nothing less than what Paul wrote to the Corinthians: "So, if you think you are standing firm, be careful that you don't fall!" (1 Corinthians 10:12). A few chapters later he reiterates the message: "Be on your guard; stand firm in the faith; be men of courage; be strong" (1 Corinthians 16:13).

Perhaps the best way to communicate my true intentions is to tell you a story.

In the 1970s and early 80s, I had several close friends associated with Oral Roberts University (ORU). The evangelist Oral Roberts, who founded the school, was a seminal figure in the

Pentecostal movement and in the world of televangelism. I never met Oral Roberts or his son Richard, but I did meet Richard's first wife Patty in 1978, as Richard and Patty were going through a difficult divorce. Our meeting was brief. We were both at the wedding of a mutual friend in Tulsa. That friend, Jan Dargatz, was the director of public relations for ORU and a gifted writer who often helped Oral Roberts write and edit his books.

Perhaps because we were at a wedding at a time when she was going through a divorce, I was particularly aware of her pain. On that weekend, I developed a deep sympathy for her and a correspondingly deep antipathy for Richard Roberts.

Over the years, I fed that antipathy toward him. I noted with self-righteous pleasure a passage in Hank Hanegraaff's book *Christianity in Crisis*. Hanegraaff documented in detail the manipulative fundraising techniques of both Oral and Richard Roberts. Particularly notorious was a time when Oral Roberts said God would "take him home" if his supporters did not contribute millions to his ministry. Richard wrote a fundraising letter that said without "the additional $4,500,000 God will not extend Dad's life." Richard Roberts went on: "Partner, we cannot let this man of God die. There is no reason for him to die."[20]

I followed these and other episodes of Richard Roberts' life with some interest. When Patty Roberts wrote her own account of living with Richard, a book called *Ashes to Gold*, she talked about some of the Roberts' manipulative practices. She singled out the "seed-faith" message for particular criticism. She said that the "seed-faith" message preached by Oral and Richard was little different from the medieval practice of selling indulgences.[21]

For all these reasons, I came to believe that Richard Roberts was a complete fraud.

Now, fast forward twenty-five years. I don't remember the exact date, but it was around 2004. I was very sick. I have allergies, and they sometimes turn into sinus infections, bronchitis, and even pneumonia. This was not a life-threatening illness. I did not have to go to the hospital. But I felt miserable for weeks. My head was stopped up and my ears were ringing. I was so short of breath that a trip up the stairs to my bedroom left me winded. On top of it all, the combination of antihistamines and fatigue completely disrupted my sleep schedule. I might need a nap at 2 p.m., but be wide awake at 2 a.m.

So it was that I was flipping around the channels at 2 a.m. when suddenly my spiritual nemesis, Richard Roberts, smiled at me from the screen. "All right," I said. "I'll give you a few minutes and see what nonsense you have to say." I fully expected Richard would give me some small and ironic entertainment value, all the while refreshing a stock of anecdotes I could use against him.

Roberts looked directly into the camera. I reconstruct what he said from memory, so it may not be exactly right, but it went something like this: "Someone out there has been sick for a long time." Okay, I acknowledged. That could be me, but 330 million people live in America. At any given moment, hundreds of thousands of people might fit this description.

This is one of the techniques of television preachers that I find so despicable and manipulative. They claim—or stop just short of claiming but nonetheless leave the impression—that they are receiving a special message from God, a "word from the Lord," as they often call it. In fact, they are merely taking advantage of the law of large numbers.

Roberts went on. "Your ears are ringing. You have a bad cough. You've been feeling miserable and you've done everything the doctors have told you to do. You've tried everything."

Well, I have to admit that he was starting to get my attention. He described my symptoms exactly.

On the other hand, my ailments were common. A Google

search of “ten most common illnesses” will take you to a list of the ten most common reasons people visit primary care doctors. Number two on the list is an upper respiratory tract infection. Number five is a sinus infection. Number six is bronchitis. And number nine is an ear infection. If I were a charlatan, these are exactly the symptoms I would describe. Chances are pretty good that these symptoms would land squarely on more than one person in any reasonably-sized audience.

But what happened next is something I still can’t fully explain. Richard Roberts looked directly into the camera and said, “In the name of Jesus, I command the ringing in the ears to stop!”

At that exact second, the ringing in my ears—a ringing that had lasted a week—instantly stopped.

I was, to say the least, astonished. I could hear popping in my ears and could feel the popping in my sinuses as they both drained of mucus and fluid. In the next few minutes, my sinuses, my ears, and my lungs all cleared.

Was this a miracle healing? I believe something definitely happened.

A healthy skepticism compels us to acknowledge that my healing could have been the result of the drugs I had been taking for a week or more. Doctors and regular users of antibiotics and decongestants can tell you they take time to work, but when they do work, they often appear to work suddenly. So was my physical healing a miracle in the strictest theological sense? A supernatural intervention in the physical world? I’m not fully prepared to answer “yes” to that question.

But neither can I say “no” either. And I do believe I experienced a spiritual miracle. God used that moment to convince me that my disdain for Richard Roberts and other faith healers is too often born of self-righteousness. I learned that day that God does indeed work in mysterious ways, and He uses whom He will.

In the Old Testament Book of Judges, we learn that God allowed Samson to slay an army of a thousand men using the jawbone of an ass. At the risk of being glib or profane, I learned that night at two in the morning that God can still use the jawbone of an ass. God is sovereign. He does not seek or require my approval to do His work in this world.

That story to say this—it is my hope that the stories and ideas that follow do not in any way quench the genuine spiritual work that God is doing in the world. As you will see as you read on, very often even the most flagrant faith-based frauds begin with good intentions.

But good intentions are not enough. We must be vigilant against self-righteousness and self-deception. We must build organizational structures and systems of accountability and transparency, so that we are saved, even from ourselves.

God is a God of Miracles and a God of Mercy, but He is also a God of Justice and a God of Good Order. Let us imitate Him in all, not just some, of these particulars.

Chapter 1

What Is Faith-based Fraud?

TV evangelists say they don't favor any particular denomination, but I think we've all seen their eyes light up in tens and twenties.

– Dennis Miller

Concerning the prophets: My heart is broken within me; all my bones tremble... The land is full of adulterers... The prophets follow an evil course and use their power unjustly. Both prophet and priest are godless; even in my temple I find their wickedness.

– Jeremiah 23: 9-11

When it comes to money, Christians get a bad rap. Evangelical Christians are among the most generous people on Earth.

Arthur C. Brooks, in his book *Who Really Cares?*, asserts that Christians out-give and out-volunteer all other religious groups, by a wide margin.[1] And they give not just to evangelistic and teaching ministries. They give to the local food pantries, to homeless shelters, to hospitals, and to all manner of other charities.

All of that giving adds up. The Center for the Study of Global Christianity at Gordon-Conwell Theological Seminary estimates that worldwide giving to Christian charities totaled $410 billion in 2009. That figure is approximately equal to the gross domestic product of Austria, the twenty-fifth richest nation on the planet. Looked at another way, $410 billion is the total gross domestic product (GDP) of the fifty poorest nations in the world combined.[2]

And 2009 was the depths of what has come to be called The Great Recession. Since then, Christian giving has gone up even more—much more. By 2015, the last year for which we have reliable data, the amount of Christian giving topped $850 billion.

Can Christians be more generous? Yes. *Should* Christians be more generous? Again, yes. The biblical minimal standard for giving is the tithe: ten percent of a person's income. The average American gives only about two percent to charity. Americans who identify as Christians give more, on average twice as much. But—given these statistics—the dirty little secret of American Christianity is that only a small number of Christians actually tithe.

But evangelical Christians are not—taken as a group—hypocrites when it comes to money. They put their money where are their mouths are. The data is clear on that point. It's true that this book chronicles the greed of many people who call themselves Christians. But it is important to realize that many of the frauds in this book would not be possible without the generosity (and, we must admit, gullibility) of Christians. For as the infamous bank robber Willie Sutton reportedly said, he robbed banks because "that's where the money is."

That's why the Center for Global Christianity also estimates that in 2015, approximately fifty billion dollars was "stolen from money that Christians give" to churches, parachurch organizations, and other nonprofit organizations.

It is worth noting early that the overwhelming majority of the one million or so Christian ministries (including about three hundred thousand churches who have filed as tax-exempt organizations) in this country are models of Christian stewardship. They do much-needed work, they do it efficiently and with limited budgets, and their leaders live frugally and modestly. These ministries are inspiring, and their leaders are unsung heroes.

More good news: the ministries you have probably heard the most about are among the good guys. The largest Christian ministry in the world, Food For The Poor, takes in about one billion dollars a year. World Vision is even larger, with 2019 revenue of $1.1 billion. In 2020, Compassion International will likely pass the one billion dollar mark.

In fact, the eight hundred largest Christian ministries in the world, according to MinistryWatch.com, take in a combined total of more than thirty billion dollars. That's a huge number. With that money, these ministries serve millions of people all around the world. Most of these organizations, including Food For The Poor, Samaritan's Purse, World Vision, Compassion International, and many others, do an enormous amount of good, and many of the men and women who work for these organizations often do this good work at great personal sacrifice.

But let's be clear: when the bad guys are allowed to operate without accountability or transparency, it's the good guys who suffer the most. The bad guys erode the confidence of donors. The bad guys force regulators to impose reporting and administrative burdens that cost all organizations. In fact, they cost the good guys more than the bad guys, because the bad guys mostly just ignore them.

So, unfortunately, the generally heroic story of American philanthropy has another side, and the rest of that story is what this book is about. Waste, fraud, and abuse in religious organizations—what I call faith-based fraud.

John Van Drunen is the former director of compliance and in-house counsel for the Evangelical Council for Financial Accountability (ECFA). He said the fifty billion dollar number mentioned above, the amount of waste, fraud, and abuse in

Christian ministry, could be even larger: "The truth is that we don't know for sure how big the number is because the overwhelming majority is unreported. But we know that it is a very big number. We also know that not addressing this issue causes a diminished witness for Christ in the world."[3]

That's why the ECFA and other organizations—under the umbrella of the Lausanne Movement—attempted to quantify the leakage and the source of the leaks in advance of The Third Lausanne Congress on World Evangelization that was held in 2010 in Cape Town, South Africa.

The causes of these leaks are not that hard to identify. "Embezzlement or fraud accounts for a significant part of the total," said Bert Hickman, a researcher at the Center for Global Christianity. "But sometimes it starts out fairly innocently with a loan to an employee that doesn't get paid back because it is improperly accounted for and then forgotten or written off."[4]

Indeed, as you will read in the pages that follow, some of the largest financial frauds in history—PTL scandal and the Foundation for New Era Philanthropy, in particular—began almost innocently, when a good idea went awry and the folks responsible for that good idea scrambled to make things right.

That's why rigorous internal controls are necessary to plug the leaks. Van Drunen said the performance of an annual audit and the creation of a truly independent board—with members who are not related to or employed by the ministry—are good places for even small ministries to start if they want to raise their financial standards.

Ron Ensminger, a partner with the Strategic Resource Group, is a part of a Lausanne committee driving this effort to, as he puts it, "plug the leaks." He said, "The 2010 Cape Town Congress is the first time in the history of Lausanne that we're embracing the resource community." That is, it was the first time that high-capacity donors were invited to the event. "If we're going to ask these individuals to significantly fund the Great Commission, we need to make sure the money is actually going to Great Commission activities."[5]

That's great. But if Christian leaders want to eradicate waste, fraud, and abuse in the evangelical church, the solutions must be top-down—as those associated with the Lausanne efforts attempt—but they must also be bottom-up. Individual donors—folk like you and me—may give hundreds and thousands of dollars, not millions. But in the aggregate, we give billions. We must also start asking questions.

Questions like those Rusty and Carol Leonard, the founders of MinistryWatch, started asking.

I'll admit straight away that if I wanted to use an example of a regular, everyday evangelical Christian to make this point, the Leonards do not particularly fit that bill. Rusty, by his own admission, never met a number he didn't like. That love for numbers took him to Temple University, where he double majored in finance and economics. He got a stock broker's license at age nineteen, and by his early twenties, he completed the daunting requirements to become a Chartered Financial Analyst, or CFA. That designation is the "gold standard" for financial analysts. Carol, though she ultimately gave up a career as an accountant to home school their three children, shared Rusty's understanding of, and passion for, economics and finance.

All of that was just a prelude for the job that catapulted Rusty Leonard into the top tier of money managers—working for the legendary investor Sir John Templeton. For more than a decade, in the late 80s and through the 90s, Leonard managed money for Templeton, ultimately serving on Templeton's Portfolio Management Committee. He managed $3.5 billion of mutual fund and separate account assets. By the time he left, he had risen to executive vice president of Templeton Investment Counsel, which was the branch of Templeton's business that managed money for high net worth clients.

Rusty and Carol Leonard had been committed Christians from an early age. And by the time they were in their thirties, they had become wealthy, so they obviously had a deep understanding of money and markets and how they worked. But it was not until Rusty started managing the assets of the DeMoss Foundation that he started seeing some blind spots in his own approach to investing.

The DeMoss Foundation was founded by the Christian philanthropist Arthur DeMoss. DeMoss made a fortune in the life insurance business that was estimated to be worth three hundred and fifty million dollars at the time of his death in 1979.[6] About two hundred million of that became the initial capital for the DeMoss Foundation. The DeMoss Foundation, in keeping with its founder's Christian values, refused to invest in companies that made money from alcohol, tobacco, gambling, pornography, or abortion.

Leonard quickly learned that staying away from those companies didn't limit financial performance. "The DeMoss account was the best performing account I had at Templeton," he said.[7]

The experience had a significant impact on Leonard. He began to realize that the biblical stewardship of money involved more than simply making money honestly and legally and then tithing your income. "When you invest in a company, you become a co-owner in that business," Leonard said. "If that business is doing bad stuff, you can't simply say you had nothing to do with it."

This more expansive, holistic view of money also began to have an impact on Rusty and Carol Leonard's own philanthropic efforts. By the mid-90s, the Leonards were able to give away fairly large sums of money, and Rusty began to realize that the way he was handling his giving was very different from the way he handled his investments.

"I wouldn't think of investing in a company, even a relatively small amount, without poring over their financial statements," Leonard said. "I went to great pains to minimize the risk of my investments, and yet here we were giving away significant sums to organizations I knew very little about. It just didn't make sense, especially since Carol and I had these unique skills to evaluate an organization's financial condition."

But when Leonard asked these ministries for their financial statements, he often met resistance. "Ministries would not give their financial statements to us, or they would want to know why we needed to see them," he said. Even those ministries that wanted to cooperate often did not have an efficient mechanism for honoring this simple request for information.

So the Leonards formed Wall Watchers, which they are reluctant to call a watchdog group. "We prefer to say that we're a donor advocate," Leonard said. "We help donors, even small donors, be more effective stewards of the resources God has entrusted to them." The primary tool for accomplishing this goal is the website www.MinistryWatch.com. On that website are profiles of about five hundred of the largest Christian ministries in the country. (Disclosure: Rusty Leonard continues as chairman of the board of Wall Watchers, and I am the president.)[8]

All of this is to say, too, that while the kinds of top-down efforts that Lausanne advocates are essential, it is donor empowerment of the kind that the Leonards are helping to create that will make a long-term difference.

Spiritual Fraud

I want to be clear, however, that this book is more than just a story of financial fraud. If it were the story merely of financial fraud, I would still be interested in writing it, and I hope you would still be interested in reading it. After all, some of these stories are absolutely fascinating in their own right.

But I am much more interested in the underlying causes of faith-based fraud. What is it about the theology and psychology of some Christians—indeed, many Christians—that allow faith-based fraud to continue? In other words:

- Why are Christians gullible, especially in light of Scripture that tells us to be "wise as serpents"? What can we learn about the spiritual lives of the communities victimized by faith-based fraud and about our own spiritual lives?
- When we do discover faith-based fraud in our midst, why are we so reluctant to decisively confront it and root it out? What do we fear?

That's why this book is at least as concerned with pastors Mark Driscoll and David Jeremiah and their book-buying schemes as it is with Bernard Madoff's billion-dollar fraud or the lavish lifestyles of Prosperity Gospel preachers. To put it bluntly: I expect pagans to act like pagans, but shouldn't those who we call the leaders of the Evangelical Church behave better?

Identifying Solutions

So what are the solutions to faith-based fraud? On the one hand, I am reluctant to answer this question at this stage in our discussion. If you have a headache, it is unlikely that the first thing you will do is call a brain surgeon. You'll take two aspirin and see if the pain goes away. A surgeon's knife seems a reasonable, appropriate solution only after you're sure you have a serious problem, and you've tried all other solutions.

My solutions, offered before we examine some of the frauds that follow, will seem like a surgeon's knife to some. And I should admit upfront: Implicit in my proposals is the assumption that faith-based fraud is systemic and not merely the province of a few bad actors.

So, in general, this book makes a case—both a biblical case and a practical, common-sense case—for the following suggestions briefly explained below: greater transparency, a self-regulating organization for ministry groups, re-regulation of the nonprofit sector, a philanthropy marketplace, aggressive Christian journalism, and a theology of work.

Let's consider these solutions here, briefly.

Greater Transparency. If you spend much time in the world of accounting or the world of journalism, you will hear this expression: "Sunlight is the greatest disinfectant." For those not used to the expression *financial transparency*, let me say that it is not a fancy, technical term. It simply means the ability to see into, and through, the finances of an organization. Today's Christian ministries have become so large and complex that the level of transparency required by law is often no longer adequate. The sunlight cannot penetrate these increasingly opaque organizations, and that is allowing disease to grow.

Greater Accountability. Christian nonprofits and churches need to take their structures of accountability more seriously. Nonprofits should have independent boards. (We recommend at least five board members, with at least three of the board members being independent.) Churches should have deacon and elder boards made up of members who are not part of the church staff.

A Self-Regulating Organization (SRO) for Ministry Groups. In the late 1970s, in part to stave off increased government regulation, the Evangelical Council for Financial Accountability (ECFA) was formed. The ECFA was and is a noble effort at self-policing, aimed at improving the standards of ethical and financial stewardship of evangelical Christian organizations.

But the ECFA has not and will not reform the Christian nonprofit industry. The most obvious limitation of the ECFA is that membership is voluntary. Many "bad guys" simply refuse to join. And many "good guys" also are not members. In fact, only about twenty-four hundred of the one million Christian ministries in America are members. Non-membership carries no stigma.

A second limitation of the ECFA is that members pay dues based on their size. The largest ministries pay the largest dues. This funding model has the effect of turning member organizations into *customers* of the ECFA. This relationship creates a direct financial conflict of interest. The ECFA has a dis-incentive to play "hard ball" with member organizations. If they do, the organizations will simply quit, with no negative consequence, since even the ECFA itself does not publicize those who terminate their memberships.[9] This conflict of interest is not theoretical. Several of the wrongdoers we mention in this book—including David Jeremiah and his Turning Point Ministries, Gospel for Asia, Ravi Zacharias International Ministries, Jim and Tammy Bakker's PTL Network, and Mark Driscoll's Mars Hill Church—were ECFA members when their wrongdoing became known to the public. In 2020, Wycliffe Associates, a charter member of the ECFA, "voluntarily resigned" while it was under review for violation of the ECFA's ethical standards. The resignation of Wycliffe Associates effectively ended the review.[10]

This inherent conflict of interest does not mean that the ECFA does not and cannot serve a positive role in the ministry ecosystem. It sets standards to which ministries can aspire.[11] It serves as a clearing house for information. It provides coaching to ministry leaders. But it cannot truly hold these organizations accountable for wrongdoing or questionable practices.

A better model would be a self-regulating organization such as FINRA, the Financial Industry Regulatory Authority. While not perfect, FINRA is a non-governmental agency providing oversight for stock brokers and trading markets such as the New York Stock Exchange. Such self-regulating organizations are common. The National Association of Realtors, the American Medical Association, the American Institute of Certified Public Accountants, and others set rules and standards for behavior, ethics, disciplinary action, and accreditation. In virtually every profession in which SROs operate, they raise professional standards while limiting governmental regulation.

I am not naïve: creating a self-regulating organization for Christian nonprofits would be a massive undertaking that would take leadership and significant funding. But if it is true that Christian ministries are losing fifty billion dollars a year in waste, fraud, and abuse, even a solution as expensive as the creation of a self- regulating organization is worth serious consideration.

Re-regulation/Deregulation of the Nonprofit Sector. Limiting governmental involvement is a strong value of this book. We do not believe additional regulation will solve the problems we identify in this book. The "bad guys" will simply add the new regulations to the list of old regulations that they are already breaking. And the "good guys" who attempt to comply will face expensive administrative burdens.

However, the last major overhaul of laws governing nonprofits took place in the 1960s, when America had less than half the number of nonprofits it has today, and before the explosion we've seen in Christian radio, Christian television, nondenominational churches, and the Internet. The rationalization of regulations to meet the realities of the twenty-first century is long overdue.

Notice, however, that I say "re-regulation" and "rationalization," not "increased regulation." We don't need more regulations, but we need smarter ones, regulations that make sense in the Internet age, an age in which producing and processing information has become both necessary and inexpensive. With a properly functioning SRO, as outlined above, or—at a minimum—requirements for greater transparency, it is possible, even likely, that while regulation might need to be re-engineered, it need not increase.[11]

In fact, Albert Meyer—who we will get to know in Chapter 5 as the whistleblower in the New Era Scandal—says that *less* regulation, not more, is the right answer. He says that government regulation "gives people a false sense of security" and gives bad actors plausible deniability. In other words, they can say, "We're in full compliance with all government regulations." This book essentially advocates Albert Meyer's position.

A Philanthropy Marketplace. Rusty Leonard believes that the long-term solution to the problem of faith-based fraud is a fully functioning, completely transparent ministry marketplace, a marketplace in which donors can make "apples to apples" comparisons between ministries before giving their money.

He uses the mutual fund industry as an analogy. Mutual funds have been around since the 1920s, but by the end of the 60s, mutual funds had only about forth-eight billion dollars. While this sounds like a lot of money, it represented only a thimblefull of money in the worldwide investment bucket.

In those days, most mutual fund investors were relatively high net worth individuals. But changes in the law and in technology caused an explosion in the number and size of mutual funds beginning in the 1970s. These developments increased the importance of independent rating services, such as Morningstar's mutual fund ratings. These rating services gave small investors much of the information that big investors had. The result: by the end of 2017, more than twenty trillion dollars was in mutual funds in the United States alone.

Leonard says the key factor in this growth was giving the small investor access to information. The increased transparency increased the confidence of all investors, small and large alike. The result was a huge growth in the number of people who became investors and exponential, not merely incremental, growth in the number of dollars invested.

Leonard believes a truly open and transparent philanthropy marketplace could result in similar growth in Christian charity. This belief led MinistryWatch to rate ministries on a one-to-five scale. It was also a decision that caused Leonard to regularly issue "Donor Alerts" when he believes a ministry is no longer managing itself in such a way as to merit donor support.[12]

Aggressive Christian Journalism. In virtually every story you will read on the pages that follow, neither the government nor church leadership brought to light the frauds. The person who exposed the wrongdoing in most of these stories was often a reporter chasing a story. In one or two cases, the source was a single whistleblower who went to a reporter when he (or she) could not get satisfaction from either the government or the church. That brings me again to a point we made in the Introduction: Aggressive Christian journalism can be a powerful antidote to hubris and fraud.

However, note that I am calling not just for journalism but *aggressive Christian journalism*. It takes both finely-tuned journalistic sensibilities and skills plus a level of theological sophistication and spiritual discernment to root out fraud in the church. As you will read more than once in this book, bad behavior is often downstream from bad theology. A journalist with an ear and mind tuned to pick up bad theology can often find bad behavior before that bad behavior becomes devastating and tragic.

A Theology of Work. As we will see over and over, one of the reasons that faith-based fraud keeps recurring is greed. But please note that I am not talking only about the greed of those perpetrating the frauds themselves. I am also referring to the greed of their victims.

I want to be careful not to blame truly innocent victims. We will encounter many of them in this book, and their stories are often heartbreaking. But in many of the cases we will examine, the victims were not truly innocent. They were Christians who wanted to get something for nothing. They had somehow developed a perverse theology, and that perverse theology often led to a perverse relationship to money and work itself. It is therefore no surprise that many (though by no means all) of the frauds in this book are proponents of Prosperity Theology.

Prosperity Theology arises when the church forgets its "first principles," and one of these is a biblical understanding of work. God is a worker. Genesis describes the creation as "work." It also describes that work variously as "good" and "very good." We are made in His image, so we are workers too. God gave Adam work to do in the Garden of Eden before the fall. Work is not a result of the fall.

But today we have a pathological relationship to work. On one extreme, we have come to view work as something that should be avoided or diminished as much as possible. Work is something we must do in order to pay for our vacations and our retirement. In other words, it is a means to an end, and that end is leisure.

On the other extreme, work becomes an end in itself. We become workaholics. We don't exactly know why we're working, but we know that we should, and we like the feelings of power and control that work gives us.

Both extremes are pathological. And both extremes are fed

by greed and the need for control. The antidote to these pathologies is a theology of work that includes the biblical idea that work is worship, and worship is work. We benefit when we worship God, but that is not why we worship God. The word "liturgy" means "the work of the people." It requires sacrifice and is done for the glory of God, not for our own benefit.

That these solutions are the right solutions may not be self-evident based on the short justification I've provided for them here, and that is why we will revisit these ideas. But I thought it only fair that you know where we're going. Now, let's get started looking at some of the more interesting frauds in history, not just because they're fascinating stories, but in order to see what we can learn about preventing these kinds of frauds from happening in the future.

Chapter 2

The Amazing Story of Charles Ponzi

I guess the only news that most people
want to hear about me is my death.
– Charles Ponzi

You will often meet with characters in nature
so extravagant that a discreet person would
not venture to set them upon the stage.
– Lord Chesterfield

It's usually best to begin at the beginning. If we were *really* to do that, we should probably start with the Ten Commandments. At least three of the Ten Commandments ("You shall not covet," "You shall not steal," and "You shall not give false testimony") deal with the notion of fraud. God took the notion of fraud seriously, and we should too.

But this book is not primarily about theology or history. So we will fast forward a few thousand years and begin our discussion of fraud in modern times with Charles Ponzi. The life and times of Charles Ponzi is a great place for us to start our discussion of faith-based fraud, because many of the faith-based frauds we are going to discuss in this book were originated, or at least popularized, by him.

What Is A Ponzi Scheme?

In its simplest terms, a Ponzi scheme is "robbing Peter to pay Paul." Victims of a Ponzi scheme are promised tantalizing returns on investment. These tantalizing returns numb what should be an investor's natural apprehension. They invest without doing the proper investigation—*due diligence*—of either the investment or the person offering it.

If the investors did their due diligence, they would discover that the real business of a Ponzi scheme is not to invest money, but to get new investors. The earliest investors are paid back not with a return on their investment, but with the money of those who invest later.

Because the earliest investors often do get paid back, they become great evangelists for the project, walking advertisements for future investors. However, because the earliest investors get not only their original investment but also a promised return, it often takes two investors to repay the original one. So if one participant in a Ponzi scheme requires two new investors, then these two require four more, and these four require eight, and so on. That's why Ponzi schemes are often called *pyramid schemes.* A single person at the point of the pyramid starts the scheme. He and the other investors quickly require a huge base of investors to support them.

Ponzi schemes, or pyramid schemes, are, by definition, not sustainable. Sooner or later, the originator will run out of new people to add to the base of the pyramid, and the entire enterprise comes crashing down.

That, in a nutshell, is a Ponzi scheme. Some of the frauds we will discuss are nothing but good, old-fashioned Ponzi schemes. Those include the fraud perpetrated by The Foundation for New Era Philanthropy and the fraudulent practices of the Stanford Financial Group. But faith-based frauds have an added element:

the perpetrators use religion to create trust. Sometimes—as in the case of New Era Philanthropy—the victims are promised that their money will do good things, such as build churches or support ministry.

Who Was Charles Ponzi?

Ponzi schemes got their name from Charles Ponzi, an Italian immigrant whose diminutive frame (5' 2") held big dreams. Indeed, Ponzi's big dreams—the "only in America" flavor of them—make him a fascinating character. "I landed in this country with $2.50 in cash and $1 million in hopes, and those hopes never left me," he told the *New York Times*.

But it is important not to glamorize Ponzi. He was a liar and a thief from the beginning, and many people were hurt by his fraud. Indeed, some struggling families, fighting for a foothold in America, never fully recovered.

Ponzi landed in Boston in 1903, and he demonstrated his discipline and intelligence by quickly learning English. His new language skills allowed him to get a job in a restaurant, eventually becoming a waiter. But the larceny in his character showed even then. He was fired after customers repeatedly complained that he shortchanged them.

From Boston, Ponzi moved to Montreal, Canada, where—in 1907—he got his first taste of big-time fraud. He naturally drifted toward the Italian community there, and he took a job as assistant teller in Banco Zarossi, a bank started by Luigi Zarossi to serve the rapidly growing Italian community. Zarossi paid six percent on bank deposits. That was double the rate of other banks, so his bank grew rapidly.

Ponzi apparently worked hard. In fact, one of the ironies of Ponzi's life is that he was smart, friendly, and a hard worker. Had he channeled these traits into legitimate businesses, he undoubtedly would have been a success. Perhaps not as big a financial success as he ultimately became, but at least his success would have been lasting. This is a characteristic of frauds that we will see over and over again in this book. They often rise because of some great skill, and fall because of some great flaw of character. They prove the old adage "character is destiny." Eventually and inevitably, fraudulent schemes collapse under their own weight.[1]

While at Banco Zarossi, Ponzi learned the ins and outs of the banking system. He also learned gaps and loopholes in the banking system that he could later exploit. Ponzi eventually rose to bank manager. In that role, he discovered how his bank was able to offer was able to offer the above-market rate of six percent—the bank invested in risky real estate deals, hoping they would mature before the depositors wanted their money back.

But many of the real estate deals the bank invested in went bad. Ponzi learned that Zarossi could not fund the outsized six percent interest payments with returns from his lackluster real estate investments. Zarossi started using new depositors' money to pay back the old depositors, hoping to buy himself time. This practice is at the center of what came to be called a Ponzi scheme: using money from new investors to pay the old investors.

The desperate efforts to buy time failed, along with Zarossi's bank. Zarossi fled to Mexico. Ponzi stayed in Montreal and tried—or at least pretended to try—to clean up the mess left by Zarossi. But Ponzi was already on the wrong path. One day, he called on a Banco Zarossi's customer and, discovering no one in the business office, wrote himself a check for nearly five hundred dollars, and forged the signature of a director of the company.

It was a brazen fraud, perhaps motivated by the desperation of being penniless. The authorities caught Ponzi almost immediately. When confronted by police, he put up no argument or resistance. He held out his hands, wrists up, to make it easy for the policemen to apply the handcuffs. He said simply, "I'm guilty." He ended up spending three years in a Canadian prison.

After his release from prison, Ponzi moved to Boston, got married, and made a half-hearted attempt to settle down. However, the lure of the big score continued to attract him. He started an advertising company, which soon failed.

But out of that company's failure came the seed of his next venture, because a few weeks after Ponzi shut down his company, he received a letter from Spain that changed his life.

It wasn't the content of the letter that changed his life. The letter was simply asking for information about his now defunct company. What caught Ponzi's attention was the International Reply Coupon (IRC) that accompanied the request for information. IRCs came into existence in 1906 in order to facilitate international business. An IRC is a coupon that the recipient can exchange for a first-class stamp in his own country. In this case, the Spaniard wanted to make it easy for Ponzi to respond to his inquiry, so he sent an IRC that Ponzi could then exchange for an international stamp. IRCs meant the Spaniard did not have to worry about sending American currency through the mail, nor go through the hassle of finding an American stamp—in Spain—for a reply. The coupon does the job.[2]

At that time, a coupon that cost only a penny in Spain could be redeemed in the United States for a six-cent stamp or cashed in for six cents. That kind of return was enough to get the gears in Ponzi's fraudulent mind spinning. Later, in 1920, he told the *Boston Post*: "I looked the coupon over. I thought . . . why can't I buy hundreds, thousands, millions of these coupons. I'll make five cents on every one."[3]

So Ponzi promised his investors a fifty percent rate of return in forty-five days and one hundred percent in ninety days. That was a return far greater than any bank, and it still left Ponzi with plenty of profit.

He took this story to the predominantly Italian, predominantly Catholic, working-class folk he knew in Boston in 1919, many of whom were fresh arrivals from Europe. They had family and friends in the "old country," so they had a passing acquaintance with IRCs. They could see how, in theory, Ponzi could make this scheme work. He soon had his first investors.

In reality, however, Ponzi's scheme was complicated and risky in the days before instant communication and efficient transatlantic transportation. Ponzi would need representatives in both Europe and the United States. If the currency exchange rates moved against him, his profits could shrink or disappear.

Even so, the profit potential was massive. It is possible that if Ponzi had bothered to set up a legitimate operation and if he had kept the operation lean and efficient, he could have paid his expenses and still eked out a profit—at least until competitors realized the inefficiencies in the market and squeezed the profits—as competitors and increased information inevitably do.

But Ponzi did not bother to tell his victims that he had none of this infrastructure in place, and he had no intention of putting it in place. He also failed to tell them that even if he had attempted to run a legitimate operation, the rates of return he was promising would have been impossible to achieve.

Defining Arbitrage

In economic terms, what Ponzi did—or pretended to do—was a form of *arbitrage*. Arbitrage is the practice of taking advantage of a price difference between two or more markets. It can be a perfectly legal and legitimate way to make money. Large international corporations, for example, might—on any given day—have money in many different currencies around the globe. They can take advantage of discrepancies in exchange rates to make money. However, the discrepancies are typically very small, and the profits on a single transaction might be just fractions of a percent. These fractions of a percent are often expressed in *basis points*. A basis point is a percentage of a percent. So, for example, twenty-five basis points would be one-quarter of one percent. Ten basis points would be one-tenth of one percent. It would not be unusual for a single transaction to yield only a few basis points of profit. However, if the transactions are in the billions of dollars, and you made many such transactions a day, it is possible to make significant profits.

Pawn shops, consignment shops, and websites such as eBay, Etsy, even PayPal, engage in a form of arbitrage. They take advantage of the price difference between two markets. If I have a rare book or a Star Trek collector's item or a musical instrument and I try to sell it among my friends, I will likely find only a few possible buyers. After all, how many people living on my street want a used trumpet? My pool of potential buyers is limited to trumpet players and only those trumpet players who need a used instrument. The demand in the market I have access to—my neighbors—is very low. The law of supply and demand says that where demand is low, the price is also low.

However, eBay aggregates such buyers from all over the world. Where demand is greater, the price is higher. As a seller, that makes me happy. eBay gets paid out of the price increase that it helps to create. Even the buyer is happy, because he has a choice where before he had no choice at all, or at least a limited choice. The buyer also has the assurance that he is paying a fair price.

We take this digression into the world of arbitrage to make this point: most financial frauds will not propose something that is completely outrageous or implausible. What makes a financial fraud successful (if "success" is the right word) is its very plausibility. Some variation of a Ponzi scheme was at the heart of the fraud at the Stanford Financial Group, New Era Philanthropy, and Heritage USA .

Earned Trust and Imputed Trust

Another important characteristic of a successful fraud is, as I suggested earlier, trust. The word "trust" and the ideas behind it may seem familiar to you, but because this notion is so important to our understanding of fraud, especially faith-based fraud, it is important to pause and examine the notion of trust.

In general, trust is built in two ways: trust is earned or trust is imputed. Psychologists tell us that earned trust is a result of *frequency of interaction* and the *making and keeping of agreements.* Trust is imputed *because of one's reputation* with other known and trustworthy people.

Let's use marriage as an example. Any man who proposes marriage to a woman within five minutes of their first meeting is likely to meet resistance and failure. Indeed, the woman will probably run away and warn her girlfriends. This is true despite the fact that many happily married couples say later they knew "from the first moment" that they would marry their spouses.

Why would they "know" from the beginning but not say "yes" from the beginning? Because trust is an essential cornerstone in a lasting relationship, and most healthy people begin new relationships with an equally healthy skepticism rather than immediate and blind trust. That is why most successful marriages follow a period of dating and courtship, a time in which the lovers learn to know and trust each other's character.

On the other hand, many cultures have arranged marriages, and these marriages are often as successful as those in cultures where marriage is by choice.[4] Why is this?

In part because the spouses come into the relationship with a level of trust *imputed* to the spouse due to existing family relationships and community bonds and experiences. A woman in an arranged marriage might reasonably expect her spouse to be faithful, a good provider, a good father, and an upstanding citizen in the community (thereby creating purpose and standing for the family) because she knows he was raised from his early youth to possess these qualities. Her own parents, whom she trusts, confirms for her that these assumptions are true. Further, the cost for him to behave in unfaithful ways is huge. So she marries a man she barely knows, and has a happy and productive life with him.

So am I advocating arranged marriages? No.[5] I am simply saying that trust is an essential element in any relationship, and we build trust in various ways. Those who engage in fraud know this, and they will do things to create an illusion of trustworthiness. They are experts in causing their victims to impute trust in them, without having to actually earn that trust through personal interaction. So, for example, faith-based frauds often claim to share a common religion, or common relationships, or common affections, and sometimes common enemies to create this illusion. That's why Charles Ponzi's first victims were fellow countrymen from the Italian-American community. He could exploit common cultural and religious ties. Also, because Ponzi's targets were recent immigrants, most of them understood the value of the IRC. When Ponzi described his scheme in his fast-talking way, his victims may not have understood completely what he said. But it at least sounded plausible. The fact that Ponzi let them invest as little as ten dollars and he promised a fifty percent return in forty-five days made the decision easier.

Greed and Charisma

Ponzi's relentless energy and confidence persuaded a few small, early investors in 1919. When these few, early investors did indeed get their money back with the promised fifty percent return, they became Ponzi's best sales people. In fact, most of them quickly realized that they could not get better returns elsewhere, so they let Ponzi keep not only their original investment but all the so-called profits as well.

The net result: money began to pour in to Ponzi's one-room office in downtown Boston. For example, by February of 1920, Ponzi's company, the Securities Exchange Company (SEC), had brought in about five thousand dollars in total. But by the end of March, Ponzi's company had more than thirty thousand dollars. The money came in at an ever- accelerating rate.

Because most of his investors reinvested their gains and he rarely paid out any returns—at least in the early days—the money just kept piling up. That is, the money that he didn't spend on himself.

Indeed, over the course of the next year, Ponzi became a remarkable figure in Boston. This diminutive man walked the downtown streets wearing custom-made suits topped by a white straw hat of a style popular at the time. He carried a cane. Pictures of him during this time showed him with a big smile and surrounded by an entourage. He bought expensive cars. He even bought a mansion with a five-acre lawn on the outskirts of town, amid Boston's old-money Brahman elite.

In the days before federally insured banks, those with substantial wealth often spread their money around to many different banks. Ponzi deposited substantial sums and was therefore well known in more than twenty banks throughout New England. Success bred success. Investments started coming from these bankers and their friends.[6]

Ponzi was relentlessly optimistic, relentlessly upbeat. This optimism is one of the reasons people were attracted to him. If you invested with Ponzi, you were smart and, now, a part of an elite community of those who had "seen the light." And—count on it—you were going to be rich. This is a page right out of the Prosperity Gospel playbook, a playbook that was also being written in the early part of the twentieth century. After all, who wouldn't want to be told that they are doing the right thing, and if they keep doing it, everything they want in life will soon be within their reach? Yes, you can in fact have your best life now.

But reality was rapidly catching up with Ponzi. He took steps to turn his scheme into a legitimate business operation. Ponzi's bid for legitimacy came in the summer of 1920, when he realized that he owed hundreds of thousands of dollars to investors, and if they all suddenly called for their money, he didn't have it.

By now he did have a reputation as a financial whiz, and people were beginning to ask what was next for him. So with the money still pouring in, he came up with a plan. He attempted to buy a significant number of shares in what came to be Hanover Trust, one of the Boston banks in which he had made significant deposits.

The president of Hanover Trust had been only too happy to take Ponzi's money, but he and the directors of the bank apparently had qualms about having Ponzi as a partner. They refused to sell him the shares he wanted.

Ponzi, though, had become—to use a phrase now common to describe modern financial crises—"too big to fail." In other words, when Hanover Trust refused to sell Ponzi shares, Ponzi threatened to withdraw all his money all at once and move it to other banks. Of course, banks are in the business of loaning money, not hoarding it, so they did not have all of Ponzi's money in the vault. If Ponzi withdrew all his money at once, the bank would suddenly have been insolvent.

Ponzi's threat forced the bank officers to acquiesce. Ponzi ended up being a majority shareholder of Hanover Trust.

Their Greed, Our Greed

I do not want to excuse Ponzi or other frauds who followed in his footsteps. They are responsible for their decisions and actions. That said, the victims in Ponzi's original scheme—and in almost all those we will discuss in this book—are not entirely innocent victims.

Many of the victims of Ponzi's schemes—for example, the officers at Hanover Trust—had a sense that what Ponzi was doing was not entirely ethical. They were willing to look the other way when Ponzi was depositing large sums of money. They asked few if any questions. But they knew something was not right. They were unwilling to become his partner until they were backed against a wall and had no choice.

It is impossible to say for sure what motivated Ponzi. Was it greed, insecurity, class envy, or something else? Whatever it was, we should not forget that many of his victims were motivated by these factors as well. The desire to get "something for nothing" is strongly rooted in the human psyche.[7]

As Ponzi's notoriety grew, he began to face scrutiny from the media. Articles critical of Ponzi began to appear in the fledgling financial newspaper *Barron's*. The articles created a brief run on Ponzi's company. However, this time Ponzi had enough cash on hand to pay the investors who wanted their money back, and that stopped the run. And Ponzi sued both the writer and *Barron's* and won five hundred thousand dollars.

But this media scrutiny marked the beginning of the end for Ponzi and his scheme. It is worth noting again the importance of media scrutiny in the downfall of almost all the frauds we will discuss. One of the themes of this book is the old saying that "sunlight is the best disinfectant," and the investigative reporters at *Barron's* were the heroes of this story—though at this point in the story, after they had been ordered to pay a half-million dollar libel settlement, it would be hard to see that.

By this time, and in order to keep the cash flowing, Ponzi hired sales representatives—a practice we will see duplicated by

Foundation for New Era Philanthropy and Allen Stanford.

In Ponzi's case, the sales people were themselves quickly becoming rich—and therefore had little incentive to blow the whistle on any questionable business practices they saw. Also, because Ponzi's own business practices were so lax, it became easy for Ponzi's employees and investors to defraud him. Investors would write Ponzi bad checks and receive one of the colored notes that Ponzi distributed to his investors. Ponzi's sales people would submit fraudulent sales in order to collect the larger and larger commissions Ponzi was forced to offer as the scheme grew.

Journalists Do The Math

The *Boston Post* published a positive story about Ponzi on July 24, 1920. That story brought more investors than ever. In fact, the day after the article appeared, people lined up around the block to give Ponzi their money. During this period, Ponzi was taking in more than two hundred and fifty thousand dollars *per day*.

It turned out, however, that the *Boston Post* story was something of a journalistic Trojan horse. Though the story about Ponzi had been positive, the *Post's* city editor Eddie Dunn had become suspicious. He assigned investigative reporters to dig into Ponzi's background. It did not take them long to uncover Ponzi's forgery conviction in Montreal and Ponzi's role at the Zarossi Bank.

The *Post* determined that if Ponzi was telling the truth about his investments in International Reply Coupons, at least one hundred and sixty million IRCs would have to be in circulation. However, the US Post Office said that only about twenty-seven thousand actually were in circulation.

The bottom line was that Ponzi could not possibly be telling the truth. It appeared that he did not even attempt to buy and sell IRCs. The evidence was easy to spot. It just took someone to do the looking, to ask a few simple questions, and to do a bit of basic math.

As we will see, that's often the case with frauds. They are usually "hiding in plain sight." They are allowed to remain "hidden" because the people who suspect something is not right are making money themselves, they think it is none of their business, or they feel powerless to make a difference.

Exploring these ideas more deeply, and seeing how they manifest themselves in frauds within the church, is another theme of this book.

Among the key lessons I hope readers will walk away with is that it is important to ask questions. Even when you are donating money to a Christian ministry or investing money with people you believe to be Christian brothers and sisters, ask the basic questions, and then ask at least a few tough questions. Good ministries (and good entrepreneurs) will welcome the questions, because they will have good answers. Tough questions are an opportunity for honest, careful, thoughtful leaders to shine.

But the bad guys avoid such questions. We will see over and over again that for want of a few basic questions—and it usually takes only a few people asking the questions—great financial and emotional calamity ensues.

Ponzi's Scheme Unravels

After the first *Post* articles, things unraveled quickly for Ponzi. A month earlier, investors had waited in long lines to deposit their money. Now investors waited in long lines to withdraw their money. Ponzi, ever the salesman, worked the line like a politician, calming nerves, even passing out coffee and doughnuts. Amazingly, even at this late date, Ponzi was able to persuade many to quit the line and leave their money with him.

However, on August 11, 1920, Massachusetts Bank

Commissioner Joseph Allen seized Hanover Trust, the bank Ponzi had co-opted, and the next day, August 12, Ponzi surrendered to federal authorities. The far-flung consequences of Ponzi's fraud quickly came to pass. In the end, almost forty thousand people, mostly New Englanders, invested money with Ponzi. Ponzi's total take: fifteen million dollars. That would be the equivalent of at least four billion in today's dollars.

These big numbers mask the individual tragedies. While it's true that many of Ponzi's investors were wealthy Beacon Hill families who could afford to lose a few bucks, the overwhelming majority of Ponzi's victims were working class folk, some of whom lost their life's savings. The phrase "lost their life's savings" is such a cliché that we forget it means children went hungry or lost the opportunity to go to school. Elderly people were robbed of dignity in their final years. Sick people were robbed of their ability pay for healthcare and died, or had their lives shortened.

Authorities attempted to recover money from Hanover Trust and return it to investors, and many of Ponzi's assets were sold to repay investors. Nonetheless, investors received, on average, less than thirty percent of the money they had invested. Some estimates are as low as twelve percent. Among the other tragic consequences, Hanover Trust and five other banks were completely wiped out, leaving hundreds of people out of work.

Ponzi faced eighty-six counts of mail fraud. On November 1, 1920, he pled guilty to a single count and was sentenced to five years in federal prison. According to Ponzi biographer Mitchell Zuckoff, "As he was led away Ponzi passed a note to the reporters in the front row: '*Sic transit gloria mundi*,' Latin for 'Thus passes worldly glory.'"[8]

He was also charged by the State of Massachusetts with twenty-two counts of larceny. The state charges surprised Ponzi. He thought his plea deal made him immune to additional charges.

He sued, a case that became known as *Ponzi v. Fessenden*, which made it to the Supreme Court in 1921. Ponzi claimed that he was facing double jeopardy, but the Supreme Court ruled that plea bargains on federal charges have no standing regarding state charges, thereby setting an important legal precedent.

After the Supreme Court decision, the Massachusetts state court trial began. Ponzi was now broke, so he served as his own attorney. Amazingly, the jury found him innocent on the first ten counts. I say amazingly, but this phenomenon, too, is one we will see again: the victims' unwillingness to admit they have been defrauded and the general public's tendency to turn these frauds into folk heroes.

But Ponzi was not home free. He was tried a second time on five of the remaining counts. This time the jury was deadlocked. A third trial on the remaining counts resulted in a seven- to nine-year sentence.

Ponzi served his sentence, but that was not the end of his career as a fraud. After getting out of jail in the late 1920s, he bounced around from one fraud to the next, eventually landing in Florida. While there, he became associated with another of the great swindles in American history. You've probably heard the expression, "If you believe that, I've got some swampland in Florida I'd like to sell you." That expression became a part of the American vernacular in the 1930s, when real-estate frauds were rampant in Florida. Ponzi was in the midst of these frauds.

Ponzi eventually fled the United States. He spent time in Europe, including his homeland of Italy. He eventually landed in Brazil. Among his last words: "I guess the only news that most people want to hear about me is my death." They got that news in 1949, when Ponzi died in a charity hospital in Rio de Janeiro.

Lessons from Ponzi

Many (though by no means all) of the frauds we will discuss in this book are some variation of a Ponzi scheme. The most basic Ponzi scheme is a classic pyramid organization, such as the Elite Church. The Elite Church encourages people to join and give money at different levels—beginning at one hundred dollars and going into the thousands of dollars. They were promised that God would multiply their gifts. The particular way God multiplies their gifts is by these early members bringing in other members, whose gifts pay the early members, and so on. The church has services at which people bear witness to how God has multiplied their gifts. These services are essentially pep rallies to recruit more members.

The Foundation for New Era Philanthropy, and the fraud perpetrated by Allen Stanford and the Stanford Financial Group also have some if not all the elements of a Ponzi scheme. As does the Heritage USA/ PTL scandal, which is perhaps the most famous of the scandals we will discuss.

The first thing to understand about pyramid organizations is, as I've already mentioned, they are unsustainable. At some point, you simply run out of people to recruit. They are inherently fraudulent. That's why they are illegal.

The second thing to remember about pyramid organizations, or Ponzi schemes, is that they often present plausible stories. Most Ponzi schemes are not flagrantly and obviously unsustainable, or no one would participate. That's why most schemes involve investments of some kind or another. Ponzi used IRCs. Jim Bakker sold memberships and the promise of use of his resort property. Bernie Madoff and Allen Stanford promised outsized financial returns based on a proprietary investment strategy. Each was different, but each was the same in that they all created the illusion or the possibility of credibility and sustainability, and that's why people were sucked in.

The Bernard Madoff scandal is a classic example. Madoff promised his investors a twelve percent annual rate of return—in good times and bad. Historically, the stock market has produced an average rate of return of eight to ten percent. And that rate is subject to ups and downs. Safer investments, such as government bonds, produce rates of return far lower. So Madoff's promise of a constant twelve percent rate of return was enormously attractive. And that number—twelve percent—was strategically selected. This rate of return was higher than investors could get elsewhere, but not so much higher as to be implausible. Also, a twelve percent rate of return, compounded annually, allows an investor to double his money in five years. These easily understandable terms turned all of Madoff's investors into his best sales people: "Invest with my friend Bernie Madoff and you'll double your money every five years." By turning current investors into sales people, one of the most important elements of a Ponzi scheme—a constant supply of new money—was in place.

The final key thing to remember about a Ponzi scheme is that they rarely hold up to close scrutiny. Ponzi's scheme unraveled when journalists started asking basic, not sophisticated, questions. A Ponzi scheme works because the victims' trust the perpetrators enough to dispense with normal due diligence.

That is why faith-based communities are ideal for perpetrating Ponzi schemes. If I have been sitting by you in church and people I trust from church have invested with you, I may feel like I have all I need to know about you. Or, on the other side of the coin, I may feel that I will damage relationships that are important to me if I ask too many hard questions. The result is the same: the hard questions don't get asked or answered.

It is because of this lack of scrutiny and accountability that some investment schemes that start out more or less legitimate become fraudulent over time. Many of the faith-based frauds we will examine—including the book-buying schemes of Mark Driscoll and David Jeremiah—began as the legitimate activities of highly respected ministries. But a lack of scrutiny and accountability over time led to behavior that ended up hurting many people.

Affinity Fraud

It's true that Charles Ponzi himself did not perpetrate a religious fraud in the way that most of the people we will examine did. Ponzi did not appeal to religion per se, but to the trust of an essentially religious people—the working class Italian Catholic community of Boston—to get his start.

I wanted to start with Ponzi, however, because he is arguably the most famous fraud in modern history. Also, in Ponzi's scheme we learn some of the basics of affinity fraud. We also begin to learn the answer to what I have come to believe is the most important question when it comes to affinity fraud in general and faith-based fraud in particular. That question is often expressed like this: "How can people be so stupid?" Slightly more charitably, the question is sometimes restated: "How can people be so gullible?" Or "Why couldn't people see this coming?"

But this question, and its answers, lead to other questions, and sometimes troubling answers.

Why, for example, do people follow and support these charlatans? Why do poor people give money so their favorite preachers can fly the world in jets? Taken to the extreme, why do people follow men like Charles Manson, Jim Jones, David Koresh, and others?

The answers to these questions reveal something about ourselves that we don't want to admit or face. What I hope you are beginning to see is that the victims of fraud are often neither stupid nor gullible. They are, however, often either greedy or needy. Again, I do not want to blame the victims of these frauds, but we must admit that those who are taken in by frauds and charlatans often have a powerful self-interest—emotional, spiritual, material, sexual, whatever—that they are attempting to satisfy.

I do not mean to diminish the wrongdoing of the perpetuators of fraud, but we should acknowledge that most frauds have few truly innocent victims. Faith-based fraud is truly a dance in which "it takes two to tango."[9]

Too Much American, Not Enough Church

At the risk of belaboring the point, we also see in Ponzi's story the importance of boots-on-the-ground journalism in exposing the fraud. Time and again, from Ponzi to televangelist Jim Bakker to John Bennett, who perpetuated the Foundation for New Philanthropy fraud, a skeptical reporter or editor is often one of the few heroes in what is essentially a tragic story.

We also begin to understand why transparency is the ultimate solution. In fact, journalism is "merely" a method by which we obtain the goal.

So we start with Ponzi because in Ponzi are many of the raw ingredients of faith-based fraud. Ponzi's first victims were those in his own Italian-Catholic community. He was flamboyant and audacious, clothing himself in the trappings of success. He was the poor boy who made good.

This story has become part of the American myth. It is a story we love to hear and to be a part of. So we must also acknowledge that in these ways and many others, Ponzi—and the faith-based frauds that follow—are quintessentially American tales. From P.T. Barnum to Donald Trump, Americans have responded to the flamboyant, the audacious. Indeed, Ponzi's fraud was based as much on misplaced hope—both his and his victims'—as it was on actual larceny.

So with these ideas in mind, we begin to understand how

affinity fraud and even the specialized version of affinity fraud we're interested in, faith-based fraud, can happen. Theologian Stanley Hauerwas said that one of the problems with the American church is that it is "too American and not enough church."[10] When we add this insight to our list of lessons about Charles Ponzi, we begin to understand why the American church is such a ripe breeding ground for all manner of fraud and excess.

Armed with these insights, let us now turn our attention from the most famous affinity fraud artist of the twentieth century to the man who will likely go down in history as the most famous religious fraud of the twentieth century: Jim Bakker.

Chapter 3

Jim and Tammy Faye Bakker Redefine Faith-based Fraud

"If Jesus were alive today, he would be on TV."

—Jim Bakker

"They [Jim and Tammy Faye Bakker] epitomized the excesses of the 1980s, the love of glitz, and the shamelessness; which in their case was so pure as to almost amount to a kind of innocence."

—Frances Fitzgerald

"The less joy you have in Christ, the more entertainment you will need from this world."

—Leonard Ravenhill

Perhaps the most famous religious fraud of the twentieth century was the Jim and Tammy Bakker/PTL scandal.

The PTL (Praise The Lord) scandal, though it happened more than thirty-five years ago, has become emblematic of faith-based fraud, and no discussion of the subject is complete without an examination of what happened in the Bible Belt city of Charlotte, North Carolina.

The basic facts are these: Jim Bakker led The PTL Network with his wife Tammy Faye. Using money donated by viewers of his program, the Bakkers created Heritage USA, a compound south of Charlotte in the suburb of Fort Mill, South Carolina. This sprawling facility included television production studios and a resort hotel. It also included an amusement park, offices, and other facilities.

But Bakker's network ultimately collapsed amid allegations of financial impropriety and sexual misconduct. When the total damages were finally accounted for, thousands of investors lost more than one hundred and fifty million dollars. These losses do not include the hundreds of millions of donor dollars that went into the nonprofit organization.

Indeed, a class-action lawsuit brought against Bakker alleged that more than one hundred and sixty thousand people gave him money. Jim Bakker ultimately spent about five years in prison and wrote a bestselling book called *I Was Wrong*.

But did he really believe that? It is hard to come to that conclusion if you look at his current activities. Today, Bakker continues on television and continues to ask for money to support his ministry and lifestyle—this time from the vacation capital of middle America: Branson, Missouri. In 2020, the New York Attorney General's Office warned Bakker to immediately stop promoting a product sold on his program's website as a cure for the coronavirus.[1] The attorney general sent Bakker a cease and desist letter to stop "false advertising" of Silver Solution on his television program. He and a guest, Sherrill Sellman, claimed that the product killed the coronavirus. The Food and Drug Administration and the Federal Trade Commission also issued warnings to Bakker.

So it is not unreasonable to ask again: Has Jim Bakker changed his stripes, or has this old dog just learned new tricks? What is even more important to ask is what does the PTL scandal tell us about American evangelicalism and the temperament of religious people in the twentieth and twenty-first centuries?

The PTL scandal also gives us a chance to examine the

dramatic effects of television on ministry. Jim and Tammy Bakker did not, of course, originate Christian television.[2] But Jim and Tammy Bakker, and many of the frauds we will examine from here on out, involve some significant television component.

This fact should cause any logical mind to ask this question: was television merely incidental, or did the celebrity and money that television brings lead inevitably to the scandals that follow?

Jim and Tammy Bakker can help us answer these questions. But before we go into any of these questions, let's start with the facts.

Before PTL Meant "Pass the Loot"

James Orsen Bakker was born in Muskegon, Michigan, on January 2, 1940. This part of middle America was conservative Lutheran and Dutch Reformed country. He and Tammy Faye LaValley met when they were both students at North Central University in Minneapolis. Even then, the young couple sensed a call to full-time ministry. They left college without receiving their degrees and immediately became itinerant evangelists, preaching and doing children and teen ministry in churches around the country.

All evidence suggests that the young Jim and Tammy, in those days, were honestly "on fire" for Christ. These were lean but good times for the Bakkers, they would later say. Ministering in a different church every week gave them an opportunity to hone their presentation skills. They could do the same "schtick" over and over till they had it down to a well-rehearsed act that, on television, journalist Francis Fitzgerald said gave them the air of being the "George Burns and Gracie Allen" of Christian television.[3]

In 1966, they settled in Portsmouth, Virginia, and began working for the Christian Broadcasting Network (CBN). Founded by Pat Robertson in 1961, CBN eventually grew to be the largest

Christian television network in the nation. But when the Bakkers joined CBN, it was still a small operation. The network's flagship program was and remains *The 700 Club*, named after the original seven hundred people who pledged ten dollars a month to keep the program on the air. The Bakkers joined the fledgling network to host *The Jim and Tammy Show.* The program was aimed at young people, and it became so successful that Jim and Tammy's celebrity was nearly as great as Pat Robertson's, a situation that was awkward for all.

So in the early 1970s, the Bakkers moved to California to begin a new program called *Praise The Lord* for the fledgling Trinity Broadcasting Network (TBN). TBN was run by another husband-and-wife team, the flamboyant couple, Paul and Jan Crouch. Once again, the Bakkers were instrumental in the creation of a Christian network that would eventually become one of the largest in the world. (MinistryWatch reported that in 2017, TBN had revenue in excess of six hundred million dollars.)

Robertson and the Crouches focused on building a television network, but the Bakkers were fundamentally entertainers and not business people, which may in fact have been the cause of their ultimate demise. Their goal was to build a program centered around their personalities that would not be carried exclusively by either CBN or TBN, but by both networks, as well as many other stations around the country. With this goal in mind, in 1975, the Bakkers moved to Charlotte, North Carolina, to begin *The PTL Club.*

Evangelicalism in the 1970s: The Jesus Movement

It is worth a digression to talk about what was happening to evangelical Christianity in America at this time.

The 1970s was a time of rapid change in the life of the evangelical church. We've already mentioned that the 1970s began the rise of the megachurch. In 1969, Larry Norman released his album *Upon This Rock*, widely considered to be the first contemporary Christian music album. We've already mentioned the founding of the Trinity Broadcasting Network and the Christian Broadcasting Network, both of which saw explosive growth through the 1970s. James Dobson founded Focus on the Family in 1977. It also owed much of its success to media, especially radio, and it became one of the largest parachurch ministries in the nation.[4]

Some of these innovations in Christian media were the result of cultural shifts in American life. The 1960s get all the credit (or blame) for a huge culture shift in American life, but it was the 1970s that saw the *Roe v. Wade* Supreme Court decision that legalized abortion. The seventies also saw an explosion in the use of drugs that made the sixties look like a church picnic.[5] And some of the changes were the result of more benign and less spectacular causes, such as changes in technology and in the regulatory environment related to the media, especially the cable television industry.

Cable television had been around since the 1940s, but from the forties to the seventies, cable television served a specific audience. Remote communities that could not pick up broadcast signals from far-away cities. They would put a community antenna on a local hill or mountain. That elevated antenna would then supply nearby homes with the television signal via cable. By 1952, about seventy such systems existed nationwide, serving about fourteen thousand people.

Ironically, this system—designed merely to give remote areas access to the same broadcast stations that cities enjoyed—ended up doing much more than that for some communities. A community antenna in the right place could pick up signals from very far away. Remote subscribers to cable systems often ended up with many more TV channel options than those living in cities.

Armed with this obvious advantage, these small and rural cable systems began to grow. Eventually, that growth posed a threat to broadcasters, who had a powerful lobby that persuaded lawmakers to place restrictions on the growth of cable.

But, in another ironic twist, one of the restrictions the FCC placed on cable, in 1969, was a rule requiring cable systems with more than thirty-five hundred subscribers to have local facilities and original programming. This rule did not drive cable systems out of business. Rather, it motivated them to expand, developing local production capabilities. A series of rule changes followed. In 1976, the FCC required new cable systems to have at least twenty channels. This ruling suddenly created a voracious appetite for cable television programming.

Proving once again the futility and unintended consequences of government regulation, restrictions designed to make it more difficult for cable systems to operate had in fact turned cable into a juggernaut.

And, once again, Jim and Tammy Bakker were at the right place at the right time.

Charlotte: God and Mammon

That "right place" was Charlotte, North Carolina, for even if the PTL Network had never come into existence, Charlotte would still hold a unique place in the history of twentieth-century American evangelicalism.

Charlotte owes its founding to Presbyterian missionaries, and it had been a center for Presbyterian and Reformed activism since before the United States was founded. German Lutherans, Ulster Scots (Scotch-Irish), and other Reformation Christians had fled Catholic regions of Europe for the New World. They went west, with the rest of the country, until they hit the Appalachian Mountains. Some crossed the mountains and settled Pennsylvania, Ohio, and beyond. But many migrated south, along what geographers call the Fall Line, that line separating the hilly piedmont from the easily traveled coastal plain. Eventually that path came to be called The Great Wagon Road, a route that is not too different from today's Interstate 85.

As these pilgrims traveled south and west, they either found what they were looking for or grew weary and stopped to put down roots. Richmond, Raleigh, Winston-Salem, Charlotte, Greenville, Spartanburg, and Montgomery all trace their history to this story of migration down the Great Wagon Road, a migration motivated at least in part by religion.[6]

Even today, we see the religious heritage of this migration. Old Salem, in Winston-Salem, North Carolina, was founded by Moravians in 1766. Lenoir-Rhyne University in Hickory, North Carolina, was founded by German Lutherans. In 1786, one of the most important and influential laws in American history passed in Richmond: the Virginia Statute for Religious Freedom. Written by Thomas Jefferson and sponsored by James Madison, the statute might be thought of as the first draft of the US Constitution's First Amendment, guaranteeing freedom of religion. It is so important that we recognize it each January 16 with National Religious Freedom Day.

Returning specifically to Charlotte. The oldest Presbyterian churches in Charlotte date from the early 1700s. Their pulpits were filled with preachers who were fiercely independent, many of them becoming part of a "black robe brigade" that led the fight for independence from England.

British General Charles Cornwallis is best remembered by history as the losing general at the Battle of Yorktown, thus ending the American Revolution. But he had earlier fought in the Carolinas and had a headquarters in Charlotte. He found the citizens of Charlotte most unwelcoming. They sometimes emptied their chamber pots from second-story windows onto the heads of British soldiers. Cornwallis eventually evacuated the town, declaring it to be a "hornet's nest of rebellion." To this day, Charlotte remains proud of this description. A hornet's nest is on the city's official seal, and the city's NBA basketball team is the Charlotte Hornets.

But in the early 1800s, the religious life of Charlotte and the country took a turn. In 1801, a revival service was held in Cane Ridge, a rural area in Kentucky. The Cane Ridge revivals attracted as many as ten thousand people—at a time when Louisville, the nearest city, had only about two thousand people.

Historians consider the Cane Ridge revival the beginning of a religious movement in America often called the Second Great Awakening. It took only a year or two for preachers who participated in the Cane Ridge revivals to make their way to Charlotte, and similar services brought Pentecostal fire to this Presbyterian stronghold.

To skip forward two hundred years is, of course, to leave much out. But it is safe to say that the twin pillars of Reformed and Presbyterian thought combined with, and sometimes in conflict with, the evangelical fervor and doctrinal confusion of the Second Great Awakening[7] explains much about Charlotte today. Understanding Charlotte's religious life helps explain much of what goes on in the religious life of America and the world.

Why? Because Charlotte became, along with Orlando and Colorado Springs, one of the cities in America to which large parachurch organizations have migrated. Today, for example, Charlotte is home to a major campus for both Reformed Theological Seminary and Gordon-Conwell Theological Seminary, as well as several other seminaries. The Billy Graham Evangelistic Association is headquartered here. Billy Graham's organization is now led by his son Franklin, who is also simultaneously the president of Samaritan's Purse, headquartered in nearby Boone, North Carolina.

Organizations such as JAARS (formerly the Jungle Aviation

and Radio Service), SIM (formerly Sudan Inland Mission), and the Bible Broadcasting Network are unknown to most of the world, but missionaries around the globe know these organizations and, in many cases, depend on them for support and even for survival. Charlotte also had a strong charismatic/Pentecostal streak running through Charlotte. Beginning in the 1970s, Derek Prince Ministries, which emphasized healing and other gifts of the Spirit, was beginning to have a worldwide impact.

In short, Charlotte was becoming a center for evangelical activity. At the same time, Charlotte was becoming a major financial services center. Charlotte, in other words, was becoming a boom town.

So it was not so unusual that Jim and Tammy Bakker would choose Charlotte for their new ministry home. In some ways, the Bakkers must have seen Charlotte as having what they likely thought of as the best of the worlds in which they had previously lived. Charlotte's Scots-Irish Presbyterianism and German Lutheranism were not foreign to this young couple who grew up among the Dutch Reformed folk of Michigan. The charismatic and evangelical zeal of many people already there made the Bakkers' landing a soft one.

And, to borrow a phrase from bank robber Willie Sutton, Charlotte is where the money is.

The Rise and Fall of PTL

Today, so many years after the fall of the PTL Network, it's hard to recall just how significant a pop culture phenomenon the Bakkers and the PTL Network were. At its height, PTL took in ten million dollars a month in contributions and other revenue. PTL never had the tens of millions of viewers it claimed.[8] Nonetheless, hundreds of thousands of people would be watching The PTL Club at any given moment, and millions tuned in to at least some portion of the program on a weekly basis.

I mentioned earlier that they were at the right place at the right time culturally, geographically, and technologically. When cable restrictions were lifted in 1972, cable systems began to proliferate. It was possible to pipe dozens or even hundreds of channels into homes. The problem, however, was that Christian TV had very little programming ready for primetime.[9] In 1975, the Bakkers jumped into that programming void.

The PTL Club, their television program, quickly landed on a hundred stations. Many of these stations asked for more programming, so *The PTL Club* quickly became The PTL Network, including a satellite system that delivered twenty-four-hours-a-day programming to cable systems around the country.

From the beginning, the Bakkers were not discriminating regarding their programming partners. Indeed, they attributed their early success to their decision not to be a "respecter of persons." They accepted programming and had guests on their program of all religious stripes, provided they were vaguely Christian. During the late seventies, mainstream evangelicals such as Billy Graham appeared on Bakker's program, but so did Pentecostal leaders such as Oral Roberts. Other guests included James Robison and Robert Schuller. These guests brought to the PTL Network the audiences of these preachers. But also appearing on PTL were pop culture stars Little Richard, Mr. T, Colonel Sanders of Kentucky Fried Chicken fame, and Gavin McLeod, who played Captain Stubing on the popular TV program *The Love Boat*.

The money began to pour in almost immediately, first in the millions and then in the tens of millions. The Bakkers struck a chord with America. Today, the daytime talk show is commonplace. If you know even a little about popular American culture, you need little explanation when you hear *Oprah*, *Ellen*, and *The View*. But daytime television in the late sixties and early seventies was dominated by soap operas and game shows.

Jim and Tammy Faye Bakker quickly competed favorably with those few talk show hosts who were on the air then, such as Merv Griffin and Phil Donahue. They had a comfortable and friendly banter, developed in those days they barnstormed churches and youth gatherings, and refined on CBN and TBN. Tammy Faye's hair and makeup were a little outrageous, but Jim would say how beautiful she looked, and viewers got the impression that Tammy Faye looked the way she looked because Jim liked her that way. Besides, her hair and makeup were only slightly amplified versions of the hair and makeup of many of the viewers themselves when they went off to their Pentecostal and Baptist churches on Sunday morning.

For millions of viewers, Jim and Tammy Faye were familiar figures, not unlike young couples they sat in pews with every Sunday. To see them on television, to know that they were speaking to millions, was in a sense a validation of themselves, and people like them.

From 1975, when Jim Bakker was thirty-five years old, until about 1984, the PTL Network appeared to be a model of rapid but regular and orderly growth. As the money poured in, the Bakkers made investments in their facilities, first building a state-of-the-art broadcast facility, and then offices. These facilities increased yet further the capacity of the PTL Network both to raise and spend money.

By 1987, when scandal brought down the Bakkers, PTL claimed to have thirteen million subscribers and assets in excess of one hundred and seventy-five million dollars, including a twenty-three hundred acre Christian theme park called Heritage USA. Heritage USA included a five hundred-room luxury hotel, an amphitheatre for staging outdoor plays, and Billy Graham's childhood home, brought from Charlotte and reconstructed piece by piece.[10]

Many film clips of old PTL shows are online. They show

classic 70s variety show fare. In fact, Jim and Tammy were often compared to Donny and Marie Osmond or even to Sonny and Cher.

Richard Ostling, the long-time religion reporter for *TIME Magazine*, wrote a profile of televangelists called "Power Glory—and Politics" for *TIME* in 1986. He described the Bakkers' affable manner: "Tammy was no great singer, and Jim no penetrating interviewer, but their TV ascent was rapid. Says their avuncular announcer, Henry Harrison: 'They were just a cute little couple that people felt good about watching.' Soon Bakker was giddily expanding religious and charitable works at home and abroad, though shunning politics."[11]

All appeared positive and prosperous, but we now know that PTL operated on the brink of collapse almost from the beginning, both financially and spiritually. The building and buying boom at PTL left the ministry tens of millions in debt by the late 70s. When *The Charlotte Observer* did a story in 1979 that suggested Bakker was diverting funds from a project to help the poor in Africa into the operating account of PTL, the Federal Communications Commission (FCC) investigated.[12]

This investigation, however, actually fueled the fire under Bakker's supporters. Just as Charles Ponzi was able to convince a jury that he was an innocent, beleaguered underdog, Bakker told his viewers that he must be doing something right because the liberal, anti-Christian, mainstream media *and* the federal government were both against him.

During this time, Christian news outlets who might be expected to take an early interest in the Bakkers were nowhere to be found. A small Christian newspaper operated in Charlotte during some of the years the Bakkers were in town, but this paper depended on PTL both for advertising dollars and circulation. In fact, the newspaper was distributed for free in the PTL Hotel.

By the time *WORLD* magazine launched, in 1986, the scandal was already public and PTL beginning to unwind.[13] *Christianity Today* recapped the coverage of others, but offered no original reporting.

I mention the absence of Christian media not to indict them for negligence of duty. I have run enough small media operations to know that such stories are not easy. They require financial, professional, and spiritual resources. But Christian publications knew long before the rest of the world what the Bakkers were up to. They were in the best position to shine a light on them. Would an early story from a Christian media outlet have prevented what followed? Would an investigative story by a Christian outlet aimed at the Christian audience that supported the Bakkers, but which also became the financial victims of the Bakker scandal, have made a difference? We will never know.

What we do know is that the *Observer's* 1979 coverage did not provide a corrective. Far from it. It seemed to contribute to Bakker's isolation and hubris. He told his viewers that it was a "witch-hunt" and they should send him more money in order to "give the devil a black eye."

In 1980, the forty-year-old Bakker—who claimed to be overwhelmed by stress and isolation—had a sexual encounter with twenty-one-year-old Jessica Hahn. Hahn claimed that she was drugged and raped. Bakker maintained that the sex was consensual, but he does not deny the event occurred.

For those of us who call ourselves Christ followers, perhaps the most tragic aspect of Bakker's story is that this obvious moral rottenness and hypocrisy did not bring down the PTL Network. Those closest to Bakker, and thousands of people who worked in the PTL/Heritage USA empire, were willing to overlook what they knew—or not ask questions about what they suspected.

It was not moral outrage, but money, that ultimately brought down the Bakker's PTL empire. At first, the way the ministry handled money might charitably be called eccentric or outrageous, but probably not illegal. The PTL ministry had purchased a three hundred and seventy-five thousand dollar oceanfront condominium and a nine hundred and thirty-five thousand dollar jet aircraft. Bakker purchased a four hundred and forty-nine thousand dollar house in Palm Springs, California, and had spent ninety-three thousand dollars on antique cars—all with bonuses he regularly gave himself. And, of course, there was the infamous air conditioned dog house for Tammy Faye's dog. (A 1981 dollar is worth about three dollars in 2021.)

Court documents made public at the time of PTL's 1987 bankruptcy listed the following expenditures:

- Rental of "a jet plane for a two-week vacation in California at a cost to PTL of $124,000, including the time it sat on the ground idle."
- While on vacation, Bakker bought two Rolls Royces for PTL and his own personal use. Bakker's cost: $58,884; and PTL's cost: $27,438. The cars apparently remained in California and were never brought to Charlotte for use by the ministry. They were apparently meant to be Jim and Tammy Faye's personal vehicles while they were at the Palm Springs home.
- "PTL spent $8,870 decorating Bakker's houseboat; spent approximately $5,900 for a multistory playhouse for the Bakker children, equipped with electricity and heat."

Again, as distasteful as these extravagances were, it is likely that they were not illegal, at least not illegal *prima facie*.[14] And to many, they were not even distasteful. By the early eighties, Bakker and other televangelists were firmly embracing prosperity theology, which said that such extravagances were a sign of God's blessing and anointing. They encouraged their listeners to give in order to get.

Television producer Phil Cooke got his start in the business working for Oral Roberts, as an undergraduate at Oral Roberts University. He has gone on to work for virtually every major television ministry. But in recent years, he has become an outspoken critic of the prosperity gospel movement and those who promote it—especially on television. Cooke is quick to mention greed as a cause for this wrong doing, but—as we discussed—the greed is not just on the part of those preaching it. Cooke also highlights the greed of those who hear the preaching:

> Many TV evangelists are rich because of greed, but not their greed. It's our greed. An earlier generation donated money to help those in need. Growing up, my mother taught us about those "less fortunate" and we gave because the Bible expressed great concern about the poor and suffering. But as I grew up, a concept came along that turned giving on its head. "Seed faith" transformed everything we knew about raising money. The original concept was actually Biblical—based on planting a seed and expecting a harvest.

Cooke believes this biblical idea has been perverted. He echoes Patty Roberts, Oral Roberts' former daughter-in-law, when he says: "Johann Tetzel, the most aggressive of the Dominican friars selling indulgences, had a saying: 'As soon as a coin in the coffer rings, the rescued soul from Purgatory springs.' It doesn't sound that different from today's 'Plant a seed to meet your need.'"[15]

Where Was the Church?

We have already asked: During the PTL scandal, where was Christian media? The unfortunate answer: Mostly absent, or indifferent, or distracted.

But Jim Bakker's transgressions were both theological and financial, so it is also fair to ask: Where was the church was when all of this was taking place?

One of the reasons I spent time in this chapter tracing the growth of Charlotte and of modern evangelicalism was to make this point: Jim Bakker's fraud would not have been possible without the aid, or at least the indifference, of Charlotte's evangelical community.

People who knew better—or should have known better—were either complicit or at least silent when much of Bakker's bad behavior was taking place. The numbers alone support this conclusion. At its peak, around three thousand people worked for the PTL Network or for Heritage USA. Many, if not most, of these people attended evangelical churches in the Charlotte area. It is likely that Bakker's sexual misconduct could have been kept within his tight-knit inner circle. It is even possible that the financial misconduct was kept to a small number of people. Possible, though we must admit, not likely. Hundreds of millions of dollars poured into the ministry. Bakker's organization, by the early 1980s, employed dozens of accounting professionals. They should have seen or at least suspected financial impropriety.

Then there's this: How is it possible that not one of the three thousnd people who worked for Bakker said nothing about the increasingly idiosyncratic theology and practices of the Bakkers? If a single one of these people spoke up about the excesses they must have witnessed, I find no record of it.

Where Was The ECFA?

The Evangelical Council for Financial Accountability (ECFA) has often been cited as an antidote to such situations as the PTL scandal, but the PTL scandal in fact represents a major failure of the ECFA. The PTL Network was an ECFA member when the scandal broke. As we will discover, many of the worst frauds and scandals of recent years were committed by organizations that were members in good standing with the ECFA. In fact, the ECFA was founded in 1979, and most of the televangelist scandals—PTL, Jimmy Swaggart, Robert Tilton—occurred after its founding. Indeed, the ECFA (for all the good it does identifying standards and educating its members) has been and continues to be inadequate to prevent the rise of significant faith-based fraud.

A brief history of the ECFA will help make this and other important points more obvious.

First, we should acknowledge that the purpose of the ECFA is honorable: its goals are to identify and promote fiscal integrity and sound financial practices among its member organizations. These are, of course, perfectly worthy goals. It is also important to note that the ECFA has done an effective job of accomplishing these goals. The ECFA document "Seven Standards For Responsible Stewardship" is a great gift to the nonprofit world. It clearly identifies standards, sets the bar, to which Christian ministries should aspire.

My point is not to say that the ECFA is bad or ineffective in its mission to set standards. My point is simply that the ECFA is a very small part of what we need to insure integrity in the Christian nonprofit sector.

It's interesting, though, that a myth has grown up around the founding of the ECFA. And that myth has done a disservice both to the ECFA and to donors. That myth is that the ECFA is the cure, the antidote, the backstop that prevents this sort of fraud. The more complete truth is that the ECFA was created as an attempt—what turned out to be a successful attempt—to prevent government regulation of the Christian philanthropic world.

In 1977, Congressman Charlie Wilson of Texas introduced legislation that terrified many in the philanthropic world. His legislation would require tax-exempt organizations to disclose financial information "at the point of solicitation." This legislation would have been tremendously burdensome to nonprofits. So burdensome, in fact, that some people speculated that Charlie Wilson was drafting the legislation specifically to limit the activities of Christian ministries.

It was a reasonable conclusion. Though evangelical Christians were credited with helping Democrat Jimmy Carter get elected in 1976, it did not take long for evangelicals to realize that the policies of Carter and the Democrats, especially on the issue of abortion, were not their own. Charlie Wilson was among the first Democrats to realize what was happening, in part because of his own political circumstances.

His circumstances are well-known to anyone who has seen the movie *Charlie Wilson's War*, which starred Tom Hanks, Julia Roberts, and Philip Seymour Hoffman. By 1977, Wilson had already developed a reputation as a drunk and a womanizer and a liberal. Indeed, his nickname was "the liberal from Lufkin." He did not run from this reputation. In fact, he reveled in it, even though his behavior caused endless headaches for his campaign staff.

One telling and typical anecdote: At the beginning of one re-election campaign, he called his beleaguered staff together and promised them that this year things would be different. "No more loose women," he told his staff with a perfectly straight face. "I've found a nice Christian girl. She's a member of the choir. Upstanding in every way. And I'm going to marry her—as soon as she finishes high school."

Wilson was joking, but his threat to regulate the nonprofit industry was no joke. Wilson's politics and lifestyle made him a target of conservative Christian critics, so he knew earlier than most politicians the growing power of the religious right. But Wilson was also a master of parliamentary procedure and a behind-the-scenes political knife fighter, skills developed in part during his twelve years in the Texas legislature before being elected to the US House of Representatives in 1972.

So when Wilson started making efforts to regulate the nonprofit sector, key Christian leaders took those efforts seriously. No matter how outrageous or onerous Wilson's legislation turned out to be, it might pass.

Senator Mark Hatfield knew this. Hatfield was a unique figure during his thirty-year tenure in the US Senate and perhaps a unique figure in the history of the US Congress. He was an outspoken evangelical Christian and solidly pro-life in all debates and votes related to abortion. However, in many other views, he was moderate to liberal. During the nuclear freeze movement of the 1970s, he allied with Senator Edward Kennedy, arguably the Senate's most liberal member. While governor of Oregon (he was elected in 1958 and served two four-year terms before being elected to the US Senate), he was the only governor in the nation to vote against a resolution supporting the Vietnam War at the annual meeting of the National Governor's Association.

So both sides had much ***not*** to like about Hatfield, but both sides also acknowledged that he was smart, politically savvy, and personally a gentle, delightful man.[16]

Hatfield's words therefore had special weight when he warned evangelicals that Charlie Wilson's proposed legislation was a threat that needed to be taken seriously. Hatfield encouraged evangelical leaders to get together and formulate a plan for self-regulation that would prevent Wilson's legislation from gaining traction. To that end, in December of 1977, a group of more than thirty evangelical leaders met, with the Billy Graham Evangelistic Association and World Vision playing key roles. But it took two years for the organization to reach agreement on its mission and charter. The ECFA officially came into being in 1979.

This history is especially significant when you remember what we have already said about PTL. PTL was investigated by both *The Charlotte Observer* and the FCC in 1979, the year of the ECFA's founding. In 1980, the Jessica Hahn affair occurred and in its aftermath, cash payments to her ultimately ran into the hundreds of thousands of dollars.

All of this might have been easy for the ECFA to explain if PTL was not a member, but in fact the PTL Network was one of the ECFA's earliest members. According to Gary Tidwell, whose book *The Anatomy of a Fraud* laid out the financial aspects of the PTL fraud:

> PTL was a member of ECFA from April 1981, until December 1986. However, on April 5, 1984, the ECFA Standards Committee, through ECFA's president, wrote to Jim Bakker that the 1984 renewal membership had been deferred until the ECFA received "accurate, complete and current information." Furthermore, the letter stated, "Because your application of membership renewal for 1984 has not yet been approved, and since the ECFA credentials and ECFA seal remain property of ECFA and may be used only in the event of an organization's good faith compliance with the ECFA standards and the organization's current membership in ECFA, PTL shall not be authorized to use the ECFA seal on any literature, films, correspondence or other fund-raising material." PTL's renewal application with the ECFA was eventually approved on August 20, 1984. [17]

During the short period in 1984—from April to August—when PTL's ECFA membership renewal was in limbo, PTL continued to represent itself as an ECFA member, and the ECFA apparently did nothing to stop it. PTL's accounting firm, Laventhal and Horwath, issued a qualified opinion regarding PTL's finances in both 1985 and 1986. A qualified opinion means that an organization's financial statements do not comply with "generally accepted accounting procedures," or GAAP.

Despite these two years of qualified opinions, PTL remained a member of ECFA almost to the very end, until December 1986. By then, largely because of the nearly one thousand articles written about PTL by the *Charlotte Observer* between 1984 and 1987, the role of the ECFA in providing any oversight or warning to the donor public was virtually inconsequential. Most critics, journalists, and historians who have looked at the PTL scandal say that the role of the ECFA was at best minimal and at worst, by allowing PTL to remain a member for so long, helped the Bakkers and their staff cover up the true extent of the fraud.

Gary Tidwell, in *Anatomy of a Fraud*, wrote: "One can only speculate, as to what might have happened had the ECFA vigorously pursued these matters. At a minimum, ECFA had a chance to prove itself as a viable self-regulating organization and, possibly, the great tragedy that occurred regarding PTL's lifetime partners might have been avoided."[18]

In a Gannett News Service article dated May 1, 1987, the president of ECFA said, "It's obvious we didn't ask enough questions or all the right ones or the answers we got weren't full answers."

In fairness to the ECFA, we must remember that the events described here took place now more than thirty-five years ago. The ECFA says it has made changes to its way of doing business to prevent such problems from recurring. It must also be noted that the ECFA was too in some ways a victim in this scandal. PTL officials either withheld information or attempted to portray that information in the most favorable light imaginable.

That said, the passing of thirty years has failed to remedy two of the most significant limitations of the ECFA. Those limitations are these: it is member supported, and there is no stigma for non-membership.

ECFA is Member Supported.

The ECFA survives on the dues of its members, and the larger the organization, the greater the dues it pays. This relationship between ECFA members and the organization itself creates an inherent conflict of interest. The ECFA has a financial incentive to overlook violations to its own code, because stripping an organization of its ECFA membership deprives the ECFA of needed income.

Of course, the ECFA is not alone in this regard. Many self-policing organizations, such as state bar associations and CPA boards, depend on the dues of their members. However, in these associations, all members pay the same price, and in these associations, the dues are relatively low and the saturation is virtually one hundred percent. In other words, if you want to practice law in Georgia, you must be a member of the Georgia Bar. So the bar has thousands of members. (In fact, in 2015, the Georgia Bar had about forty-five thousand members.) The bar association's financial health does not depend on a few member firms. However, the ECFA's financial health depends heavily on a relatively small number of the largest Christian ministries in the country—and in 1986, PTL was one of those organizations.

No Stigma for Non-Membership.

To practice law, you must be a member of the bar, but you need not be a member of the ECFA

> to operate as a nonprofit, and the overwhelming majority of Christian ministries in the nation are simply not members of the ECFA. The ECFA has about twenty-five hundred members, out of the nearly one million religious nonprofits in the United States, and the overwhelming majority of these are at least nominally Christian organizations. That's a fraction of a percent who are ECFA members. It is true that among the largest Christian organizations, ECFA membership is more common. However, even among that group, it is by no means universal. Of the eight hundred or so ministries listed on the MinistryWatch.com website (which are generally the largest Christian organizations in the country), fewer than half are ECFA members.

In short, the ECFA might yet evolve into the self-regulating organization (SRO) that I introduced in the opening, but it has so far not been able to fill that role, and it did not prevent the PTL scandal, nor many of the scandals that have followed.

The Math Didn't Work

What the ECFA could not accomplish, the *Charlotte Observer*'s Pulitzer Prize-winning reporting did. The articles, written by an investigative team led by Charles Shepard and Mark Ethridge, focused on the centerpiece of Bakker's empire: Heritage USA, a sort of Disneyland for Christians.

The main fundraising tool used by Bakker was a one thousand dollar lifetime membership to Heritage USA. The membership gave buyers a three-night stay at the hotel each year, as well as other benefits. As fundraising plans go, this was not a bad one. Colleges and universities use a similar technique when they make tickets to popular sporting events available first to their large donors. Permanent seat licenses which give their holders early access to ticket purchases at sporting events work in a similar way, as do timeshares. So, once again, we see that what eventually becomes a fraudulent scheme started out as something completely legal and reasonable, only to go badly awry over time.

This train went off the rails when the lifetime memberships were dramatically oversold. Bakker had been clear that only twenty-five thousand lifetime partnerships would be sold in the first hotel (The Grand) and thirty thousand lifetime partnerships would be sold in the second hotel (The Towers).

However, according to court documents, Bakker and others sold 66,683 partnerships in the Grand and 68,755 partnerships in the Towers. Furthermore, of the $66.9 million raised for The Grand, only 52 percent was used for construction expenses. Of the $74.2 million raised for The Towers, only 15.4 percent was used for construction.

The balance of the funds was drawn down almost instantaneously to meet daily operational expenses at PTL, including executive compensation. These facts formed the basis for the charges of wire fraud and mail fraud that ultimately sent Bakker to prison. According to Gary Tidwell, The Grand Hotel was oversold by at least July 7, 1984, and The Towers was oversold in May 1986. On both dates, PTL was a member in good standing of the ECFA.

Reconstructed, But Unregenerate

Amazingly, then and now, some people believe that Bakker got a raw deal. Consider, for example, *WORLD's* May 25, 1987, story that describes a family from Clearwater, Florida, the Spikeleto family, who bought at least four of the timeshares. "We don't have any regrets," said Rudy Spikeleto. In fact, when Jerry Falwell Sr. replaced Bakker as head of PTL, in a too-little-too-late attempt to clean up the mess, the Spikeletos said they were disappointed.

The *WORLD* article goes on: "They just wish Jim Bakker himself could come back, because his record at dealing with crises in the past indicates he could handle this one, too. Even the reports that $92 million is missing do not concern many of those visiting here. They assume Bakker did something appropriate with the money; their trust is eerily total."

Indeed, people such as the Spikeletos did give Bakker a second chance. Today he is in Branson, Missouri, and he has a new wife and a new television program. In January 2008, he moved into a six hundred-acre development called Morningside. It is hard to see the compound in Branson and not think that after all these years, Bakker has finally created in Branson what he tried to create in Fort Mill.[19]

On television he still peddles everything from doomsday prepper food to—in 2020—a solution that regulators say he claimed would cure the COVID-19 virus. But Bakker remains brazenly undeterred, once again. He stopped selling the "Silver Sol Solution" on his program, but he did so only after the FTC and the FDA threatened legal action. He blames "certain government agencies" for his troubles. "While I strongly disagree with the idea that these statements were in context anyway misleading," he told his television audience in March of 2020, "in response to these government agencies, and after prayerful thought, we have suspended offering silver solutions."

He added, "My heart is broken. We know this is an inconvenience to those of you, our partners, who regularly use the Silver Sol Solution. It has tore up a lot of our viewers. I am so heartbroken."

Bakker once again—as he did in the 1980s—painted himself as a heroic figure in a spiritual warfare, committed again to "giving the devil a black eye": "It's just like there is warfare. If there has ever been warfare in this country, it is right now."

Chapter 4

Todd Bentley Takes the Money and Runs

In his arrogance the wicked man hunts down the weak, who are caught in the schemes he devises.... His ways are always prosperous; he is haughty and your laws are far from him... His victims are crushed, they collapse. They fall under his strength.
—Psalm 10: 2, 5, 10

Silence in the face of evil is itself evil: God will not hold us guiltless. Not to speak is to speak. Not to act is to act.
—Dietrich Bonhoeffer

Christopher Fogle, of Cedar Rapids, Iowa, loved to fish. It was a break from his fast-paced, twenty-five-year career with the Perkins Restaurant chain.

But when Fogle got cancer, his relaxing trips to the lake with his children had to end. Not being able to fish with his kids was a devastating blow for the active forty-five year old. But for Todd Bentley, television preacher and self-proclaimed healer, Fogle's story was an opportunity.

Todd Bentley is a self-described faith healer. His so-called

Lakeland Outpouring was a months-long series of healing services in the spring and summer of 2008 that attracted hundreds of thousands of people to a huge tent in Lakeland, Florida. The meetings eventually ended in scandal, with Bentley admitting to an inappropriate relationship with an employee, as well as to alcohol abuse.[1]

But at the height of the revival, I gave Bentley a chance to talk about the healings he claimed were happening in Florida. I asked Bentley, through a spokesperson, for a list of people who had been healed at the services, healings that—if confirmed—would indeed "proclaim the glory of God." I was told when I made my first request that Bentley was out of the country. However, after six weeks and more than a dozen requests, I expected that no list would be forthcoming.[2]

So I was surprised when the ministry eventually sent me a list of thirteen names. Chris Fogle was number twelve on what I came to call "The List," which had not only the person's name, but a brief description of what happened to him. Next to Fogle's name was this note: "Healed through the Outpouring and is back to fishing."

I received the list on August 8, 2008. I used The List—plus search engines and a subscription to a background checking service—to track down the names, to talk with many of them, and to get their side of the story Todd Bentley was sharing with me.

However, when I Googled Chris Fogle's name, I didn't find a phone number. I found an obituary.

Two weeks before I received The List from Todd Bentley, on July 22, 2008, Christopher A. Fogle—according to the Keokuk (Iowa) *Daily Gate City*—"left this life . . . after a courageous battle with cancer."

In fact, a close review of The List I received revealed more problems. Christopher Fogle was not the only person "healed" who is now dead.

Take the story of Phyllis Mills, of Trinity, North Carolina. I called her on April 22, 2009, to hear the testimony of her healing. She did not pick up the phone. Instead, a polite but subdued family member told me, "Phyllis passed away a few days ago." She paused, as if not believing the cruel and ironic timing of my call, an irony I immediately grasped when she said, "In fact, we're on our way to her funeral now."

I apologized for the timing of my call, told her I was sorry for her loss, and quickly got off the phone.

A few days later, when Phyllis Mills' obituary appeared, I discovered that she was sixty-six at the time of her death, had lung cancer, and was undergoing aggressive treatments. This was in direct contradiction to the note on The List, which said she was "healed at the revival." Mills "was taking radiation, but was sent home," according to notes on Bentley's List, with "no trace of cancer in her body."

Another problem with Bentley's List is that some of the healings on it, even if legitimate, didn't happen at Bentley's services. Consider, for example, Gaila Smith, fifty-three at the time I interviewed her in 2009. She lived in Yerington, Nevada. She had breast cancer ten years earlier at forty-three and got a total mastectomy at that time.

But the cancer had spread to her liver. Over the next decade, she endured more rounds of chemotherapy, the latest one ending in December of 2008. She eventually attended a women's conference, where "God touched me," she said.

If she was healed at the women's conference, why had she ended up on Todd Bentley's List? Because she later attended Bentley's meetings in Lakeland. When she was there, Bentley instructed the crowd, "If you have experienced a miraculous healing, come forward."

Smith went forward and told her story. But she ended up on this list that Bentley was claiming credit for. Beside Smith's name was this note: "Healed of breast cancer that had spread to liver. Totally healed in Florida, all scans are now clear."

Not only did the healing not take place at the Outpouring, Smith later admitted to me that the scans are not clear after all.

"The doctors tell me that my numbers are going up," said Smith, who told me that she too had a healing ministry.[3]

In fact, she was one of several people I interviewed from Bentley's List, people Bentley said had been healed at his gatherings, who themselves led healing ministries. By claiming that they were healed at a Bentley rally, it is hard to discount the possibility that they were hoping to bask in Bentley's celebrity.

Further, Gaila Smith held to the notion that she was well even in the face of evidence her cancer was spreading. When I asked her how she could say she was healed even as her doctors were telling her the cancer was spreading, she said, "We don't buy into that. That's a fact, but it's not the truth. The truth is that I've been healed."

In the end, though, reality triumphed over wishful thinking. On May 30, 2012, Gaila Smith died of the cancer of which Todd Bentley claimed she had been "totally healed."

Not all of the healings claimed by Bentley were from life-threatening illnesses. In these cases, the claims of healing are more difficult to prove or disprove.

Take, for example, Leigh Ann Ansley, then forty-three, from Birmingham, Alabama. Bentley's List says she was "healed of severe knee damage from an accident. Has had 4 knee surgeries, but still had pain. Healed in the worship service and even her knee scar is disappearing. Also healed of migraines."

When I contacted her, Ansley confirmed that she had attended the Lakeland Outpouring for about a week, and she confirmed that she did ask for prayer for an old skiing accident. She said that after the prayers, the knee "was not as stiff" as it had been. As for the headaches: "I still have migraines," she admitted. Ansley was one of the few on the List who had not followed Bentley's activities after the Lakeland events. When she learned about subsequent problems with drinking and his divorce and remarriage, she said, "That's not good. In fact, that's pretty bad. I was wondering what happened to him."

Keith Tuplin was one of only two men on The List. Tuplin pastors what he calls a home church in Montego Bay, Jamaica. He had heard of Bentley's fall from ministry, and he said, "It grieved me. Saddened me. What he did is very hard to justify." But Tuplin was steadfast in his belief that God had used Bentley to heal him of flat feet. "I had pain in my feet for many years," he said. In fact, The List said Tuplin, then fifty-seven years old, had suffered through "forty years of flat-footedness." Tuplin said the "pain instantly disappeared" after a "word of wisdom" at one of the Lakeland Outpouring services.

Did his feet change? Could his doctors see any change in them?

"No," Tuplin answered. "I can't see any change in shape. I just feel much better. And I'm not the kind of guy who goes to a doctor much."

After months of phone calls, internet searches, and emails, I was eventually able to get through to twelve of the thirteen names on The List. I could not confirm a single, independently verified example of healing. Where medical evidence was available, as in the cases of Fogle and Smith, the evidence was clear that, in fact, no healing had taken place. In the case of Tuplin and others, the evidence was ambiguous, at best.

And, one presumes, these people were the best examples Bentley and his team could offer.

Regarding Bentley's fall from ministry, Tuplin said, "God uses who He chooses to use. God used Todd to heal me." Nonetheless, Tuplin admitted that he was concerned to see Bentley back in ministry so soon. "What he did is very hard to justify, restoration or not."

Tuplin and Gaila Smith are not the only two who claim to be "healing ministers" themselves.

Gina Weatherby, a personal trainer from San Angelo, Texas, says she was healed from scoliosis, a curvature of the spine. Again, though, it was not at the Lakeland Outpouring, but at a women's conference where Bentley "was ministering" in February 2008. She said that her pain has "gone away." She also said that she now is involved in healing ministry. "I'll just be going along," she said, "and my hands will get hot. I'll pray for whoever is nearby."

How does Weatherby feel about Bentley's fall? "As a minister myself, it makes me very humble. It's a reminder that anyone can get caught up. Especially when God is using you, it's hard not to get caught up in it and believe you're special," she said, with what I took to be unintended irony.

So do these stories prove one way or the other that Todd Bentley is either a healer or a fake? Does it mean anything that less than a year after the conclusion of the Outpouring, two people on a list of just thirteen "healings"—a list provided by the ministry itself—are dead, and a third died just a few years later? Or that the rest of the stories don't stand up to even the most common-sense questions?

Dr. Michael Brown said it does matter. Brown is the author of *Israel's Divine Healer*, considered one of the definitive examinations of how healing takes place in Scripture. He personally believes in supernatural healing, but he also says a healthy skepticism about most healing stories is a sign of wisdom and discernment.

Brown said the fact that this list was presumably the best

Bentley's ministry had to offer is a special cause of concern. "If you're going to make claims of healing on a very public, even international, stage, you'd better have your documentation in place," Brown said.[6] "God can and does heal. But our experiences should not shape our theology. Instead, our theology should be the lens through which we evaluate our experiences. And our theology should be based on Scripture."

Bentley's stage was huge. Supporters claimed hundreds of thousands of people attended the Lakeland Outpouring and hundreds, if not thousands, of people were healed. Many of them remained loyal to Bentley, even as evidence mounted that his healings were not legitimate and the behavior in his personal life disqualified him from ministry.

By now, we know that this kind of blind loyalty is not unusual. We saw the same phenomenon with Ponzi and Bakker and we will see it again in the stories ahead.

We also saw it in Lynn Breidenbach, the spokesperson for Bentley who provided me with The List. Breidenbach was herself the co-pastor of a charismatic church near Lakeland, Florida, and a relentless cheerleader for Bentley throughout most of the Lakeland Outpouring. But a few years after the Lakeland meetings came to an ignominious end, Breidenbach herself died of cancer, at age fifty-seven. Breidenbach had been active in local politics, and she had a spokesperson of her own, Permelia LaLonde. LaLonde said, "We don't regret our time there at all. We saw many miracle signs and wonders. The Lord knew what was going to happen, but he chose Todd anyway. And there are still fires burning all over the world. How can you argue with that?"[7]

Restored, but Unregenerate?

Meanwhile, on March 9, 2009, less than a year after scandal ended the Lakeland Outpouring and Bentley's marriage, Bentley remarried—to a former employee. He moved to Fort Mill, South Carolina, to undergo a restoration process under the direction of charismatic ministry leader Rick Joyner, whose ministry had purchased the old PTL/Heritage USA site.[4]

Bentley's restoration process, under Rick Joyner, lasted less than a year. It is worth pausing a moment here to talk about restoration of fallen Christian leaders. Many of the faith-based frauds we are discussing in this book and many more we are not discussing in detail but whom have been in the public eye (including Ted Haggard, the former pastor of New Life Church and former president of the National Association of Evangelicals) have found a restoration process to be their path back from disgrace to continued ministry.

The idea that God can and does use broken people, even traitors, after He restores them to wholeness is thoroughly biblical. But what is a valid, biblical restoration process, and did Todd Bentley's process qualify?

First of all, it is important to acknowledge that a moral or legal failure should not necessarily or permanently disqualify a person for future Christian ministry. The God of the Bible is a God of forgiveness and restoration. Scripture is full of examples. Moses, David, and Paul were murderers. (To be completely accurate, I should say that Paul was "merely" an accomplice in Stephen's murder.) David was also an adulterer. Jesus himself prescribed a restoration process for the fraudulent tax collector Zaccheaus (Luke 19). Peter denied Jesus three times, but was ultimately restored after a poignant scene in which Peter had to face the man he had betrayed and confess his love to him three times. The list goes on.

In our own time, we have heard the stories of gangbanger Nicky Cruz, Watergate conspirator Chuck Colson, and others. God used them all mightily after they were caught in sin.

So the idea of being restored from a place of disgrace to a

place of fruitful ministry is a biblical one. But what are the necessary and sufficient conditions for restoration? And did Todd Bentley's restoration process under Rick Joyner qualify? Scripture does not outline a formula, but Scripture does provide some guidelines.

True Repentance. The word *repentance* means to "turn from." So a condition for restoration to ministry means that the old, sinful, fraudulent behavior must truly be history. Any minister who repents, even if that repentance is sincere, who puts himself back in a situation similar to the one in which he first fell—as Jim Bakker and Todd Bentley have done—deserves to have the sincerity of his repentance, or at least the quality of his judgment, questioned.

The Passage of Time. One demonstration of repentance is to let time go by with no recurrence of the old behavior. How much time? Again, Scripture gives us no clear guideline. When Moses murdered the Egyptian overseer, he fled Egypt and was in exile for forty years. Saul converted sometime between AD 33-36. It is possible he had as many as fourteen so-called lost years between the date of his conversion and any record of public ministry. Many scholars believe these lost years were not lost at all, but were a part of Paul's discipleship process.

On the other hand, Peter denied Jesus on the night prior to Jesus' crucifixion and was restored to full fellowship with Jesus just days later. However, that restoration was dramatic and heart-rending for Peter, and happened in the presence of Jesus himself. It is fair to say that neither Bentley, Bakker, nor any of the people we discuss in this book offer a similar example.

Recompense. It is possible that one of the reasons that Peter was restored so quickly after his denials was the unique opportunity Peter had to reaffirm his love for Jesus. Jesus asked Peter three times—one time for each of Peter's denials—"Do you love me?"

Peter affirmed his love three times and received from Jesus a specific instruction: "Feed my sheep." When the tax collector Zaccheus turned to Jesus, he said he would restore four-fold the money he had fraudulently taken from others.

Recompense is more complicated when the fraud is spiritual. How can Todd Bentley provide recompense to the families he claimed to heal? These are men, women, and children who were given false hope, whose emotional and spiritual lives were pawns in his quest for money and power. How many of these men and women rejected medical help because Bentley led them to believe that seeking help was a sign of doubt? I don't know the answers to these questions, but common sense tells me that a sincere and public apology and the humility that such an apology requires would be a necessary start.

Accountability. A restoration process must include ongoing accountability. A person who has defrauded the public has demonstrated by the fraud itself that his judgment is flawed. Even someone who is sincerely repentant is suddenly not flawless in his judgments and discernment. It's possible that the spiritual and emotional pathologies that led to the scandal (especially if the sin is a sexual sin) might take years to fully heal. A restoration process should include accountability to others, either a church body or wise individuals who have no other agenda than to restore the fallen person to full fellowship with Christ and His church.

Barriers of Protection. We should also concede that even after a full restoration process, certain areas of ministry might remain permanently off limits to the restored person. It would be folly for even a restored pedophile to be a youth minister. Sincerely repentant and fully restored financial frauds, because of the powerful work God has done in their lives to restore them, might make great speakers who can testify to God's grace and healing, but does it make sense to put them in charge of the church's money? Probably not. Sin has consequences, and even restored sinners should have barriers of protection around them to ensure that they are not tempted by those sins for which they have a demonstrated weakness, not to mention the protection these barriers provide to potential new victims.

Todd Bentley's restoration process exhibited almost none of these qualities. To take just one example: even Rick Joyner admitted that Bentley's remarriage was "wrong and premature." Bentley was out of the pulpit for less than a year. And during his restoration process, Bentley and Joyner put regular video conversations between them on the Internet. Bentley and Joyner followed a process that does not even remotely resemble the one outlined above.

Back On The Platform

Almost immediately after Bentley's fall and "restoration" in 2009 and 2010, he was back on the platform. By late 2010, Bentley had rallies in Texas, Tennessee, Michigan, and Haiti. And from 2010 to present, he has maintained his Fresh Fire Ministries in Fort Mill, South Carolina.

As for accountability: virtually none. His board of directors has only four people: Bentley, his wife Jessica, Rick Joyner—the man who led what many consider Bentley's "restoration" process—and Darryn Belieu, the former worship leader at The Secret Place, the church Bentley served—as of 2020—as pastor.

Because of ongoing irregularities in his ministry, a 2019 panel of charismatic leaders, under the leadership of Dr. Michael Brown, determined that Bentley "is not qualified to serve in leadership or ministry today."

It's not clear if the panel led by Brown will finally have an impact on Todd Bentley's ministry. The statement the panel released on Brown's Facebook page admitted as much:

> Unfortunately, what's missing in the modern church is often the combination of relational and organizational accountability, which would ensure each minister's ability to navigate turbulent emotional, organizational, and spiritual waters. We pray that Todd would find such relational and organizational accountability, and it is our hope that this will become the norm, rather than the exception, for other leaders in the days ahead.

In the meantime, Bentley continues in ministry and he and his colleagues went on the offensive against the Brown-led panel and statement. Michael Fickess, a colleague of Bentley and one of the keynote speakers at his so-called Secret Place Conferences, posted a video saying he "wholeheartedly, unapologetically rejects" the findings of what he calls the "tribune panel." He posted the video on January 2, 2020, and in the first twenty-four hours, it had received more than ten thousand views, indicating that even Bentley's surrogates can still draw a crowd.

If anything brings Bentley into submission, it is likely to be financial restraints rather than spiritual or organizational ones. 2017 is the last year for which financial statements are available for Bentley's Fresh Fire USA ministry. That statement showed Bentley and his wife Jessica combined for an income of $169,327. That would be great money for most American households, but it was a significant pay cut from the Bentleys' prior year of $192,176. To compound the problems, Fresh Fire's expenses exceeded revenue for each of the past three years. The losses now total $84,678. These losses mean the ministry has a negative net worth. Its liabilities now exceed its assets by $48,972.

These financial realities may be why Bentley started a side business in 2019. Long known for his flowing beard, in September he announced a company that promises men products that will up their "beard game." The online company sells beard oils and other beard and skin grooming products.[5]

And those who think Todd Bentley has gotten a dose of humility by recent events should consider the name of his new enterprise: Magnificent Man.

Chapter 5

John Bennett and the Foundation for New Era Philanthropy

"I have betrayed you."
—John J. Bennett

"You may choose to look the other way, but you can never again say you did not know."
—William Wilberforce

The PTL and Todd Bentley scandals we've discussed so far should have been easy to spot for those with even a modicum of spiritual discernment. That was why we took a side trip in the last chapter to discuss prosperity theology. It is often at the theological level, not the financial level, that problems show up first. Financial, sexual, and organizational improprieties are often downstream from theological error.

That's why those chapters won't be our last excursion into the world of prosperity theology. That particular theology is at the root of many of the frauds in this book. In fact, one of the theories of this book is this: ***faith-based fraud is almost always predictable, and bad theology is that predictor.***

Bad theology inevitably, if not immediately, produces bad behavior. Theologians like to talk about orthodoxy (right doctrine, or right beliefs) and orthopraxy (right practice, or right behavior) as if they are different categories, but in some ways they are intimately related. Bad doctrine eventually produces bad behavior, just as bad behavior (Romans 1 teaches us) compels us to jettison sound doctrine.

A shorthand way of saying that is this: Ideas have consequences, and bad ideas have victims.

If these principles are true, then I would reiterate a principle we have already discussed: journalists and watchdog groups that are distinctively Christian can play a particularly important role in helping to keep the church on the path of integrity. That's because a discerning Christian journalist has the ability to spot not only financial or legal improprieties, but also theological ones before they have manifest themselves in bad behavior.

The PTL scandal, we can now see, was a case in point. *The Charlotte Observer* had little interest in Jim Bakker's prosperity theology. They became interested in him only after his theology began to manifest itself in financial and legal improprieties. But, as we asked earlier, what might have happened if a Christian journalist had investigated Bakker first? If someone who knew Bakker's theology wasn't in the main stream of Christianity had paid attention, might it have provided a corrective?

It's hard to know. Evangelical Christianity is in a melancholy state, as is Christian journalism. Christian whistleblowers and the journalists who tell their stories are rarely celebrated. More often they are branded as troublemakers.

But, assuming such people existed then, it is also possible that such an investigation, done early and in a responsible, professional manner, might have averted one of the great religious and financial scandals in American history, a scandal that contributed materially to the erosion in confidence of the evangelical church, including its ideas, its institutions, and its leaders.

Then again, maybe not. For it is also true that we are all flawed human beings, subject to the reality of original sin. As an old hymn that we (alas) no longer sing much in the contemporary evangelical church powerfully observes: "Prone to wander, Lord I feel it. Prone to leave the God I love." Even those who have sound theology are not immune from the temptations of the world, the flesh, and the devil.

That is why transparency and accountability are two other important themes of this book. And that brings us to the next scandal. One that has a very different character from the PTL debacle.

Something New Under the Sun?

It's hard to imagine a person more different from Jim and Tammy Faye Bakker, or Todd Bentley, than John G. Bennett Jr.

Faith-based frauds like Bakker, Bentley, and others in this book are flamboyant and seem to come alive in the spotlight. That, indeed, was also Charles Ponzi's modus operandi.

Bennett, on the other hand, was the quintessential behind-the-scenes player. He was friendly and outgoing, but serious, a successful businessman. He lived an affluent lifestyle, but not a flamboyant one. He was active in his local church and counted evangelical leaders such as Tony Campolo and Dr. Jack Templeton, son of legendary investor Sir John Templeton, among his friends.

But the Foundation for New Era Philanthropy, Bennett's brainchild, was a Ponzi scheme that operated for six years, from 1989 until 1995. It victimized some of the most respected institutions in evangelical Christianity. In fact, it seems that one of John Bennett's motivations was not so much money, but influence, a chance to be in the "inner circle" among evangelicalism's elite. The New Era scandal survived for so long in part because it was the opposite of the PTL scandal. In fact, even its very name—New

Era—seemed to signal that what it was doing was not going to be business as usual.

In essence, the New Era scheme worked like this: John G. Bennett Jr., a prominent Christian businessman, told his friends, Christian donors, they should give money to the Foundation for New Era Philanthropy rather than to their favorite charities. Why should they do so? Because the money would be matched after three months and New Era would then make the contribution to the charity, only the contribution would be doubled.

How could Bennett and New Era do this? Bennett claimed to have anonymous benefactors who were matching the money. This process allowed these anonymous benefactors to give away large sums of money and maintain their anonymity. And it allowed the smaller donors to double the gifts they wanted to make to ministries they loved.

Bennett started New Era in 1989 by asking his friends to give him relatively small amounts of money that they had already planned to give to charity. He basically said, "Why give your favorite charity five thousand dollars today when you can give them ten thousand dollars in three months?" Bennett was affable and forthcoming when confronted with questions. The most obvious question: How could he double the money in three months? His answer was clear and direct: The anonymous donor.

But other questions remained. Why didn't the anonymous donor just give away his money anonymously, perhaps using Bennett as an intermediary to ensure his anonymity? The answer to that question, Bennett said, is that the matching funds scenario was more strategic, more leveraged, for the anonymous investor. Charities too often come to depend on big "sugar daddies." This strategy insures that the anonymous donor never gives more than half of a large gift. That's good for the organization. It forces the organization to continue to work to develop its base of donors.

Another question: Why does Bennett and New Era need to hold the money for three months before distributing it to the charity? The answer to that question too was straightforward and sensible. When you give away large chunks of money, you need to do due diligence. Is the charity legitimate? Do they have all their paperwork in place? Are their government filings up to date? The recipient organization must, in essence, be approved to receive the money. The requirements were not onerous, but they were necessary, Bennett said. Holding on to the donor money for three months allows that process to be completed. It is sort of like earnest money in a real estate transaction.

Another matter vital to donors was what happens when the anonymous donor's money runs out. This question was the one on which Bennett was the most vague. He said he had more than one anonymous donor. How many? That answer changed over time. The story that seemed to last the longest: nine donors. Bennett explained the changing story by saying that other anonymous investors heard about the original few and wanted to be a part of this process.

And, of course, there was this obvious implication: It was possible the money would run out. Get it while the getting was good.

In 1989, Bennett convinced a number of donors to give him relatively small amounts of five thousand dollars, in most cases. In January of 1990, Bennett made the promised payouts. Both the donors and the recipient organizations were delighted.

What Bennett didn't tell anyone is that Bennett himself was the anonymous donor. Until then, Bennett had made his living as a consultant, and he had been a successful businessman and a generous giver himself. On this occasion, he simply channeled his personal giving through New Era. This gift, in January 1990, appears to be the last legitimate transaction the Foundation for

New Era Philanthropy made.

This is a key point. In fact, it is one of the aspects of the New Era scheme that is most interesting from a psychological point of view. Bennett never had an anonymous donor, so this was fraud from the very beginning. But, interestingly, anonymous donors did, in fact, come forward, even in the early stages of the scheme. In other words, Bennett's idea of allowing anonymous donors to match the gifts of others actually had some merit. It might have worked. William Simon, the former secretary of the treasury, whose net worth at the time of his death was about five hundred million dollars,[1] asked to be one of the anonymous donors, but Bennett never responded.

Why? The most obvious explanation is that Bennett intended to commit fraud from the very beginning. He had no intention of turning New Era into a legitimate business or philanthropic operation. Bennett may have feared the anonymous investors would want more control or disclosure than Bennett was willing to offer.

Whatever the reason, these initial transactions in 1990 were the beginning of a fraudulent scheme that went on for five years, longer than most schemes of this type. When these first few donors saw that the plan actually worked, or at least from their perspective appeared to work, they were anxious to tell their friends. Some of them were quick to "double down" themselves, giving yet more money to New Era. Just as in Charles Ponzi's original scheme, the money began to flow.

The Foundation for New Era Philanthropy nonetheless remained relatively small until 1993, when donors to the Philadelphia Academy of Natural Sciences gave two hundred and fifty thousand dollars to New Era, which New Era then matched. Donations of this size do not go unnoticed, even in a large and moneyed city such as Philadelphia. Soon the Philadelphia

Public Library, the Philadelphia Orchestra, and the University of Pennsylvania joined the program.

It is important to remember that New Era was a classic affinity fraud. That is, the victims had either a direct affiliation with Bennett, or they were separated by no more than one or two degrees. In the early days, that meant that most of the organizations involved with New Era were from the Philadelphia area, Bennett's home town.

And Bennett was also an evangelical Christian. As the word got out about what Bennett was doing, and as people saw its apparent success, others wanted in. The list of ministries involved with New Era began to read like a who's who of evangelical organizations. Eventually, more than one hundred and eighty evangelical groups became involved, including many Christian colleges. Among the organizations involved with The Foundation for New Era Philanthropy were Wheaton College, The Biblical Theological Seminary, CB International, Covenant College, John Brown University, and International Missions, to name just a few.

From New Era's beginning in 1989 until the quarter-million-dollar gift to the Philadelphia Academy of Natural Sciences in 1993, all seemed to be going pretty well with New Era. But the Philadelphia Academy, and the attention that gift attracted, dramatically increased New Era's appetite for cash. For a while, Bennett was able to keep up by increasing the minimum donation qualifying for a match from five thousand dollars to twenty-five thousand dollars. This change allowed him to match the earlier, smaller gifts with newer and larger gifts.

But eventually all the small matches cycled through New Era, and he faced the prospect of now having to match these newer, larger gifts. Bennett met this challenge in several ways. First, he lengthened the waiting period between donation to New Era and the time the gift was matched and distributed. The waiting period went from three months to six months to nine months to ten months. By the time he made these changes, so many donors had seen their gifts matched, and so many organizations had received money, that no one questioned the process. Everyone was benefiting, or so it seemed.

But it wasn't enough. That's when Bennett took another page from Charles Ponzi's playbook. He created a sales force, offering representatives ten percent of the money they raised. However, when he did this, Bennett stepped over a bright ethical line. The Association of Fundraising Professionals has long said it is unethical to offer fundraisers commissions or bonuses. This development was a major turning point in the Foundation for New Era Philanthropy's journey.[2]

But it was easy to see why Bennett didn't have trouble finding sales reps or raising a lot of money. The sales rep had a fairly easy pitch to a potential donor: give to New Era Philanthropy and they'll double your gift to the ministry you love. The result of this pitch, and this sales commission scheme, is that the sales representatives sometimes came from the ranks of the very donors and organizations who were unknowingly participating in the scam. But these sales reps—the former development officers of the ministries receiving the doubled gifts—brought their donor lists with them, and for a while, they kept the money flowing into New Era.

A Surreal Twist

Bennett developed a third way to keep the scam going, and this development caused New Era to take a surreal turn.

Remember, from 1989 until 1993, New Era had been matching (rather, claiming to match) donor gifts with the funds of the anonymous donor. And while that claim was completely fraudulent, it at least had the effect of motivating donors to give.

As New Era grew, its appetite for cash grew. Delaying payments and recruiting sales people brought short-term relief, but only compounded the long-term problem. Bennett was looking at a growing mountain of liabilities. He needed much more new cash than his sales people could generate from individual donors, even very wealthy donors.

Bennett solved this problem, at least temporarily, by allowing organizations to donate to themselves, often out of their endowment funds. This practice was highly irregular, and it should have caused at least some of the Christian organizations to ask questions. Christian organizations could see and appreciate the logic of the original scheme. The original scheme allowed relatively small donors to leverage their money with the resources of the anonymous megadonor. And the megadonor in effect used the smaller donors, in effect, to do due diligence on the ministries. It was an unusual scheme, even an unlikely scheme, but John Bennett knew that it would appeal to the evangelical mind. And he was right.

But allowing the organizations to donate to themselves dramatically undercut the benefits of the original plan. Indeed, it undercut the very ethos of the original scheme. Why would the anonymous donor match funds that the charity already had? What was the good of that?

But by this time, 1993, New Era had been operating for several years. Many wealthy Christian people, and others who were not so wealthy but who were in influential positions with Christian organizations, had seen New Era work. By now, New Era had all the trappings of an established and reputable organization, including fancy offices and glowing testimonials from respected evangelical leaders. Remember our discussion from the introduction: Frauds require trust, and trust can either be *earned* or *imputed*. Bennett had managed to create both.

So no one asked questions. Whatever skepticism the leaders of Christian organizations may have had—indeed, should have had—was buried under the lure of easy money. Once again, as was the case with Ponzi and Bakker, ***it was not just the greed of the frauds that allowed the schemes to continue, but the greed of the Christian leaders themselves.*** Or perhaps it was fear—the fear of being left out of a scheme from which so many of their peers were benefiting.

Given these circumstances, it is not hard to see why some of the smartest folk in the Christian world got sucked into the New Era scandal. The plan seemed elegant, even leading edge. And at least up until 1993, Bennett had not sought publicity, had gotten both new donors and new recipients completely by word of mouth, and made some donors feel that they were on the inside of something new and important. That created a sense of urgency to act before others diluted the effectiveness of the idea.

But all of these qualities aroused the suspicion of one Albert Meyer. He was a part-time professor at Michigan's Spring Arbor College, working in the financial office to make ends meet. Meyer took one look at the Foundation for New Era Philanthropy and recognized it as a classic Ponzi scheme.

But would anyone listen?

Albert Meyer Stands Alone

Neither Spring Arbor College nor John Bennett knew what they were getting into when they ran into Albert Meyer.

Albert Meyer was a young South African accountant. He had earned his stripes in the accounting profession with the South African branch of the global firm Deloitte & Touche. But Meyer wanted to come to the United States, so he came to Spring Arbor College to help build the school's accounting department. Because young professors at small Christian colleges are not at the top of the pay scale, Meyer earned extra money by working in the college's business office.

When Meyer worked for clients of Deloitte & Touche, Deloitte billed those clients about one hundred dollars an hour for his time, but at Spring Arbor, "I was making about nine dollars an hour," Meyer said. "And I was glad to have it. I needed the money."[3]

Meyer was doing fairly routine work, primarily bank reconciliation. In other words, he made sure that the accounting records of the college agreed with the statements coming from the bank. Reconciling a bank statement is tedious, exacting work, which requires checking off hundreds or even thousands of items.

Every business is different, but in most businesses, you'll see the same kinds of transactions over and over again, in more or less the same amounts. Accountants are trained to pay special attention to the anomalies.

That's why one transaction stuck out to Albert Meyer. It was a wire transfer to the Heritage of Value Foundation for $296,000. "Why are we sending a wire transfer to this foundation?" Meyer asked himself. "What was the urgency that required a transfer?"

Meyer said he asked himself these questions, but he was "reticent to ask others. I was a foreigner then. I didn't know how my questions would be received. After all, I was just reconciling the bank statement."

But the wire transfer and what his response should be gnawed at him. In these days before online search engines, Meyer had to go to the college's library to satisfy his curiosity. In Spring Arbor's library, he found a directory of foundations. The listing with the closest match was the Heritage Foundation, a large Washington, DC, thinktank that is well-known and respected among conservatives. But he found no Heritage of Value Foundation.

"It occurred to me that someone might be trying to get us to confuse the two or to believe there might be a relationship between the two," Meyer said.

So he dug further. It turns out that the Heritage of Value Foundation wasn't even an organization. It was a DBA, short for "doing business as." DBAs are common in business and can save time and money. If I own Smith's Tire Repair Shop, I might also register a DBA "Smith's Tire Repair" or "Smith's Repair Shop" so I can deposit checks from busy customers who might not get my name exactly right.

So who owned the DBA for Heritage of Value Foundation?

Meyer called the editor of the directory. It turned out that the Heritage of Value Foundation was a DBA for John Bennett's Foundation for New Era Philanthropy.

The editor had also found that listing strange, so he contacted Bennett and had lunch with him. The editor then told Meyer, "Bennett doesn't want the publicity. He keeps his cards very close to the vest."

Meyer, as an accounting professor, knew well the history of Ponzi schemes. When he learned about the secrecy of New Era and Bennett's disdain for publicity, he said, "That was a massive red flag. Publicity is what killed Ponzi." Indeed, as we have seen, publicity or, more precisely, scrutiny by journalists and subsequently by the public, has again and again proven its value in rooting out fraud.

Had John Bennett studied the frauds of the past? Was he taking steps to avoid being caught?

Perhaps, but maybe this case was different. On the one hand, Meyer could appreciate any individual or organization that does good work without attempting to get a lot of glory. When it comes to charity, the Bible teaches, "Don't let your right hand know what your left hand is doing." (Matthew 6:3)

On the other hand, bad guys also often avoid publicity and the scrutiny it brings.

All of this added up to a situation in which Meyer knew he had to act. "If you were a chemistry professor and you saw the maintenance department using a banned chemical to clean graffiti, you can't say nothing. You can't say, 'That's not my responsibility.' You have to speak up."

So he did. Meyer went to his boss at Spring Arbor College. He at first asked basic questions about the organization. His boss showed Meyer marketing material from the Foundation for New Era Philanthropy, including the suggestion of an anonymous donor.

She added, "We think the anonymous donor is John Templeton." Templeton, Meyer knew, was one of the richest men in the world. He was a legendary investor and philanthropist known for funding Christian causes and institutions. "Sir John" had religious views that might be called eclectic.[4] But his son, Jack, was an evangelical Christian and a friend of John Bennett.

Meyer was told, "We apply for the grant. Bennett invests the money in safe government bonds, and the return pays his overhead." Bennett then returns the money, matched by the money from the anonymous donor.

Doing The Math

If the original situation smelled fishy to Meyer, these explanations smelled even fishier.

"I asked why we had to send Bennett the money," Meyer said. "Why not just put it in an escrow account?" An escrow account is an account over which an independent third party has responsibility. For example, when you purchase a home, you must often bring money with your offer to buy. That money is called "earnest money." It tells the seller that your offer is serious, or in earnest. That earnest money goes into an escrow account—a special account until the sale of the house is complete. Escrow accounts are, in other words, common financial tools, and the money could as easily have been held, and invested in safe financial instruments, from an escrow account as from Bennett's accounts.[5]

Meyer was also puzzled by the explanation of the scheme itself: that the money was invested in "safe government bonds." Government bonds are safe, but because they are safe, they pay low interest rates, and the short-term bonds that Bennett would have to be investing in would pay particularly low rates, probably less than five percent. Meyer calculated the interest at five percent on the $296,000 he had seen when he was doing the bank reconciliation. That's less than fifteen thousand dollars per year. And Bennett said he would hold the money for only ninety days. The interest generated would be less than four thousand dollars.

Meyer had been told that this interest income was what supported the operations of New Era. But Meyer could easily see that this was not enough to support an organization. The only way to support an organization the size New Era had become would be to have hundreds of millions of dollars under management.

But if New Era was doing what Bennett said it was doing, the money should be going out about as fast as it was coming in. At any given moment, very little money actually earned interest. If Bennett was really paying back the original investment in just ninety days, or even in six months, there would simply not be enough investment capital at New Era at any one time to throw off enough cash to pay for the overhead.

So Meyer went back to Spring Arbor's controller with his suspicions. "I didn't say, 'This sounds like a Ponzi scheme,'" Meyer said. "But I did suggest that things did not make sense."

The controller heard Meyer's concerns and did not disagree with them, but she said the transaction had been approved by the board of directors of the college. So Meyer wrote to the board chairman, who wasn't convinced by Meyer's arguments, but he was sufficiently troubled that he said, "We're going to see Mr. Bennett."

A True New Era?

One reason it was not easy for Meyer to get anyone's attention about his concerns over New Era was because, at least for a fairly long while, it truly looked as if the Foundation for New Era Philanthropy might really be ushering in, well, a new era in philanthropy.

After all, the early investors got their money back with the promised returns. And it was the 1990s, a decade in which the gross domestic product of the United States grew by fifty percent. Massive fortunes were being made in technology and other arenas. Bill Gates started the Gates Foundation in 1994 with two billion dollars. In 1993, George Soros founded the Open Society Foundation, which has since given away eleven billion dollars. The notion that John Bennett had an anonymous billionaire behind him was plausible. It is also important to note that the investors in the New Era scheme were careful, circumspect people. The people and organizations who made up the evangelical movement were neither the Pentecostal firebrands from which Bakker and Bentley came nor the mainline Christianity of the established denominations, so named because in the eighteenth and nineteenth centuries, they were the churches on the "main line" of the trolleys or streetcars of such cities as Boston and Philadelphia.

Twentieth century evangelicalism was in some ways a middle path between these two streams. In the early days of the evangelical movement, especially in the post-World War II era, evangelical organizations were young, entrepreneurial, and—at least some of them—highly successful. Parachurch organizations such as Focus on the Family, Young Life, Campus Crusade for Christ, and others became hundred million-dollar organizations. World Vision and Compassion International are now one billion-dollar organizations.

The 1970s and 80s saw the rise of the megachurch, churches

with more than two thousand in regular weekly attendance. In fact, in 1970, the US had only about a dozen protestant megachurches. By 2020, the country had more than three thousand such churches.

The evangelical movement did not have the same degree of institutional infrastructure as the mainline church, but that infrastructure, at least informally, was growing. And many of the people in the movement knew each other. These were the people and the institutions John Bennett targeted.

That's one reason Albert Meyer took his concerns to the Evangelical Council for Financial Accountability.

The ECFA has grown to about twenty-four hundred members, but in 1995, it had only about five hundred members. Nonetheless, Albert Meyer thought it could help, thought it *should* help.

"They are supposed to be a watchdog," Meyer said. Indeed, more than fifteen years later, when I interviewed him for this book, Meyer remains particularly critical about the ECFA's role in the scandal. "They were caught with their pants down," he said. (The ECFA maintains that it is not a watchdog group, but an "accreditation agency" that promotes "financial integrity.")

Meanwhile, the more Meyer looked into New Era, the more he became convinced it was a fraud, and exposing the fraud became almost an obsession. He wrote to the SEC, the American Institute of Certified Public Accountants, the IRS, and the *Philadelphia Inquirer*, which had started doing positive articles about Bennett and New Era. Meyer wanted the *Inquirer* to know the whole story.

"They all blew me off," he said.

Meanwhile, what Meyer had suspected was rapidly coming to pass. If "publicity killed Ponzi," as Meyer had said, it was also killing John Bennett and New Era. After the two hundred and fifty thousand dollar matching gift to the Philadelphia Academy of Natural Sciences, New Era got increased attention. Other organizations became interested in investing, but the scrutiny also increased. Some investors wanted to see evidence that Bennett was investing in government bonds. So Bennett showed them bonds. What he didn't say was that he was showing the same bonds to everyone.

Meyer still didn't understand why Spring Arbor College had sent the money to the Heritage of Value Foundation, so he asked to see evidence that the money was being held. Officials at New Era told him that Prudential Securities held all the money.

"I called Prudential Securities," Meyer said. "They had never heard of the Heritage of Value Foundation." Meyer learned that the Kenosha, Wisconsin, office of the firm was the home of all of New Era's accounts. This was another red flag for Meyer. Why would a small local office be responsible for hundreds of millions of dollars? It just didn't make sense.

One thing that did make sense, given the perverse logic of Ponzi schemes, was that during this time (1993 to 1995), Bennett was going on something of a spending binge. What was once a small, word-of-mouth operation had become a marketing machine. Bennett's sales team got not only (unethical) commissions, but also expensive, glossy marketing materials. With his sales staff flying around the country, Bennett bought a stake in a travel agency. All New Era travel flowed through the travel agency, and the profits from the travel agency went to Bennett himself.

New Era, meanwhile, was sinking more deeply into debt. A growing staff at his Radnor, Pennsylvania, office processed incoming money, but little money was being paid out. The activity there grew to a near frenzy—a late-twentieth century version of Charles Ponzi's Boston operations.

All this time, Meyer kept making phone calls, asking questions, and often facing discouragement. After Spring Arbor College made its first investment and was repaid with a matching gift a few months later, a member of Spring Arbor's staff literally waved the check in Meyer's face, as if to say "I told you so."

Meyer eventually discovered that Wheaton College had a copy of New Era's financial statements. The financial statements were obviously incorrect. All the people and organizations who gave money were listed, but according to Meyer, "there should have been millions or even tens of millions of dollars in liabilities" on the financial statements.

Months turned into years, but Meyer's persistence eventually paid off. One of the reporters Meyer had called when he started uncovering problems with New Era was Steve Stecklow of the *Wall Street Journal*. By 1995, New Era was beginning to unravel, and Meyer would feed Stecklow each new development. Stecklow did a meticulous job of reporting the problems at New Era, in part by following the trail that Meyer had blazed.

As a final step in the reporting process, Stecklow visited the offices of New Era on May 10, 1995. "When Steve got to Bennett's office," Meyer said, "there was pandemonium."

That was a Wednesday. The following Monday, May 15, 1995, Stecklow and *The Wall Street Journal* published the first of what would be a series of articles critical of the Foundation for New Era Philanthropy.[6]

That same week, Albert Meyer received his vindication. In quick succession, the Foundation for New Era Philanthropy was sued for forty-four million dollars for a loan it had failed to repay to Prudential Securities, and then it filed for Chapter 11 bankruptcy protection. The filing documents said that New Era had assets worth about eighty million dollars, but liabilities in excess of five hundred and fifty million dollars. The liabilities that Meyer had been saying all along should have been on the financial statements were finally disclosed.

The ECFA quick ly realized that the New Era scandal was

particularly troubling for the evangelical community. Many of the organizations involved were either ECFA members or organizations that were a part of the evangelical movement. After the scandal came to light, the ECFA stepped in to help member organizations reclaim their money. The ECFA asserts that ninety percent of all moneys were returned to their original investors.

But Albert Meyer said, "That's completely wrong. First of all, nowhere near ninety percent was recovered. Secondly, why should the ECFA take credit for that? That money was stolen property. It had to be returned with or without the ECFA. The ECFA was embarrassed that they did not take early warning signs more seriously and tried to deflect attention from that mistake."

That said, it is true that the ECFA did attempt to facilitate the return of money to the original donors, and it is true that a significant portion of the money did get returned. But if anyone deserves credit for this, the credit should go to leaders such as Hans Finzel.

Finzel was the president of a Colorado-based ministry called WorldVenture, which does relief work in the poorest sections of the world. Finzel was newly appointed to that job when he first heard about New Era. "It looked like an exclusive club that I might be able to join," Finzel said.[7]

Finzel asked around and heard nothing but praise for New Era. Other evangelical leaders called Bennett a visionary who had created a new kind of philanthropy. According to the *Wall Street Journal's* Stecklow, Bennett "claimed he was giving away more money than the Rockefellers, and for a time that was true."

So Finzel and many other organizations were sucked in, from "tens of thousands to hundreds of thousands to millions," Finzel said. "We had grown to depend on this money."

Finzel learned about *The Wall Street Journal* story over the weekend, before it broke on Monday morning. "At first I didn't believe it," he said. "But then I read the story. It was one of the most disappointing days of my life. My biggest emotion was embarrassment."

Finzel realized immediately that the money WorldVenture had received "was dirty money." Finzel also thought that he would probably lose his job. "I was new. I figured this would be enough to do me in," he said. "So in a way it didn't take any courage to do the right thing. I figured I had lost everything anyway."

To Finzel, the right thing was for WorldVenture to pay back to the original donors the millions of dollars it had received from New Era. And though it took years, WorldVenture did just that.

Finzel's board stood by him. He continued in his role as president for more than fifteen years, retiring as one of the elder statesmen of the evangelical movement. He now teaches leadership to others. When he left WorldVenture, it had an annual budget of more than twenty-five million dollars, and was thriving.

The Psychology of Wealth

If you look only at the courageous behavior of men like Albert Meyer and Hans Finzel, it would be easy to think this is a "feel-good" story in which all ended well. But that is not the case. Tens of millions of dollars vaporized in wasteful spending and abuse. One factor in the loss of money was the increasingly opulent lifestyle of Bennett himself. In filings from the subsequent lawsuits, it became apparent that Bennett took at least eight million dollars for himself.

It is also important to remember that while Finzel and some other organizations stepped up and did the right thing, many of the organizations returned only that money that they hadn't yet spent.

That's why Albert Meyer and the ECFA have very different views of how much money was returned. The ECFA has maintained through the years that it helped repatriate as much as ninety percent of the money to its original owners. Albert Meyer scoffs at this idea. He says that it might be possible that ninety percent *of the money that had not been spent* was repatriated. But many organizations had already spent the money and were simply unable, or refused, to follow the high road of Finzel and WorldVenture. Also, Meyer further derided the notion that the ECFA facilitated the repatriation of funds. Meyer said, "The law required the money to be returned."

In the end, however, and for whatever reasons, of the $354 million that ended up being paid in to New Era, about $135 million was never returned to its original owners.[8]

In some ways, the biggest tragedy of the scandal surrounding the Foundation for New Era Philanthropy was that there really was the seed of a great idea in it. Bennett knew that from a purely statistical point of view, rich people are generally well educated, hard working, and risk averse.[9] The American legend is seasoned with stories of the wildcatter, the go-for-broke, bet-the-farm, risk-taking entrepreneur. And there are a few of those, to be sure. But the overwhelming majority of millionaires in America made their money themselves over a fairly long period of time—ten to forty years. They accumulated their money as a result of hard work and thrift. They are not showy people.

And when it comes to their giving habits, they are especially not showy. Previously, I mentioned Arthur Brooks' *Who Really Cares?* That book provides the statistical data for this conclusion: A direct relationship exists between a theologically conservative Christian faith and charitable giving, and most of the giving is done "below the radar."[10]

The Bible says that when we give we are not to let the left hand know what the right hand is doing (Matthew 6:3). So when Bennett told potential donors to the Foundation for New Era

Philanthropy that the funds were being matched by an anonymous donor, they found this story plausible. Indeed, many of them found the entire system not merely plausible, but virtuous. They admired the über-wealthy anonymous donor for avoiding the limelight, and they welcomed the opportunity to invest their own relatively small sums alongside him. So in an ironic but very real sense, Bennett used the theological sophistication of his victims against them.

Bennett's behavior raises an interesting question: Did he start out to defraud his donors and the recipient organizations, or did he start out with good intentions and things simply got out of control?

When Bennett's case eventually came to trial in 1997, Bennett's lawyer, Gregory P. Miller, argued the latter. Bennett was on a "mission from God to change the world," Miller told the court. "He was not motivated by greed, but by an unchecked religious fervor." Miller also said that a 1984 automobile accident had left Bennett brain damaged.

But Richard Goldberg, the US attorney who prosecuted the case, said this defense was nonsense. He called the defense "worthless in theory" and "untrue for Mr. Bennett" in particular, especially the part about brain damage. Tests Bennett took after the accident showed "no brain damage at all." Miller ultimately withdrew this questionable line of defense, and a plea bargain was struck. Bennett went to jail later that year, on September 22, 1997, for what was—at the time—the biggest charity fraud in history. He was sentenced to twelve years, and he spent ten of them at Fort Dix Federal Correctional Institute before being released to a halfway house on September 11, 2007. He remained there until March 2008, when he was released. Bennett refused repeated requests to be interviewed for this book, saying he was writing a book of his own about the experience.

So did Bennett intend to commit fraud? Some people who have looked closely at the case say no. "I'm not sure Bennett set out to commit a fraud," attorney Seth Perlman said. "I think the situation got away from him. These things aren't necessarily set up to defraud charities or the public, but the philanthropic community is about power and reputation . . . not so much about money. And that's very enticing."[11]

Interestingly, the ECFA helped lead an effort to rehabilitate Bennett's reputation.

"The community that he hurt on this thing has come back and petitioned President Clinton and President Bush to pardon him," ECFA President Paul Nelson told the *NonProfit Times* in 2005, adding that he had personally sent a letter on behalf of Bennett. "Many caught in this thing have come back and said the man has paid his price. He's no longer a threat."[12] Of course, the ECFA had egg on its face as a result of the scandal, so it makes some sense that it would promote a narrative that concluded "all's well that ends well."

Albert Meyer, however, was not convinced. "This was a Ponzi scheme from the beginning."

And, indeed, it's hard to argue against Meyer. It's now obvious that he never had an anonymous investor, so that was a lie from the very beginning. And when anonymous donors came forward, such as William Simon, who wanted to participate as anonymous donors, Bennett never responded. Now we know a possible reason why. If Bennett had let Simon or anyone else into the inner circle of his dealings, his cover would have been blown almost instantly.

On the other hand, if Bennett had been aggressive at recruiting Simon and other anonymous donors, it's possible that New Era might have succeeded legitimately. But that is a possibility now lost to history.

Bennett's own lavish lifestyle suggests motive for the fraud.

Jerri Williams, an FBI investigator who helped build the case against Bennett, suggested another motive: "What he got out of this was power. He got access to top people in a world [in which] he cared about being seen as a top person himself."[13]

Lessons from New Era

A key lesson here is not complicated, and one we have heard before and will hear again: If it is too good to be true, it probably is.

Another key lesson is also one that is a theme of this book: Donors and ministry leaders should insist on transparency.

A third lesson is related to the first two: Ask tough questions. A credible person or organization will welcome the tough questions because tough questions give credible people an opportunity to demonstrate that very credibility.

WorldVenture's Finzel says now that his failure to get answers to tough questions was the key to his organization getting sucked in. "We asked questions like 'Who are the anonymous donors?' but we were told the money would stop coming if we looked into who they were," Finzel said. He now knows that this lack of transparency should have been a red flag.

At the risk of making an obviously self-interested statement, we should reiterate yet another lesson: Hard-nosed investigative journalism played a key role in exposing this fraud. Christian media should have had the inside track on this scandal and could have reported on New Era long before the *Wall Street Journal* and the *Philadelphia Inquirer* found this story. As it was, by the time this story spilled out of the Christian community and made its way into the mainstream media, the fraud was already massive and the damage was already great.

Another lesson worth mentioning here is that a lust for

power sometimes takes the form of being one of those "on the inside" or "in the know." This desire can be just as seductive and destructive as the lust for money or sex. This lust for insider status appears to be the primary motivator both for Bennett and for many of those who ultimately became victims of his fraud.

Because so many of the early participants received large paydays, they were reluctant to ask too many questions. The role of Albert Meyer is particularly important. And that brings us to another lesson: ***one person can make a difference.***

In fact, it would not be an overstatement to say that what was at the time considered the largest religious and financial scandal in American history was brought to light by the persistence of a part-time accounting professor who relentlessly asked a few key questions. And those questions amount to little more than "where did the money come from?" and "where did it go?"

Such questions reflect a clarity of purpose, the same kind of clarity of purpose we discussed earlier, when we noted NASA's Gene Krantz and his instruction to "work the problem."

And it was not just Meyer's clarity of purpose that made the difference. Personal courage should not be overlooked. Meyer reasonably believed that he might lose his job when he started asking questions. Indeed, the president of his own college told him to keep his mouth shut.

But the accounting professor knew the math simply didn't work, and he was right. In fact, the president of Spring Arbor College eventually called Albert Meyer and said, "You were right all along. We should have listened to you."[14]

So how do we prevent such frauds in the future? Some might think that it would be additional regulation. Meyer, for his part, doesn't believe additional regulations are the right answer. "Regulation creates a false sense of security," he said. "People think the SEC, or the IRS, or someone, is making sure that things are OK. But it was just that false sense of security that created this problem. The SEC, the IRS, the ECFA—everybody failed. Regulation is counterproductive. Transparency is the only answer. Give people all the information they need to make informed decisions, and let people decide for themselves."

Whatever Happened To Albert Meyer?

Since we are giving Albert Meyer his well-deserved last word on this chapter, it's only fitting that we learn what happened to him.

Given this debut for the young accountant, it is probably not surprising that Albert Meyer's work uncovering fraud did not end with the Foundation for New Era Philanthropy.

In 1996, he joined Martin Capital Management as a portfolio manager. During this time, he questioned Coca-Cola's accounting practices, questions that led to reforms there, and resulted in yet more publicity for his forensic accounting skills, including a front- page story in the *New York Times*. The case has also become a case study at Harvard Business School.

At the end of 1998, Behind the Numbers, an investment research company, hired him as a research analyst. Meyer's report on Tyco International was the first published assault on the company's accounting and governance practices, practices that in 2002 led to the resignation of Tyco's president, Dennis Kozlowski. Kozlowski was ultimately convicted of larceny and sentenced to prison. He was granted conditional release on January 17, 2014.

In part because of his work uncovering the New Era fraud, Albert Meyer was awarded the Michiganian of the Year award. In 2005, the American Accounting Association honored Meyer with the Accounting Exemplar Award.

He now runs an investment firm in Dallas called Bastiat Capital, named after the nineteenth-century economist and philosopher Frederic Bastiat, who advocated for limited government and free markets. It's fitting that Albert Meyer would name his firm after Bastiat, because Bastiat's last words, uttered on his deathbed in 1850, were words that guided Meyer during the New Era scandal: "The Truth." And to make sure he was understood, Bastiat gathered himself one last time and with great effort repeated, "The Truth."

Chapter 6

Prayers, Ponzis, and Profits: Bernard Madoff and Allen Stanford

"Well, uh, yes, yes. I have to say it is fun being a billionaire."
—Allen Stanford

"It was one big lie."
—Bernard Madoff

Now listen, you rich people, weep and wail because of the misery that is coming to you. Your wealth has rotted, and moths have eaten your clothes. Your gold and silver are corroded. Their corrosion will testify against you and eat your flesh.
—James 5: 1-3, 5

The people we have discussed in the past few chapters—the Bakkers, John Bennett, and Todd Bentley—might be broadly grouped together in a single category: ministry frauds.

In other words, the Bakkers, Bentley, and Bennett focused on Christian audiences. They told their victims that the money they gave will go to Christian ministry.

In this chapter, we will look at a different species of faith-based fraud. Bernard Madoff and Allen Stanford were not particularly religious people, but—like Charles Ponzi—they used their contacts in the religious community to create their empires, and, in the end, many well-meaning religious people and organizations were severely damaged.

We'll begin with Allen Stanford.

Number 205

Number 205. "Two-oh-Five." That's what some of (former) Texas billionaire Allen Stanford's colleagues and friends started calling him in 2008 when he was named number 205 on *Forbes Magazine*'s list of the four hundred richest people in the world.

Soon after he was named on the list, he appeared on CNBC, the financial network. Anchor Carl Quintanilla asked him, "Is it fun being a billionaire?"

Allen Stanford, then fifty-eight, laughed and answered, "Well, uh, yes, yes. I have to say it is fun being a billionaire."

But it got a whole lot less fun on February 17, 2009. That was when the SEC said Stanford and his accomplices had been operating a "massive Ponzi scheme," had misappropriated billions of dollars of investors' money, and had falsified the Stanford International Bank's records to hide their fraud.

The SEC was blunt in its assessment: "Stanford International Bank's financial statements, including its investment income, are fictional." Also named in the complaint were Laura Pendergest-Holt, Stanford's chief investment officer, and James Davis, Stanford's chief financial officer (CFO).

The Rise of Allen Stanford

So how did Allen Stanford go from being a student at Baylor University to one of the richest men in America to one of the biggest frauds in the history of American finance? It is, in some ways, a classic Texas-sized story—with equal parts opportunism, hard work, and religion.

The basics of Stanford's rise to the ranks of the super wealthy are not so hard to follow. Stanford's father owned a small but profitable insurance agency, and when Allen graduated from Baylor, he took a job in the family business. When the oil bust of the mid-1980s crushed the Houston real estate market, Stanford swooped in, buying distressed properties, using money from his father and from friends.

By the mid-90s, Stanford had made his first hundred million, as well as many millions more for friends who invested in his deals. Stanford began investing in real estate and other ventures in Antigua, a tax haven, and he eventually moved there. In Antigua, his massive investments and civic involvement motivated the island nation's leaders to recommend Stanford for an honorary knighthood, which he received in 2006. After that, official communications from Stanford Financial Group and other ventures he owned would refer to him as "Sir Allen Stanford."

Because Stanford had made so much money for so many of his friends in those early days in Texas, it was easy for him to get them and others to invest in subsequent ventures.

After he moved to Antigua, Stanford grew fond of the sport of cricket. So he bought a professional cricket team, and then a league, and he changed the rules of this five-hundred-year-old, tradition-bound game. A single cricket match can sometimes go on for days. Under Stanford's new rules, a match was less than four hours long, suitable for television. Stanford bragged in the pages of *Forbes* that he hoped to turn cricket into a major television sport and make himself another fortune in the process.[1]

It was just the sort of grand vision that causes excitement—and the sort of hubris that causes apprehension. So it helped that Stanford recruited his college roommate, James Davis, to be his CFO.

A "Straight Arrow"

Davis came from the small town of Baldwyn, Mississippi, southeast of Memphis. He had a reputation as being a "straight arrow." Jimmy Davis, as his friends called him, was a man who projected small-town values. He often opened business meetings with prayer.[2]

The both-feet-on-the-ground reputation of Jimmy Davis calmed investors and associates of Allen Stanford, who had become increasingly flamboyant as his wealth grew. Stanford owned jets and yachts. His personal life was also becoming increasingly chaotic. Stanford once told his staff that his priorities were "God, family, and me." But he ended up separating from his wife and fathering six children with four different women.[3]

Jimmy Davis was the antidote to that apprehension. Having a guy like Jimmy Davis on staff calmed people's jitters.

Danny Horton, the mayor of Baldwyn, told me, "Mr. Davis was a real asset to our city." In fact, though Allen Stanford was a Texan, and Houston was Stanford's headquarters, Davis made the unusual decision to keep his own office in Memphis, in part so he could remain active in Baldwyn's civic life.

Mayor Horton said, "Mr. Davis moved back into the same home that had been in his family for generations, and he bought and renovated several buildings here. He had a love and a passion for the rural community."

Davis even taught Sunday school at Baldwyn's First Baptist Church, and it was there that a teenager, Laura Pendergest (now Pendergest-Holt), came to his attention. Horton told me she is "a fine young lady from a fine family" who went off to "The W," which is what locals call the Mississippi University for Women.

The W has a reputation for being precisely the place where "a fine young lady from a fine family" would go. For generations, it had been a kind of finishing school for girls from Mississippi's elite families. The academics are respectable, but not overly rigorous. The tuition was stiff enough to accomplish what the academics could not: keep the neighborhood from going to pot. The W had traditionally produced the "perfect professional's wife." In recent years, it had produced a few top professionals of its own.

One of whom is Laura Pendergest, who pursued a degree in math education at The W. She joined Stanford Financial Group soon after graduation. Under the mentorship of Jimmy Davis, her former Sunday school teacher, she rose quickly through ranks. By the time she was thirty, with no specialized financial education except what she was able to pick up on the job, she became the firm's chief investment officer and occupied an office next to Davis' in Memphis.

She was not a certified public accountant (CPA), nor did she hold the chartered financial analyst (CFA) designation.

David Baglia spent more than twenty years as chair of the department of accounting at Grove City College, a Christian college in Pennsylvania. He now chairs the accounting department at Campbell University. Baglia said, "The requirements for these designations are rigorous, but these designations are fairly common for this level of responsibility. The fact that the chief investment officer at such a large firm didn't have these designations or other similar designations is unusual."[4]

Rusty Leonard was more blunt. "It was a recipe for disaster," said Leonard, himself a CFA who, as you may recall, managed money for the legendary investor Sir John Templeton.

The fact that Pendergest-Holt and Davis first met in church was not that unusual for Stanford Financial Group. Religious faith, personal connections, and church ties were common at Stanford. The story about Jimmy Davis having met Laura Pendergest-Holt in church became a part of the oral culture at Stanford Financial Group. Many of Stanford's employees were recruited as a result of relationships in church or Christian organizations.

In 2005 and 2006, Stanford caused waves in the financial planning industry by bulking up its US network of financial planning offices. In just a few years, Stanford had a network of almost thirty offices, mostly in the Southeast, and more than a hundred advisors. Many of the organization's leaders were outspoken Christians who recruited other like-minded financial advisors, according to Greg Leekley, who was a consultant to Stanford during the heyday of the recruiting process. "We weren't trying to set up a Christian financial planning practice," Leekley told me. "And we weren't looking for just Christians. But when you know the same people and have the same beliefs, the trust comes more quickly."

Baglia said that such affinities are not necessarily unusual or improper, but they do sometimes lead to sloppiness in the due diligence process. "We're comfortable working with people we know and have an affinity with," Baglia said. "But that does not absolve us of the responsibility of due diligence."

Anyone looking closely at Stanford might have also been concerned by the nepotism. In part because Jimmy Davis still kept close ties to Baldwyn, Mississippi, nepotism soon developed. Pendergest-Holt's sister married Ken Weeden, Stanford Financial Group's former managing director of investments and research. Pendergest-Holt's cousin Heather Sheppard was an equity specialist.

Further, when the case eventually came to trial, testimony revealed that at different times, the "straight arrow" Jimmy Davis was perhaps not so straight. He had maintained affairs with both Heather Sheppard and Laura Pendergest-Holt, his protege.

But most of the information about all these convoluted and sometimes sordid relationships did not become public until much later. While Stanford, Davis, and Pendergest-Holt were building the business, they presented to the world an image of small-town Christian values. Once again, we see opportunities for fraud and abuse because the *imputed trust* placed in people who had not *earned* trust as a result of professional training and years of experience.

Auditors sometimes talk about the "smell test." If something doesn't smell right, that doesn't mean it's rotten, but it does mean you should do a bit more sniffing around.

In retrospect, Baglia said, all of these circumstances should have been warning signs. But when you're on the inside and the money is flowing, human nature makes it tough to call a timeout and ask hard questions. "Our accounting society has a t-shirt that says, 'In God We Trust. All Others Subject To Audit.' That's good advice, even when you're dealing with Christians."

Stanford's "Black Box"

Such advice seems obvious now, but in 2005, this advice was easy to ignore. At Stanford Financial Group, the money was flowing. The main source of revenue was Stanford's ***certificate of deposit***, or CD.

A certificate of deposit is a common, popular investment vehicle. Most CDs are offered by banks, credit unions, and thrift institutions (often called savings and loan institutions). In many ways, they are like a savings account, but with two important differences. When you put money in a savings account, you can put even a very small amount in, and you have immediate access to that money. You can deposit it one day and withdraw it the next.

CDs require you to leave your money in for a set period of time. The minimum amount of time is usually around six months, though one-year CDs are the most popular. Longer-term CDs are also common. For this reason, CDs are sometimes called time deposits. Another difference between CDs and savings accounts is that CDs usually require a minimum investment, often five hundred dollars or more. The larger the investment, and the longer you are willing to leave your money untouched, the better the interest rate you will get. So-called jumbo CDs usually require an investment of one hundred thousand dollars or more.

Because of these qualities, banks are usually able to offer interest rates on CDs that are slightly higher than the rates they offer on their regular savings accounts. Investors and savers who will not need their money for long periods of time, such as those saving for college or retirement (or wealthy people who don't need their money to live but don't want to lose it), like CDs because they give a guaranteed, risk-free rate of return. In fact, if you buy a CD through your local bank, it is treated as a deposit by federal regulators and is insured by the Federal Deposit Insurance Corporation (FDIC).

So how do the banks make their money? They take the money that is invested in CDs by individual investors and they combine that money and make larger investments in financial instruments that offer slightly larger returns, financial instruments that are available only to large investors.

For example, a bank might take one thousand dollars from you and offer you a guarantee of five percent interest if you let them keep your money for a year. The banks could then combine your money with the money of many others and make a one hundred thousand-dollar investment in a financial instrument that pays a guaranteed seven percent interest, but which won't take small investments from individual investors. At the end of the year, you get your one thousand dollars back, with five percent interest. The bank has made only two percent, but the bank made it with your money, and the bank is handling millions or billions or—in the case of large financial institutions—hundreds of billions of dollars.

If this description sounds familiar, it's because this is another form of arbitrage: taking advantage of the different prices in different markets. As I said when we first introduced this subject in our discussion of Charles Ponzi and his IRCs, arbitrage is perfectly legal, but it can be abused.

Before Allen Stanford came along, the CD market was one of low risk and small profits. After banks pay their own expenses, they might make as little as one percent per year on CD products, but the business is worthwhile because literally trillions of dollars in CDs are bought and sold each year.

Stanford's CD product was different. At a time when other CDs were offering six to eight percent, Stanford was promising ten to twelve percent on its CD product. The Stanford Financial Group said that they were investing in safe and easily sellable ("liquid") financial instruments, such as government bonds and stock market funds. They said that they were able to offer the higher interest rates because they accepted only large investments. This reduced transaction costs.

But Stanford also admitted that a certain percentage of funds went into what it sometimes called a "black box." It suggested that the money in the black box produced outsized investment returns without significantly affecting the risk of the overall fund. Stanford maintained that it couldn't tell investors what was in the black box because that disclosure would destroy its competitive advantage.

Again, this lack of transparency should have been a warning signal. Rusty Leonard said, "With a 'black box model' the manager is essentially saying 'trust us, we know what we are doing.'" At this point in our journey, it should be increasingly apparent that Stanford's "black box" shares much with New Era's anonymous donor and Charles Ponzi's IRCs: Mysterious, but plausible—if you don't ask too many questions.

Thousands of investors should have known better. Even more culpable are the hundreds of investment advisors Stanford had recruited. But they all turned a blind eye to the warning signals and focused their eye instead on what the SEC later called "improbable, if not impossible" rates of return. Eventually, at least fifty thousand investors poured at least eight billion dollars into Stanford Financial Group's CD products.

Riding High

With that kind of money flowing in, life was indeed good for Allen Stanford, Laura Pendergest-Holt, and Jimmy Davis. Because Allen Stanford had moved to Antigua to avoid taxes and pursue his newly discovered passion for cricket, many of the day- to-day operations of Stanford were run not from Stanford Financial Group's headquarters in Houston, but from Jimmy Davis's office in Memphis. This geographical dislocation further allowed wrongdoing to proceed without oversight and scrutiny.

What most of the organization did not know was that it wasn't just Stanford investing in Antiguan real estate or television-friendly cricket matches. It later came out that much of the money used for these investments came from investors in Stanford's CD products. These were the investments Stanford hoped would produce the outsized returns he needed in order to pay back his investors. Stanford invested at least fifty million dollars in his cricket enterprise, and—to his credit—the 2008 Stanford 20/20 Tournament that took place in the West Indies attracted a worldwide television audience of about three hundred million.

The large contingent of evangelical Christians within Stanford also led the company to invest in Christian-themed activities and investments. Stanford invested in a film called *The Ultimate Gift*, which has a Christian message. The movie eventually turned out to be a good investment for Stanford, costing less than ten million dollars to produce and market, but eventually generating more than thirty million dollars in revenue, including DVD sales.

These investments made from Stanford's "black box" turned out okay, but others did not, especially after the financial crisis hit in 2008. Billionaire Warren Buffett is reputed to have said, "You don't know who's swimming naked until the tide goes out." It turns out that when the financial tide went out during the Great Recession, Allen Stanford was exposed. The money that individual investors had been pouring into Stanford's CD products was not being reinvested in safe, liquid instruments. That money was invested in risky and illiquid enterprises.

All of these details about the risky investments and Allen Stanford's personal life were carefully guarded by the evangelical Christians in Stanford's organization who used his investments in Christian activities, as well as the Stanford Financial Group's support of St. Jude's Children's Hospital, to project a high-integrity, family-friendly image.

But the fraud complaints and lawsuits started flying in 2009. An amazing story started to unfold.

The Unraveling of Stanford Financial Group

A February 17, 2009, civil complaint first made Stanford's fraud public.[5] This complaint recounted in detail a February 2009 meeting in an airport hangar in Miami that included three Stanford employees, who became cooperating witnesses. These three met with Pendergest-Holt, two unnamed Stanford executives, and an attorney.

Pendergest-Holt revealed to these employees/informants that assets in one portion of Stanford's portfolio had decreased in value from eight hundred and fifty million dollars to just three hundred and fifty million dollars in about seven months. (Remember, we were still in the so-called Great Recession, when asset classes of all types had lost value.) At another meeting several days later, one of the soon-to-be cooperating witnesses "broke down crying because of the revelations" and threatened to go to authorities.

The complaint continues: "Soon thereafter, Attorney A walked over to (the confidential informant) and suggested they begin to pray together."

To add to the drama, on the day the complaint containing this story was made public, Allen Stanford went missing. A nationwide search and a media frenzy ensued. Federal marshals raided Stanford's offices in Houston and Memphis. The Dallas office of GodTube, one of the Christian businesses in which Stanford had invested, was searched by federal authorities.

Charlotte, which had served as the backdrop for the PTL scandal, also played a bit part in the Stanford saga. Stanford Financial Group had an office in Charlotte with more than twenty-five employees, most of whom had recently moved—and brought their clients—from Bank of America, Wachovia, and other Charlotte-based financial institutions. That office was subsequently shut down, throwing those employees out of work.

Also in Charlotte, The Film Foundry, the company that produced *The Ultimate Gift*, found itself cash starved. Even though its projects with Stanford had been profitable, much of those profits, in the millions of dollars, were held in Stanford accounts that were now frozen by federal authorities.

Sharing the Film Foundry building in Charlotte's fashionable South End Historic District was the Open Finance Network (OFN), co-founded by Greg Leekley, the man who had helped Stanford recruit Christian financial advisors. Stanford had invested more than ten million dollars in this technology startup and had pledged millions more. In part because of Stanford's participation, OFN had ultimately been able to raise more than twenty-five million dollars in venture capital over a five-year period. The company's technology was on the verge of being market ready. In fact, it had just started producing revenue. However, it was not producing enough to take care of its more than one hundred employees. With Stanford's assets now under the control of a federal judge, cash infusions to OFN stopped. Virtually all one hundred employees lost their jobs overnight. Stories such as these were played out all across the country.[5]

Authorities eventually found Allen Stanford in Fredericksburg, Virginia, three days later, with his girlfriend. (Stanford was not yet divorced from his wife Susan, whom he married in 1975, and with whom he has a grown daughter. However, they had been separated by this time for more than a decade.) Stanford's attorneys said he was not fleeing, but had simply "relocated" there with his girlfriend.[6]

According to a press release from the Justice Department issued soon after Stanford was found in Fredericksburg, the case was built with contributions from the FBI's Houston Field Office, Internal Revenue Service-Criminal Investigations and the US Postal Inspection Service. It was prosecuted by attorneys from the Washington, DC, Criminal Division's Fraud Section.

Having this kind of investigative firepower leveled against you is big trouble, not just for Stanford but for Laura Pendergest-Holt and James Davis, those two former pillars of Baldwyn, Mississippi, First Baptist Church. Davis originally remained tight lipped in apparent solidarity with his old Baylor roommate. He cited his Fifth Amendment right and refused "to testify or provide an accounting . . . or produce any documents related to the matters set forth in the Commission's complaint."

But Pendergest-Holt's quick ascent from The W to a lofty title and a salary of as much as one million dollars a year was followed by an equally quick descent. The eminent prospect of trading her pearls and high heels for an orange jumpsuit shocked her into cooperating with authorities. She was arraigned on criminal charges in a Houston court on February 27, 2009, just a week after the first civil lawsuits against Stanford were made public. She was charged with obstructing the government's investigation of Stanford. Prosecutors had asked for bail to be set at one million dollars, but Pendergest-Holt's attorneys successfully argued that because her assets were frozen, as were the assets of thousands of Stanford investors, she could not make this bond. It was ultimately set at three hundred thousand dollars, of which she had to produce thirty thousand dollars. She made bail and was released, though she was required to wear an ankle monitor, a fashion accessory not much in vogue among the polished graduates of the Mississippi College for Women.

These events cracked Laura Pendergest-Holt's high-gloss veneer. Her attorneys announced a couple of weeks later, in March 2009, she was "fully cooperating" with authorities. James Davis, her old mentor, ultimately said he too would cooperate.

Their cooperation lightened their punishment considerably. On June 21, 2012, Laura Pendergest-Holt pled guilty to obstructing an SEC investigation. On September 13, 2012, she was sentenced to three years in prison, followed by three years of supervised probation. She obtained her full freedom on April 23, 2015. On January 22, 2013, Davis was sentenced to five years in jail, followed by three years of supervised probation. He also had a judgment of one billion dollars against him. Jimmy Davis left prison on July 24, 2017.

Their cooperation helped investigators build an ironclad case against Allen Stanford. On June 19, 2009, the Justice Department unveiled criminal charges against Stanford and four other officials at his Stanford Financial Group, as well as against Leroy King, administrator of the Financial Services Regulatory Commission on the island nations of Antigua and Barbuda, where the company had its headquarters.

So less than a year after being Number 205 on *Forbes'* list,

FBI agents took Stanford into custody. He ultimately became prisoner number 35017-183.[7]

But much drama remained before Stanford's conviction. While in custody, he got into a fight with other prisoners, who beat him severely. His lawyers said the beating had given Stanford amnesia and made him unfit to stand trial. That argument didn't work, so they said Stanford was addicted to anti-anxiety drugs that impaired his judgment and made him unfit. That worked long enough to get Stanford weaned off the drugs. Stanford's lawyers used the time to sue the FBI and the SEC for $7.2 billion, claiming that it was not Stanford's fraud and mismanagement that caused billions to vaporize, but the "Gestapo" tactics of federal law enforcement.

While all these machinations delayed proceedings, they could not prevent the inevitable. Finally, on March 6, 2012, after a trial that lasted six weeks, it took the jury only three hours to convict Allen Stanford.

On June 14, 2012, Stanford was sentenced to one hundred and ten years in prison. Prosecutors had sought a longer sentence, calling Stanford a "ruthless predator" and someone who "lived a life steeped in deceit." Unless something extraordinary happens, Allen Stanford (no longer Sir Allen Stanford after his knighthood was stripped) will die in prison.

But for many people swindled by Stanford, Davis, and Pendergest-Holt, the prison sentences bring no comfort. A full ten years later, most of Stanford's victims have seen little or no money recovered. Angela Shaw's family lost millions. She told CNBC in 2019, on the tenth anniversary of Stanford's arrest, "The only true justice Stanford's victims could ever see is in getting their savings back. Sadly, all they have seen and can expect to see is a few pennies on the dollar."[8]

Mad About Madoff

Like Allen Stanford—or, more specifically, like Jimmy Davis and others around Allen Stanford—the other key figure we're discussing in this chapter, Bernard Madoff, also used his contacts in the religious community to betray the trust of those in that community. Also like Stanford and Charles Ponzi before him, he used later investors to keep the earlier investors happy. While Charles Ponzi may have given the Ponzi scheme its name, it took Bernard Madoff to elevate the Ponzi scheme to the level of a near art form.

Indeed, in March 2009, when Madoff finally pled guilty to eleven federal crimes, the full measure of his fraud became clear, and the bottom line was this: Bernard Lawrence Madoff, born April 29, 1938, now holds the dubious distinction of having perpetuated the largest Ponzi scheme in history. The court-appointed trustee responsible for sorting out the mess estimated that more than eighteen billion dollars had been lost by investors. If you count the gains that the investors thought they had but which, in fact, had been merely fabricated, the total losses approached sixty-five billion dollars.

So this was certainly a fraud, the largest in American history.

But a faith-based fraud?

Absolutely. As we will see, Bernard Madoff used his contacts in the Jewish communities—beginning in New York, then in Florida, and then around the world—to attract investors.

And there is another reason to take a close look at the Madoff fraud. As we have mentioned earlier, one of the questions always asked after a fraud is exposed is this: "How could people be so gullible, so naïve?" In the Madoff fraud, however, we see that some of the richest and most savvy investors in the world were taken in. How could that happen?

Certainly greed played a role, but we also look at another motive. That other motive, which may even be more powerful than financial greed, is the longing for community, or at least to be in the "inside circle."

If you were a Madoff investor, you were part of an exclusive inner circle. We see this phenomenon over and over, but we discussed it most fully in reference to the New Era scandal. John Bennett and Bernard Madoff—indeed, even Charles Ponzi and Jim Bakker—provided a sense of belonging. You were part of the in-crowd, the cool kids, the smart set.

To help us understand this motivation more, let's first look at the man at the center of the madness.

What's a Nice Jewish Boy Like You . . .

Madoff was born into a Jewish family in the Queens borough of New York in what in some ways was the perfect year for a striving, upwardly mobile entrepreneur: 1938. Though born in the Great Depression, the Depression was not a part of his personal experience. He was too young to serve in either World War II or Korea, and too old for Vietnam. But the peace, stability, and economic prosperity created in part by these wars were the milieu in which Madoff made and lost billions. His was a life of wealth without any real sacrifice.

Madoff's first foray into the financial world came when he founded Bernard L. Madoff Investment Securities in 1960, just after his graduation from Hofstra University. The company got its start buying and selling so-called penny stocks. Penny stocks are not necessarily stocks that cost a penny, but stocks that are very cheap, sometimes selling for even less than a penny. They are stocks for which no ready market exists. That is to say, they are not listed on any of the major stock exchanges, such as the New York Stock Exchange. So firms such as Madoff's are sometimes called "market makers." If you wanted to buy or to sell penny stocks, you could go directly to Madoff's company.

But the stock prices were low and the companies being traded had very small market capitalization, or total value. They are sometimes called microcap stocks. So for Madoff to make money, he had to charge higher commissions than normal stock brokers, and he had to be extraordinarily efficient. The 1960s were the very beginning of the era in which computers were used on Wall Street. Madoff's firm was in the forefront. It developed innovative computer technology to handle the trades.

It's important to note that penny stocks occupy a special niche in the investment world. They are not illegal, but they are less regulated than the stocks of more established companies, the stocks traded on the major stock exchanges. Proponents of penny stocks say the microcap market provides capital for companies, especially technology companies, too new and too innovative for traditional stock markets. Over the years, the microcap markets have produced just enough success stories to keep this myth alive. Sun Microsystems and Sprint/Nextel had their roots as microcaps.

But because the stock prices are so low and so thinly traded (relatively few people buying or selling the stock on any given day), they are subject to price manipulation.

A simple price manipulation scheme might look something like this: imagine a stock trading for a penny that trades infrequently, once a week or so. A manipulator buys one million shares of this stock for ten thousand dollars. If this same buyer "bids" two cents a share the next day, he will likely find plenty of sellers, because that's twice the price the stock was just yesterday.

So our manipulator purchases more shares, though this time not nearly as many, perhaps another one hundred thousand shares, one-tenth the amount he purchased the day before. Because he paid twice the price per share, this transaction costs two thousand dollars. He now has twelve thousand dollars into the stock, and he owns 1.1 million shares.

But a few people are beginning to notice. Why did the stock double in price in a single day? Does somebody know something others don't? I'd better buy a few shares just so I don't miss out. And, of course, people who already own the stock are happy for the price jump. Some of them decide to sell at the higher price and make a profit.

But human psychology begins to override the fundamentals of the company itself. For every person who decides to sell their stock for a profit, others feel validated in the decision they made to purchase the stock, or perhaps they just get greedy. Whatever the reason, many of them are no longer willing to sell at two cents a share. They now want three cents. Buyers now paying attention to the stock price are willing to pay, because the stock is still very cheap. Even at three or four or five cents a share, it's a good deal if the stock eventually goes up to a dime—or a dollar. More buyers notice. They notice, in part, because firms like Bernie Madoff's firm, so-called "market makers," are calling everyone they know to tell the story. A frenzy ensues. The stock does hit a dime, then a dollar.

But wait. Do you remember our original buyer, the guy who got the ball rolling? He now owns 1.1 million shares of a stock worth a dollar a share: $1.1 million and all that money in a matter of weeks or months with only a twelve thousand-dollar investment.

Such blatant, easy-to-follow manipulations rarely (if ever) occur just as I've described them. They can be too easily seen as manipulations, and manipulating stock prices is illegal. Today, both market pressures and regulations tend to prevent such schemes (though not always, as the GameStop stock manipulation of 2021 demonstrated).[9] But what is not unusual is for investors with a high tolerance for risk, or money they're willing to lose, or both, to buy and sell small-cap stocks in the hope that a relatively small movement in the stock price will produce a large profit.

And there's one more thing to note: every time a stock changes hands, whether the transaction produces a big profit or a big loss, the broker gets a paycheck. And by the 1980s, Bernard Madoff was one of the biggest brokers of such transactions in the world.

Many people consider the promoting of penny stocks unethical, even when it's legal, because the buying and dumping of penny stocks do little to help build the companies these stocks represent. The purpose of stock ownership is to provide capital for a company's growth and development. Stock owners are not owners of a piece of paper. They are part owners of a company. Certainly from a Christian point of view, this kind of ownership carries with it a responsibility of stewardship.

But such notions are mostly lost in the stock market generally and in the penny stock world in particular. Indeed, operating in this netherworld of the financial services industry often becomes a refuge for the ethically challenged. Despite that, or perhaps because of that, Bernard Madoff thrived. His firm became the largest market maker at the NASDAQ, the stock exchange that ultimately grew out of small-cap stocks, and became one of the largest market makers on Wall Street.

But what really turbocharged Madoff's cash machine was the wealth management arm of his company. As Madoff's brokerage business grew, his clients made money and needed someone to manage it for them. Madoff quickly moved into that arena. Like Ponzi and Stanford before him, Madoff promised outsized returns—in excess of twelve percent—year after year. And like Stanford, Madoff claimed a "black box" methodology he wouldn't reveal, saying that to reveal the methodology would destroy his competitive advantage.

As the cash rolled in, Madoff began to take on the trappings of success and respectability. By 2009, Madoff had an ocean-front residence in Montauk on Long Island, as well as a home on the Upper East Side of Manhattan, valued in a 2009 filing at seven million dollars. He had a home in France, and a mansion in Florida, where he also kept a fifty-five-foot fishing yacht. The list of outsized assets goes on.

Madoff could buy cars and boats and real estate. Buying respectability is a bit more complicated. Philanthropy is one way to do that. Political contributions were another. Madoff began to make contributions to the Democratic Party. He was not a mega giver, but he was a steady giver, and he seemed to calculate his giving so that he gave just enough money to give him access to the politicians—and the big donor events and parties that would allow him "face time" with current and prospective clients.

Democratic Senator Charles Schumer, Madoff's own senator from New York, received about thirty thousand dollars from Madoff over the years. In total, Madoff gave about two hundred and forty thousand dollars to federal candidates between 1991 and the time the scandal was publicly revealed in 2008. These candidates included Senators Barack Obama and Hillary Clinton, and US Representatives Charles Rangel and Vito Fossella.[10]

Did all of this money buy Madoff special treatment from legislators and regulators? We have no direct evidence of that. But that possibility is one more reason regulations are inadequate to fight fraud, said Albert Meyer. Even those regulators who are honest are bound by a bureaucracy that prevents them from moving nimbly enough to catch bad guys. For these reasons, Meyer says flatly, "Regulators can't be trusted."

Weeping and Gnashing of Teeth

Bernard Madoff's fraud was devastating to his clients, and its sheer size had ripple effects through the economy has a whole. But it was particularly egregious and damaging for reasons quite apart from its sheer size.

First, Madoff was a former chairman of the NASDAQ. While he may have begun his career on the fringes of the financial services industry, he had moved into the mainstream. Indeed, he had become an establishment figure. If a guy like Madoff could be so crooked for so long, can anyone be trusted? Madoff 's fraud raised questions about the integrity of the entire financial system.

In fact, a Cornell University study published in 2017 found that "people who knew Madoff's victims or who lived in areas where victims were concentrated lost trust in the financial system and dramatically changed their behavior." According to the study, these investors "yanked $363 billion from the financial advisers they had entrusted—even though many of these advisers had nothing to do with Madoff."[11]

This study quantifies what even casual observers knew: Bernard Madoff's fraud sent waves through the already jittery financial markets in 2008. The Madoff scandal made material contributions to the Great Recession of 2008-2009. Not only did sixty-five billion dollars in wealth vaporize from the personal net worth of thousands of investors, but the erosion of confidence caused by the Madoff scandal hit both Wall Street and Main Street hard.

Another group hit hard was Jewish charities. Take, for example, the Robert I. Lappin Charitable Foundation, which has financed the trips of hundreds of Jewish youth to Israel. Soon after news of the Madoff scandal broke, the group posted a stark message on its website: "The programs of the Robert I. Lappin Charitable Foundation and the Robert I. Lappin 1992 Supporting

Foundation are discontinued, effectively immediately. This includes Youth to Israel and Teachers to Israel. The money used to fund the programs of both Foundations was invested with Bernard L. Madoff Investment Securities and all the assets have been frozen by the federal courts. The money needed to fund the programs of the Lappin Foundations is gone."[12]

They were not alone. The JEHT Foundation, which supports reform of the criminal justice system, said it would also shut down because its largest donors were Madoff investors. The Chais Family Foundation, which gives about twelve and a half million dollars each year to Jewish causes in Israel and the former Soviet Union, laid off its staff and shut down after losing eight million dollars with Madoff. This closure would also cause other ripple effects: The United Jewish Communities and the American Jewish Joint Distribution Committee were among its main beneficiaries.

For Madoff, the fraud unraveled quickly. On December 10, 2008, Madoff confessed to his two sons, Mark and Andrew, what he had done. In what was a courageous decision—but one which must also have been heart-wrenching—they immediately went to the authorities, who arrested Madoff the next day. On June 29, 2009, Madoff was sentenced to one hundred and fifty years in prison, the maximum allowed at his age, which was then seventy-one years old.

At his sentencing, he said, "I have left a legacy of shame, as some of my victims have pointed out, to my family and my grandchildren. This is something I will live in for the rest of my life. I'm sorry."

For the forty-eight hundred investors who had been victimized by Madoff, who had lived most of his life in luxury, Madoff's words and his life sentence were small consolation. Madoff's victims suffered far more than he has. Among those victims were his own sons. On December 11, 2010, exactly two years after Madoff's arrest, Mark Madoff died by suicide.

Lessons from Madoff and Stanford

The massive frauds of Bernie Madoff and Allen Stanford contributed to the financial crisis of 2008 and 2009. The federal government eventually had to pour seven hundred billion dollars in the economy to keep it from a complete meltdown. So it is not an overstatement to say that every single American taxpayer—at least indirectly— was a victim of Madoff and Allen Stanford.

One of the lessons of these two stories is that the damage such men cause is not isolated merely to a few rich investors who could afford to lose the money. Thousands of people who were not wealthy lost money. Some lost their life savings. Thousands of people lost their jobs as a direct or indirect result. Scores of nonprofit organizations lost financial contributors and, in the case of Madoff's victims, some of those nonprofits were driven out of existence altogether.

In a nutshell, the damage these scandals caused is profound and, as in the case of Mark Madoff's suicide, tragic. Mark and Andrew Madoff had done the right thing in turning in their father, but it is inconceivable that their actions did not exact a tremendous emotional and spiritual toll on them. In fact, when Mark Madoff died, one press report said he had grown despondent after carrying for two years the "toxic burden of a name that meant fraud to the world."[13]

A second lesson to be found here is the same lesson we have found elsewhere: Transparency is the only sure-fire way to avoid such scandals.

Both Stanford and Madoff led investors to believe they had a black box of proprietary information and techniques that earned them returns no one else had been able to duplicate. In both cases, their claims ended up being false. Once again, we learn that secrecy is the forerunner of disaster. Transparency is the cure for fraud.

Finally, we see yet more evidence for Albert Meyer's contention that government regulators can't be trusted to prevent such frauds. Indeed, Madoff and Stanford operated in one of the most heavily regulated industries in the world. Yet they still found out a way to "game" the regulators.

Given that, Meyer would not be surprised by this final irony: Both Madoff and Stanford were well-known contributors to politicians in both parties. But Madoff, as I said earlier, had a favorite, New York's Democratic Senator Charles Schumer, who received at least thirty thousand dollars from Madoff since 1992.

What I did not mention earlier was this: Schumer is a senior member of the Senate Banking Committee, one of the bodies that is supposed to be watching the financial services industry.

Chapter 7

Let a Thousand Toxic Weeds Bloom

"Christians have fallen into the habit of accepting the noisiest and most notorious as the best and the greatest. They have learned to equate popularity with excellence."
—A.W. Tozer

Until now, we've highlighted fraudulent schemes that were massive, notorious, well known—at least well known in their day. It might be easy to say that these frauds are interesting, and even instructive, but they are, for the most part, special cases. After all, the vast majority of Christians give most of their money to their local church or to local ministries they know. It might be easy to walk away from what we have discussed so far with a single, simple rule: ***Don't give to organizations you don't know.***

That's not a bad rule. It's also likely not enough. The local church itself is not immune from fraudulent schemes. Sometimes local church leaders succumb to temptation and perpetuate these schemes, and other times the local church is a victim of schemes that involve money entrusted to them by their members. The simple math here is this: wherever money is at stake, the possibility for fraud exists. And the larger the pot of money, the greater the temptation.

That's why we're now focusing on local churches and

common frauds that have been perpetuated there. It is important to note before we dive in that the few brief stories I recount here are truly just a representative sample. During the years I wrote about charities and philanthropy for *The Charlotte World*, *WORLD*, and MinistryWatch, I heard about some new fraud or scandal involving a local church almost every week of the year, only a few of which I was able to cover.

I steadfastly maintain it is still true that the vast majority of churches and ministries behave with integrity. But not all, and even the ones that are behaving with integrity face constant temptations.

That's why it's worth looking at a few stories that are perhaps not so well known as the ones we have dissected so far, in hopes of learning how to avoid the pits into which these Christian leaders fell.

"I'm Amazed People Believe This Stuff"

Legend has it that P.T. Barnum once said, "A sucker is born every minute."

If that's true, it's possible that Harvey Dockstader Jr. was out to find them all, and he did it in ways that were so outrageous, ways that so obviously are not aboveboard, that you wonder how anyone fell for them—yet they did.

Perhaps the first thing you should know about Dockstader is that for two years he was running his scheme from prison. He was convicted of running an illegal pyramid scheme in Harris County (Houston), Texas, in 2006, and sentenced to two years in jail.[1]

Dockstader's scheme was an odd mix of an old-fashioned chain letter, a multilevel marketing organization, and prosperity theology.

His organization, Elite Activity, recruited pastors into the organization, who then recruited their flocks. The new recruits gave money to the organization—in amounts as small as fifty dollars, but in some cases as large as one thousand dollars a month. The money goes to those at the top of the pyramid, with those at the bottom getting nothing—unless they are able to recruit more people below them. The organization sells nothing, has no products or services. It exists purely to get more people to join the network.

"It's a classic pyramid scheme," said Valerie Turner, the assistant district attorney who prosecuted Dockstader. "A pretty straightforward case."

But this pyramid scheme has a twist. Any pyramid scheme that is able to stay in business long has to have a twist, because pyramid schemes are patently, explicitly illegal. So this one maintained that payments into the pyramid scheme were not investments or purchases or dues or fees, but gifts.

This pyramid scheme essentially represented itself as a new kind of religion, and new recruits were told they are embracing a "belief system of giving." And like much prosperity gospel teaching, recruits were promised a massive "harvest" on the "seeds" they planted. The website declared, "You can receive $800, $2,000, $4,000, $8,000, $16,000, $32,000, and $48,000 in gifts—Over and over again!!"[2]

According to prosecutor Turner: "It always amazes me that people fall for these schemes, but they do. We see them pop up from time to time."

One of the interesting aspects of this one, however, is that despite the fact that Dockstader was in prison until May 2010, his organization continued to operate, and during that time, it officially claimed to be a church: The Elite Resurrected Church. People who contribute money are "members" of the church.[3]

Though the "church" had a website, finding a live person who was willing to speak for the organization was difficult. When

I first reported on the Elite Church, Dockstader was in jail, and Dockstader's attorney was the pastor of the Elite Resurrected Church. He didn't respond to my attempts to contact him.

However, Jean Small, of Portsmouth, Virginia, said she has been involved with Elite for seven years, and claimed it had more than half a million members. She said, "It became a church to overcome legal issues and because it's a belief system. That belief is that you have to give to get." This single sentence encapsulates the worst form of prosperity theology.

Though Dockstader is white, the overwhelming majority of the people involved in the Elite Resurrected Church are not, and many of them think their involvement is somehow an exercise in black empowerment. Jean Small, for example, said, "I was in the civil rights movement in the sixties. Now I'm in the gifting movement."

Her claim of half a million members was hard to substantiate, though it's clear that from 2005 to 2010, the group had something of a heyday. Just as Charles Ponzi initially targeted the Italian community in Boston, so did Elite often work in insular ethnic communities or poor minority communities. Brazilian pastors in Boston, for example, embraced Elite Resurrected after an article about it appeared in a Portuguese-language newspaper targeting the Brazilian community.[4] Elite also spread in Mormon communities in Utah before voluntarily shutting down its Utah operation after a citation from the Utah Division of Consumer Protection.

Jane Driggs, president of the Utah Better Business Bureau, told me that such scams often start out with people recruiting their family and friends, and if a few people start making money—even if it is at the expense of others—people start to believe that they can too. Driggs said it is not surprising that such scams often spill over into religious communities because they prey on people's inherent desire to believe. "People just want to believe," she said.

"Unfortunately, you have to be careful what you believe in."

For a couple years after Dockstader got out of jail, he was still finding believers to follow him. He formed a new organization called Connecting Us All International, and for a few years, until about 2013, he was up to the same activities, and many of the people involved were the same ones who worked with him before.

Connecting Us All International was a weird amalgam of the same "theology of giving" that was a part of Elite, but also has positive thinking and New Age philosophies blended in. As of 2020, the Facebook for the page was still active, though it had no posts more recent than 2011. Those posts were motivational and inspirational sayings.

Dockstader himself re-settled in Utah.[5] He has been involved in a variety of business ventures—including multilevel marketing—in a Fundamentalist Latter-Day Saints (FLDS) community that has many residents that still practice polygamy. In fact, the *Salt Lake City Tribune* identified Dockstader as "a veteran network marketer who is a member of a polygamist group in Centennial Park and owns a health-food store in neighboring Colorado City." He told the paper that "network marketing" is great for people in the FLDS Church. "It teaches how to be social, how to deal with their bottled-up fears. From that perspective, it's therapeutic. They may not make money, but they'll blossom if they participate," he said.[6]

He was also involved for an undetermined amount of time with a crypto-currency network called BitClubNetwork, an organization its website says has mission "to help YOU cash-in on Bitcoin as it becomes a mainstream global currency." However, in December of 2019, the leaders of the BitClubNetwork were arrested for perpetrating a $722 million scam. Federal authorities said BitClubNetwork was, in fact, a classic pyramid scheme.[7]

The Tip Of The Iceberg

When Rusty Leonard and I started writing about faith-based fraud for *WORLD*, I originally thought we might run out of interesting stories. We would tell the ones we knew about, and we'd then struggle to find more.

Alas, such was not the case. Once we started writing these stories, we started getting emails and phone calls from readers who would often begin the conversation with some variation of this statement: "If you think that story was outrageous, you should hear this one." The person would then go on to recount yet another outlandish faith-based fraud. And sometimes they came from some pretty unlikely places, and that unlikeliness sometimes made them the most tragic.

Such was the case when we came across the story of New Horizon Fellowship—a story that ended tragically, with the tearing apart of a church and with many people losing their life savings.

The story begins with one David Talbot, who seemed like a trustworthy Christian businessman to the members of New Horizon Fellowship, a new church starting up in Wyckoff, New Jersey. He talked the talk of an evangelical Christian, said Bill Werner, one of the elders at New Horizon.

But according to Werner, and eventually according to the attorney general of the State of New Jersey, he may have talked the talk but he didn't walk the walk. That is if you don't count a perp walk: Talbot was sued by New Jersey because he "operated a fraud" by selling over five hundred thousand dollars in unregistered securities "which promised high yield returns."

The complaint, filed in the Superior Court of Bergen County on August 8, 2009, further alleged that Talbot and two co-defendants "appealed to investors' religious beliefs because some investors were told a percentage of the profits were going to charitable purposes, including to purchase a church."

That church? The very same New Horizon Fellowship, which is now defunct. Most of the people who lost money in the scheme were members of the church, who, according to Werner, were offered "crazy returns of thirty percent a month." Werner said he considered the offer in 2007, but he became suspicious when Talbot couldn't explain where the money would be invested or how the returns could be so great. "Talbot said it was a secret, and that if the word got out, it would kill the deal," according to Werner.

It's worth observing that, if you've read this far, you already have a very strong suspicion that this deal is a fraud. But in case I haven't been clear so far, let me be clear here: any investment deal that offers returns that appear too good to be true—and "crazy returns of thirty percent a month" certainly fall into that category—is likely a fraud. Secondly, any person who says he cannot disclose how he is making that money—who claims, as did Madoff and Stanford, to have a "black box"—is also likely a fraud.

Talbot, however, was apparently a winsome guy with a way with words.[8] He became involved in the local Christian community by telling people he was a recent convert to Christianity. He certainly seemed to have the zeal of a new convert, and he also appeared to be a successful businessman.

He further impressed upon the members of New Horizon with what appeared to be his connections and celebrity status. He had recently persuaded legally and financially troubled NFL quarterback Michael Vick to turn over his financial affairs to him. Vick had been one of the highest flying professional athletes in the world. In 2006, *Sports Illustrated* estimated Vick's annual income to be in excess of twenty-five million dollars.

But a series of run-ins with the law eroded Vick's endorsement income. Those run-ins culminated with his conviction on charges related to dog fighting. He began serving time in a federal prison in late 2007.

Talbot claimed he was offering spiritual guidance to the disgraced Vick. It was a story that added to Talbot's evangelical credentials, and it was part of the picture of himself that Talbot painted for New Horizon members. Only later did a Virginia bankruptcy court remove Talbot as Vick's advisor. Allegations later emerged that Talbot took fifty thousand dollars of Vick's money. But during the time Talbot was at New Horizon, he appeared to be scrupulous and successful.[9]

It's now obvious that Talbot was simply constructing an elaborate con.

The civil complaint against Talbot and associates Robert Schroy and Kenneth Simmons alleged that "at least ten investors" were defrauded. Werner believes, though, there could be many more and that the total amount of money could be much more than the five hundred thousand dollars in the August 8, 2009, complaint, possibly in the millions.

"At our church alone, I know it is above one million dollars," Werner said. "I know one woman who invested three hundred thousand dollars. She told her mother in Alabama, who invested and got her friends to invest. The amount from Alabama is greater than the amount from New Jersey."[10]

And there was more. Schroy and Simmons became associated with an organization called Jesus Rallies in Chicagoland, Inc., which authorities investigated after complaints that similar investment schemes had been discussed with Christian investors in Chicago and other parts of the Midwest.

Talbot's lawyer was a high-profile celebrity defense attorney, Jeffrey Lichtman. Lichtman managed to win a dismissal of murder conspiracy charges against organized crime boss John Gotti Jr., a case that elevated him to national stature.

Lichtman, though, was unexpectedly media shy on this case. He failed to respond to my repeated requests for an interview.

However, Lichtman did respond to the *Bergen Record* shortly after the original complaint was filed: "If this was a fraud, why is it that the great majority of the investors . . . don't believe they've been defrauded?"

This question—or one very much like it—shows up again and again when one looks at faith-based fraud. Many of Jim Bakker's victims have never admitted that they were defrauded. As we learned in earlier, some of those who lost money with Bakker are now contributing money to his new Branson-based operation. Why are even the victims of faith-based fraud reluctant to seek the truth and pursue justice?

Bill Werner, the church elder who refused to invest with Talbot has one plausible answer to that question. "People are afraid to come forward. After all, first, you lose your money and then, if you come forward, you hold yourself up to ridicule for being so gullible," he said. "Who wants to open themselves up to that insult after you've had a pretty big financial injury?"

But eventually, at least some of Talbot's victims got over their embarrassment. They talked, and that's what led to the August 2009 charges against Talbot.

By then, Talbot had already been named as a defendant in another lawsuit. The Department of Labor sued Talbot, Michael Vick, and another of Vick's advisors, Mary Wong, for $1.35 million. The Labor Department said the three of them improperly tapped into more than one million dollars from the former NFL star's marketing company's retirement plan.

Talbot was eventually barred for life for acting as the trustee of a retirement plan, or from working in the securities industry in any capacity in New Jersey. But I have not been able to find that he ever served any jail time for his fraud of the New Horizon church members, or any of the other fraudulent activities with which he was charged. Robert Schroy was, however, sentenced to forty-six months in prison in 2013, and he was ordered to pay $1.5 million in restitution.[11] However, court documents indicate that neither Schroy, Talbot, or Simmons had enough assets to re-pay the victims.

The Christian Industrial Complex at Work

In this chapter we are highlighting the fact that it is not just the large, sensational frauds such as PTL, New Era, Madoff, and Stanford that we should guard against. As New Horizon Fellowship demonstrates, the local church is not immune. New Horizon Fellowship also highlights the particular vulnerability of building funds to fraud.

Building funds offer special challenges to churches. First, a relatively small church, which has appropriate safeguards in place to handle regular weekly or monthly contributions, may not have experience to deal with the large amounts of money that suddenly come in during a building campaign.

Secondly, when church leaders want to raise money for building programs, they often turn to companies that specialize in church fundraising—to folks outside the church. After all, most churches rarely embark on building campaigns. Many pastors and church leaders will go through entire careers and never be a part of a building campaign, or participate in only one or two.

So it makes sense to bring in a company that does this sort of thing every day, can help you through the process, and tell you what works and what doesn't work. And I want to emphasize that many fundraising companies have long and honorable histories of helping churches and Christian ministries raise funds effectively and with great integrity.

But where we find large sums of money, we also find at least the possibility of fraud. That takes us to our next story, the story of a company called Alanar.

Alanar represented itself as a full-service financial company for churches involved in building campaigns. It turned out many churches signed up for Alanar's services. The company ended up handling more than one hundred and twenty million dollars from one hundred and fifty churches, large and small. More than eleven thousand investors put money into Alanar projects. But Alanar too ended up being a Ponzi scheme, and its owners ended up going to prison for diverting more than six million dollars of those funds for themselves.

How A Church Bond Works

Before we unpack the story of Alanar, let me explain a bit about how church bonds work.

Each building campaign is different, but many building campaigns involve asking members for multiyear pledges. These kinds of fundraising campaigns are pretty straightforward. The member is essentially giving the money to the church, but not all at once. A typical campaign might have a member pledge three thousand dollars over a three-year period. At the time of the pledge or soon thereafter, the member gives the first thousand-dollar gift. This initial gift and the pledges that accompany them then allow the church to go to a bank and borrow enough money to build the church. The church then pays the bank back with monthly payments not unlike an individual homeowner might pay mortgage payments.

The bank is usually happy with this arrangement.[12] Because members have paid the first third (or fifth, in the case of a five-year pledge) in advance, the bank is getting a significant down payment. If the bank ever did have to foreclose on the church, they would own a piece of property worth much more than the amount of money the bank has at risk.

Plus, the bank knows that honorable people have already pledged the other two-thirds. Also, most churches build because they are growing. The new building will allow the church to grow more, bringing in more members—and that translates into more donors. When all goes well, such a system allows the building to go up quickly while the debt is kept to manageable levels. In three to five years, many fast-growing churches have paid off their buildings.

And it must be said that most of the time it does go well. You will occasionally hear about a high-profile church that defaults, but hundreds of thousands of church buildings have been built using this relatively conservative—and successful—financial model.

But some churches elect another financing route: they sell bonds. Bonds, as we learned, are promises to pay. In other words, they are a form of debt. But a church bond allows a church to be in debt not to a bank, but to its own members. You might think that sounds like a bad thing, but it can be a good thing—again, if handled properly.

Let me explain.

In the example above, a member gives three thousand dollars over a three-year period. For a middle-class family, such a gift—given over and above normal weekly gifts to the church—might be the very most that family can give. Most families have only so much they can give away.

But it is also possible that this same family is saving money, and has been saving for years. A family that has only a few thousand dollars to give away might have tens of thousands or hundreds of thousands in savings or investment accounts—such as college accounts or retirement accounts.

Indeed, for many middle-class and upper middle-class families, the amount of money in the "investment bucket" is often much larger than the amount of money in the "giving bucket."

But here's the rub: the family already has a plan for that money. Retirement. College for the kids. Whatever. That's why the family usually has that money invested in relatively safe financial instruments, such as blue-chip stocks, or bonds with guaranteed rates of return.

So why not buy church bonds?

The family that can give only three thousand dollars might be able to purchase bonds worth several times more than that from the church. Remember, a bond is a promise to pay. So the church issues the member a piece of paper, the bond itself, that says when the church will pay back the bond, usually with some small rate of interest. As in the example above, the church gets the money it needs to build the building. The difference is that the church doesn't make monthly payments to a bank. It makes payments to its members instead.

Wait a minute, you might be saying. The members aren't supposed to get paid back for three to five years. And you are right. That's where a bond company, sometimes called a specialty finance, or church finance, company comes in.

A bond company is an expert in this process. It will make sure that the church complies with the laws associated with the sale of bonds, and the bond company usually trains the leadership of the church in how to sell the bonds to its members. The bond company actually issues the paper bonds and holds the money the members invest until the church needs it for the construction. Then the church makes payments to the bond company rather than to a bank.

The bond company holds and invests the money until it is time to pay back the members, three to five years later. As before, if all goes well, everyone is happy. The church gets a building, the members get their money back, with some interest (usually slightly less than they could get elsewhere, but the money was used for a good cause).

The bond company often gets an upfront fee that is added into the cost of the building, and sometimes the bond company earns some of the interest—the difference between what they were able to earn on the money and what they had to pay back to the members. But banks would have similar charges, so such fees are considered reasonable.

When all is said and done, bond companies usually make between five and seven percent of the total amount financed. That may not sound like a lot, but in the early 2000s, a medium-sized church might spend more than five million dollars on an education building or a new, larger worship center. To manage such a deal, a church bond company might make in excess of two hundred and fifty thousand dollars.

The process I have described here, or some variation of it, is a common one. It takes place hundreds, if not thousands, of times each year.[13] The overwhelming majority of these projects go well, and the overwhelming majority of the companies involved in these projects are run by honest businesspeople.

Of course, this process—even when it works well, without fraud or scandal—glosses over significant philosophical and theological problems. For example, while Scripture doesn't forbid debt, it strongly warns against it (see Proverbs 22:7; Romans 13:8). I've become convinced that one of the reasons Scripture warns against debt is because churches in debt begin to make decisions based on the debt. Programs are initiated or terminated based on their ability to help the congregation pay off the debt, not based on obedience to God or the needs of the community that church has been planted to serve.

That discussion is beyond the scope of this book, but what is very clearly relevant to the scope of our conversation is this: Where there are big pots of money there are great temptations. And yielding to that temptation is what happened to Indiana-based Alanar, who once again enters our story.

Alanar Agonistes

Alanar—as I said—billed itself as a full-service company.

That was a significant selling point to church leaders who might otherwise have found the process of a fundraising campaign daunting. A part of Alanar's service included training the leaders of client churches to sell bonds to fellow church members. In Alanar's training, church members were advised to open meetings with prayer, quote Scripture during the sales call, and "never sell the facts, sell warm stewardship and the Lord."[14]

For Alanar, the plan worked for nearly twenty years. It worked, in part, because Alanar did just enough of what it said it was going to do that it threw skeptics and investigators off its trail. In the case of Alanar, as has been the case of other Ponzi schemes we have discussed, Alanar was able to create a story that seemed plausible to its hearers, even though it ultimately proved to be false.

Eventually, though, Huntington County (Indiana) Prosecutor Bob Hunley filed ten separate felony charges against the leaders of Alanar: former pastor Vaughn Reeves and his sons, Chip, Chris, and Josh. The charges accused the Reeveses of diverting at least six million dollars for personal use.

But it took years for Alanar to be brought to justice. When charges finally were filed on June 30, 2009, Hunley said, "This is a day a long time in the making. I'm glad to hold Vaughn Reeves and his sons accountable. People trusted their life savings to these men. Investors felt they were helping to build churches, not buy the Reeveses expensive homes, fancy cars, airplanes and swimming pools."

Hunley's office alleged and ultimately proved that Reeves and his sons set up an elaborate network of companies, at least eight in total. One company, Churchman's Capital Group, apparently was the company that took money from churches and issued the bonds. Churchman's Investment Corporation was the name of an online brokerage account at E*Trade.

The network of accounts and the constant transfer of funds between the accounts allowed the Reeves family to keep up the deception for years. Again, the deception depended on Alanar having some measure of success. In fact, between 1988 and 2005, at least one hundred and fifty churches were built and many bondholders were repaid.

However, during almost all of that time, it is now clear Alanar was paying early investors with money coming in from newer investors, in the style of a classic Ponzi scheme. And just like Charles Ponzi, Reeves apparently was able to get early investors to invest their money again. That meant that in some cases, Alanar never actually had to pay out cash to investors. In 2005, when authorities finally took action, the first action was not a criminal charge, but an injunction by the SEC. The injunction ordered Alanar and all related entities to cease operations.

It was at this point that Alanar started to unravel. Because Alanar could not take in any more money, it became quickly obvious what was going on.

Even so, it took nearly five years after that initial SEC action to bring the case against Reeves to fruition. But that day came, and it came on October 21, 2010, when a Gibson County jury convicted Vaughn Reeves Sr. on nine out of the ten felony counts of aiding, inducing, or causing securities fraud. While the trial lasted almost two weeks, it took the jury just four hours to reach a verdict. Prosecutor Bob Hunley said, "This is a great day for the investors who lost so much. They have been waiting a long time for their day in court, and today they finally got it."[15]

Prosecutor Hunley might be excused for his enthusiasm at calling it a "great" day because for him it was a hard-won legal victory. But for the investors themselves, it was more of a bittersweet day. It was clear even then that millions of dollars would likely never be returned to their original investors, to say nothing of the interest they were supposed to receive.

The court appointed attorney Bradley Skolnik to manage what was left of Alanar's operations in 2005, and what he took over was a mess. Some churches were built and some early investors did get their money back. However, other investors, some of whom had poured their life savings into Alanar's bonds, were left with little recourse.

Because some churches were still making payments on their bonds, Skolnik was able to return some money to investors. At least eight of the churches were in some stage of foreclosure proceedings when Skolnik took over. One of the reasons: the churches' leaders were seduced by the Reeveses into building bigger than they could afford. Several of these churches lost their buildings, which was a tragedy for these congregations, though the sale of these buildings yielded more money that was eventually distributed to shareholders.

In December 2010, Reeves was sentenced to fifty-four years in prison. At the time of his sentencing, more than thirteen million dollars had not yet been recovered.[16]

Skolnik and another court-appointed receiver, Michael Rusnak, spent another four years trying to get money back to the original investors. The last two million dollars went out in September of 2014. At the time, Rusnak told the Associated Press, "It's something that just goes on so long, I think everyone is glad to see it over." But he admitted that the final disposition was not fully satisfactory because he had to foreclose on churches, and even those foreclosures didn't make investors whole. "Believe me, it's painful," Rusnak said. "Sometimes, we had no choice."[17]

Of the more than eleven thousand people who invested in Alanar projects, about three thousand people received little or no money back. But that number is an abstraction until you hear the story of Karen Lamb, of Terre Haute, Indiana. She told the

Associated Press that she had invested fifty-five thousand dollars in Alanar bonds, and she had so far received back only about six thousand dollars.[5] Sam Robinson of Farmersburg, Indiana, invested three hundred and eighty thousand dollars He said he has received only a small portion of it back. Robinson was on hand for the closing arguments in the Reeves trial. "They always talked about God and helping churches to build," Robinson said. "I'm still stinging over the loss of my savings."

Before the judge, Lena Martin, handed down her verdict, she highlighted Steve Duncan, who lost so much money that he could no longer afford medical insurance or medical treatment. As a result, he lost his eyesight. "This has ruined my life," Duncan told Judge Martin, "and the lives of many others."

As for the Reeveses: Two of Vaughn Reeves' three sons spent time in prison, though they are now out. A third son avoided prison, but had to repay about one million dollars as part of a plea agreement.

As of 2020, Vaughan Reeves is still in prison. His projected release date is December 31, 2035. If he makes it to his release date, he will be ninety-one years old.

Lessons Learned: What to Do When Confronted With Fraud?

Bill Werner, the elder in the now defunct New Horizon Fellowship, raised an interesting point that we have already talked around, but which now is a good time to address directly: What should Christians do when confronted with fraud in the church?

When it comes to frauds in the church, people are often afraid to come forward. Werner said that people are afraid to appear gullible. They are embarrassed. Others feel that such matters are "family matters" and should not be settled in the civil courts. They often cite 1 Corinthians 6:7: *"Actually, then, it is already a defeat for you, that you have lawsuits with one another. Why not rather be wronged? Why not rather be defrauded?"*

On the face of it, this looks to be a fairly clear injunction against suing others. Crown Financial Ministries, one of the nation's most respected evangelical ministries, says this: "As American citizens, we have the legal right to sue if we feel that we have suffered loss. As Christians and fellow believers, however, our primary purpose is to serve God. Thus, we give up our rights to God. In so doing, rather than going to the courts of this world with an issue of personal injustice, we must turn only to God regarding the personal injustice and leave the results to Him."

Both this verse and the Crown advice contain much wisdom. But it is also evident that this advice is not absolute. Crown Ministries goes on to say this:

> On the other hand, if somebody brings a suit against you, you have a right to defend yourself. Paul defended himself against unjust claims throughout the book of Acts (16:37; 22:25; 25:11). Although Paul did not attack his accusers or attempt to extract any compensation from them, he did vigorously defend himself against their claims, several times even reciting Roman law applicable to his case. As long as our motives are right and we are not seeking retribution, we can defend ourselves.

Or take this example: We read in the book of James that it is "true religion, undefiled before God, to look after widows and orphans in their time of need." Imagine, for example, that an insurance company refuses to pay a widow her fair and just payments upon the death of a husband? I would argue that a lawsuit is not only allowed but, if all other options are exhausted, it is all but required in order to give this widow justice.

In the early years of the homeschooling movement, lawsuits were often necessary tools used by Christian families against their local governments to secure for parents what they perceived to be their biblical rights to bring up their own children in "the nurture and admonition of the Lord."

And even if you are willing to give up your right to a lawsuit against someone who has defrauded you, that does not mean you have no responsibilities in the face of fraud. If someone, even someone who claimed to be a Christian, committed a crime in your presence, or a crime against you, do you not have the right, even the responsibility, to report that crime? I say the answer to that question is an emphatic yes.

I would further argue that the biblical admonition not to sue or not to report frauds to criminal authorities is further mitigated by the fact that many of the frauds I have seen are perpetrated by people who may claim to be Christians, but whose very claim of Christian faith is itself demonstrably fraudulent.

That said, in all such matters we should proceed with humility. After all, who truly knows another person's heart? Men of true faith can do truly dishonorable things. The theologian Reinhold Neibuhr once said that the doctrine of original sin is the only one for which we have empirical data. Indeed, I often say to myself and to my friends that when I want to see evidence of the doctrine of original sin, I look in the mirror.

Nonetheless, God establishes civil governments. They are legitimate tools to bring about justice. As Christians, we can and should use these tools to bring to justice those who would defraud widows, orphans, the poor, and others.

And, as this chapter makes clear, opportunities for fraud are not available just to the Bakkers, Bennetts, Stanfords, and Madoffs of the world.

They are all around us.

Chapter 8

What Would Jesus Fly?

The deadly doctrines disseminated by prosperity preachers pose the greatest threat to Christianity from within.

—Hank Hanegraaff, *Christianity in Crisis: 21st Century*

Johann Tetzel, the most aggressive of the Dominican friars selling indulgences had a saying: "As soon as a coin in the coffer rings, the rescued soul from purgatory springs."
It doesn't sound that different from today's "Plant a seed to meet your need."

—Phil Cooke, *The Last TV Evangelist*

Up until now, we've mostly discussed organizations and activities that might broadly be called financial frauds. But another species of fraud exists that we might call theological fraud.

This fraud includes many prosperity gospel preachers, some of whom we've already mentioned, including Jim Bakker. They do not directly promise a return on investment, as Charles Ponzi or Allen Stanford did. They tell people that their own prosperity is from God; their poverty is because they haven't given enough.

In some ways you have to admire the brazen directness of the prosperity gospel preachers. They tell you up front: If you give money to me, I'm going to buy mansions and planes. I'm going to stay in first-class hotels. I'm going to live high on the hog.

And their followers oblige.

A Prosperity Gospel Primer

The prosperity gospel goes by many names. It is sometimes called the "health and wealth" gospel or "prosperity theology" or "name it and claim it" theology. Because prosperity theology is a do-it-yourself theology, not bound by a creed or historical biblical orthodoxy, it is difficult to say with certainty what a particular prosperity preacher believes.

This very do-it-yourself quality is one reason prosperity theology has had resilience within modern evangelicalism. Prosperity gospel preachers flirt with the boundaries of theological orthodoxy. They can and often do claim to be misunderstood if they actually step over that theological boundary. Joel Osteen, Benny Hinn, Oral Roberts, and many others have all made statements that were clearly heretical and, in some cases, made them repeatedly, only to retract them later when the criticism of those statements became severe.[1]

That said, the clear impression we get from a close study of them is not that they are actively promoting heresy. They are actively promoting themselves, and the heresy is a by-product.

In general, prosperity theology is a belief that God provides material prosperity and physical health to those He favors. A corollary to this definition is this: Material prosperity is a sign of God's favor. An important way of seeking God's favor is to "plant seeds" of faith, usually in the form of financial gifts to the prosperity gospel preachers themselves.

To oversimplify to the extreme, Biblical theology teaches that Christians have been richly blessed by God's unmerited favor, His grace, and we seek to be a blessing to others—by giving and service—as acts of worship and gratitude. Prosperity theology teaches that God's blessing is a result of our giving. It teaches that you give to get. It teaches that "you can't out-give God." It teaches that our giving unleashes God's favor.

Proponents of the prosperity gospel use, and misuse, certain key passages from Scripture:

- Bring the whole tithe into the storehouse, so that there may be food in My house, and test Me now in this, says the Lord of hosts, "if I will not open for you the windows of heaven and pour out for you a blessing until it overflows." (Malachi 3:10 NASB)
- But you shall remember the Lord your God, for it is He who is giving you power to make wealth, that He may confirm His covenant which He swore to your fathers, as it is this day. (Deuteronomy 8:18 NASB)
- I have come that they may have life, and that they may have it more abundantly. (John 10:10 NASB)
- Beloved, I pray that you may prosper in all things and be in health, just as your soul prospers. (3 John 2:4 NASB)

In the late twentieth and early twenty-first centuries, we have seen the prosperity gospel all around the world. It may even be the dominant theology in some parts of South America and Africa.

But it is also fair to note that it is an American export. The relationship between faith and prosperity is particularly rooted in the American experience. Consider, as one of many examples, a resolution of the Second Continental Congress that asks God to "be graciously pleased to bless all his people in these colonies with health and plenty, and grant that a spirit of incorruptible patriotism, and of pure undefiled religion, may universally prevail."[2]

It is important to note, though, that one expression in this resolution, written by William Livingston, separates his brand of theology from modern prosperity theology, and that phrase is "pure undefiled religion."

That phrase is an unmistakable echo of James 1:27. In the King James Version of the Bible that Livingston would have surely known, that verse says "Pure religion and undefiled before God and the Father is this, to visit the fatherless and widows in their affliction, and to keep himself unspotted from the world." The New International Version, more familiar to us in the twenty-first century, says this: "Religion that God our Father accepts as pure and faultless is this: to look after orphans and widows in their distress, and to keep oneself from being polluted by the world."

A complete theological critique of prosperity gospel theology is beyond the scope of our conversation. Several excellent theologians and writers have written sound and readable critiques of prosperity theology. Michael Horton's *Christless Christianity* and Hank Hanegraaff's *Christianity in Crisis* come immediately to mind. I commend those books to you.

Let me simply say here that the position of this book is the prosperity gospel is a false gospel and that its proponents have departed from the way of biblical Christianity. The basis of this conclusion derives at least in part from the very verse above, which gives us a definition of "true religion." Practitioners of true religion use their resources to look after orphans and widows, and they keep themselves from being polluted by the world. Practitioners of the prosperity gospel are often at the other end of the spectrum. I would also observe that prosperity theology is self-contradictory, and that fact exposes it as fraud. In other words: If it is true that God always and inevitably returns financial seeds sown with an abundant financial return, why would not these very prosperity preachers immediately sow the money they are given into the lives of others rather than on the material goods for themselves? Their very behavior, their lavish expenditures on mansions and airplanes, and their stockpiles of cash are the clearest indicators that they don't believe what they're preaching. Otherwise, they too would be giving away all they own in anticipation of an even greater return.

So, again, a complete debunking of prosperity theology is a book for another day. For now, we'll turn our attention not to the theology but to one of the more public and ostentatious vanities of the prosperity preachers. Nowhere is the practice of prosperity theology more evident than with those preachers who use private jets to do their work.

Up, Up, and Away

Billionaire Warren Buffett became one of the richest men in the world by knowing what adds value to a corporation and what does not. And one of the things that does not, he has argued for years, is a corporate jet. They're a luxury in almost every case, a necessity for only a few, and he would often rail against them in the annual reports of his company, Berkshire Hathaway, and elsewhere.

That's why, when Berkshire Hathaway finally bought a corporate jet in 1989, he only half jokingly called it "The Indefensible."[3]

But try telling that to Fred Price, Creflo Dollar, Jesse Duplantis, Benny Hinn, or Kenneth Copeland. They are among the more than thirty churches and Christian ministries that have luxury jets, according to an investigation into the use of luxury jets I conducted for *WORLD*, using data provided to me mostly from the Dallas-based ministry watchdog Trinity Foundation.[4] According to Ole Anthony, founder of the Trinity Foundation, the ownership and use of luxury jets are among the surest indicators that donor money is not being used for ministry purposes.

"There are incredible abuses of these corporate jets for personal use," Anthony said. "Mind-bending abuse that they do with impunity."

Using ministry resources for personal use is prohibited by IRS regulations, but the IRS almost never investigates tax-exempt organizations. Of the more than one million tax-exempt organizations in the country, less than ten thousand get audited each year—that's one tenth of one percent. And the number audited many years is closer to five thousand.[5]

When a media organization uncovers abuses of an executive jet for personal purposes, Anthony said, the televangelists say they've reimbursed the ministry. "But it's just a claim," Anthony said. "They are not required to, and almost never do, provide anything that resembles real documentation of the claim."

This data is why such men as Albert Meyer say regulation, beyond requirements for complete transparency, is not the answer.

"Government regulations give people a false sense of security," Meyer repeats like a mantra. And regulations that are not enforced are particularly dangerous. They allow ministry leaders to say, as televangelist Kenneth Copeland said during the height of the Grassley investigations, "If we're breaking the law, why haven't they found anything?" The net effect is a small but very real erosion in the rule of law in the nonprofit sector and in the country generally.

One possible fix to this abuse would be for all ministries, including churches, to release their Form 990s. Or, at a minimum, to require organizations that want to call themselves churches to actually be churches. In recent years, more and more ministries are claiming to be churches. They do not perform any of the traditional functions of churches. They do not hold Sunday morning services. They do not perform weddings or burials. They do not administer sacraments. But they call themselves churches so they do not have to release their Form 990s to the public.

Most of the prosperity gospel preachers hide behind the

church exemption, but—increasingly—other Christian ministries that had previously released their Form 990s to the public are hiding behind that exemption as well. Among them: Ravi Zacharias International Ministries, Wycliffe Associates, Cru (formerly Campus Crusade for Christ), TransWorld Radio, Liberty Counsel, and Focus on the Family.

Requiring all ministries to be more transparent would not necessarily end the practice of using corporate jets, but it would make the use of such jets more obvious to donors, who could then make their own decisions about whether they wanted to support such ministries.

Jet Setting with Jesse Duplantis

A look at the flight records of televangelist Jesse Duplantis provides a telling glimpse into this world.

Duplantis was once one of the charismatic movement's stars. He is not as well known outside of those circles as Kenneth Copeland, Benny Hinn, and the other members of the Grassley Six investigated by Senator Charles Grassley from 2007-11. Nonetheless, this Louisiana-based televangelist—who in his youth was a guitarist in various heavy metal rock bands—has been preaching since the late 1970s. He is known for his Cajun accent and his exuberant style and humor, as well as for his shock of silvery-white hair and his taste for high-end jets.

Over the years, he has owned several. But as I was preparing this book, his chariot of choice was a Falcon 50. It is fast, with a top speed just below the speed of sound, thanks to its three jet engines. In fact, it is the only plane in this class with three engines and is considered a "super-medium" or "long-range" plane, capable of almost three thousand miles between refuelings. That gives it the capability of flying literally around the world. When Duplantis bought the plane in 2006, he wrote in his ministry's magazine that it was an "amazing tool for world evangelism" and he thanked his partners for making the purchase possible. To drive that point home, in September of 2006, he took the plane to Russia for a series of meetings and preaching events.

An examination of flight records compiled by the Trinity Foundation revealed that from April 2006 to March 2008, Duplantis made 469 flights—an average of almost one every week day—and logged hundreds of thousands of miles on his Falcon 50. Three of those trips were to Las Vegas, and four of them were to Hawaii. On one of the Hawaii trips (May 14-22, 2007), he took a side trip to American Samoa. On another one (February 23-March 7, 2007), he engaged in a bit of island hopping in Hawaii, making at least a half dozen flights within the Hawaiian Islands during that trip.

"It's almost impossible to imagine that all these trips could have been ministry trips," said Trinity Foundation's Ole Anthony. In May 2018, news accounts erupted yet again about Duplantis' jets. He was asking his followers to donate money so he could purchase a new fifty-four million dollar Dassault Falcon 7X. He said during his fundraising for the jet that he needed a new one—which would be at least the fourth one his ministry has owned since 2006, that he was "just burning them up for the Lord Jesus Christ." He also said, "I really believe that if Jesus was physically on the earth today, he wouldn't be riding a donkey. Think about that for a minute. He'd be in an airplane, preaching the gospel all over the world."[6]

Duplantis' ministry has made other public attempts to defend his aircraft. Michael Wright was the director of marketing for Jesse Duplantis Ministries. He said, "We've sent our schedule to Delta and other airlines and asked them if they could get us where we need to be, and they can't. They can't get us from point A to B to C to D at the times we need to be there. For us, the plane is a necessity."

But perhaps his most bizarre rationale for the jet came in 2016, when Duplantis was a guest on Kenneth Copeland's television program. Here a partial transcript of their exchange:

> **Copeland:** Oral [Roberts] used to fly [commercial] airlines. But, even back then it got to the place where it was agitating his spirit. People coming up to him, he had become famous, and they wanted him to pray for them and all that. You can't, you can't manage that today. This dope-filled world, and get in a long tube with a bunch of demons. And it's deadly.
>
> **Duplantis:** It works on your heart, it really does.[7]

Fred's Price

Jesse Duplantis is by no means the only power user of executive aircraft. In a seven-year period (2000 to 2007), a Gulfstream jet (with a retail sticker price of about thirty-seven million dollars) used by evangelist Fred Price filed plans for more than seven hundred flights.

For many years, until he died of COVID-19 in early 2021, Fred Price was perhaps the most flamboyant and unapologetic proponent of the prosperity theology in the country. For thirty-five years, he was the pastor of Crenshaw Christian Center in Los Angeles. Under his leadership, Crenshaw became one of the nation's first predominantly African-American megachurches. In 2009, at age seventy-seven, he passed the reins of leadership to his son, Fred Price Jr., then age thirty.

The church continued to grow, but in June 2017, Fred Price Jr. resigned as pastor, apologizing for "serious personal misjudgments which have affected my life and my family." Fred Price Sr., then in his late eighties, resumed duties as pastor. Through it all, the church has continued to grow and in 2018, claimed twenty-eight thousand members.

Still, Fred Price's theology is as suspect as his use of donor funds. Here are a few representative examples.

- Do you think that the punishment for our sin was to die on a cross? If that were the case, the two thieves could have paid your price. No, the punishment was to go into hell itself and to serve time in hell separated from God.[8]
- If you've got one-dollar faith and you ask for a ten-thousand-dollar item, it ain't going to work. It won't work. Jesus said, "according to your faith," not according to God's will for you, in His own good time, if it's according to His will, if He can work it into His busy schedule. He said, "According to your faith, be it unto you." Now, I may want a Rolls Royce, and don't have but bicycle faith. Guess what I'm going to get? A bicycle.[9]
- The whole point is I'm trying to get you to see—to get you out of this malaise of thinking that Jesus and the disciples were poor and then relating that to you thinking that you, as a child of God, have to follow Jesus. The Bible says that He has left us an example that we should follow His steps. That's the reason why I drive a Rolls Royce. I'm following Jesus' steps.[10]
- Because I talk about finances and prosperity a lot, I have been called the 'prophet of prosperity.' Personally, I like the title. It is what God has called me to do—to teach His people that He wants them prosperous. Too many Christians have a challenge with the idea of material prosperity. They can go along with prospering in every way except financially. It is a shame that they are so ignorant of their covenant rights. For example: Some folk have heard me say that I think I am worth a million dollars a year in salary, and that made them uncomfortable. They

> mentioned that another renowned Christian leader has worked diligently over the years and receives very little salary. They became indignant that I would have the nerve to make such a statement. My comment to them was that maybe the other person does not think he is worth a million dollars a year, and that is not my fault. As a man thinks in his heart so is he.[11]

The following is an excerpt from Dr. Price's book *Higher Finances*, taken from his website:

> We need to realize that when God tells us to believe that we receive what we pray for, it is because what we are praying for is already in existence in the spirit world. Our believing we receive what we pray for causes that thing to come out of the spirit world into this physical world. I like to refer to this as the duality of existence. Everything exists in two forms—first of all in spirit form, then in physical manifestation form. It is faith that makes the transfer from the spirit world into the physical world. Your healing is there, your new home is there, your new car is there, peace is there, and deliverance for your children is there. But you have to reach out into that spirit world and claim your Covenant by saying, 'In the name of Jesus, I believe that I receive it.' Maintain that confession, keep standing by faith on God's Word, and the thing you are believing for will come to pass in your life.[12]

Again, though this book is not specifically about theology, it is impossible to ignore the theology of prosperity gospel preachers such as Fred Price, Jesse Duplantis, Kenneth Copeland, and others. That theology departs from historical Christian doctrine. They, arguably, serve a different god, a god who is not the Sovereign God revealed in the Bible. Their god's power can be released only with the permission of humans.

In that sense, we humans (these preachers suggest) have power over God. We are gods ourselves. If you think that is an overstatement, consider this excerpt from a sermon by Creflo Dollar, one of the more popular prosperity gospel preachers, and one of the preachers investigated by Senator Charles Grassley as part of the so-called Grassley Six:

> **Dollar:** If horses get together, they produce what?
> **Congregation:** Horses!
> **Dollar:** If dogs get together, they produce what?
> **Congregation:** Dogs!
> **Dollar:** If cats get together, they produce what?
> **Congregation:** Cats!
> **Dollar:** So if the Godhead says 'Let us make *man* in *our* image,' and everything produces after its own kind, then they produce what?
> **Congregation:** Gods!
> **Dollar:** Gods. Little *g* gods. You're not human. Only human part of you is this flesh you're wearing.

Now, it seems almost too easy and too obvious to point out that this idea, that we can be "as gods" (Genesis 3:5 KJV) is precisely the promise with which Satan tempted Eve in the Garden of Eden.

You might reasonably be wondering what does this theology lesson have to do with owning corporate jets? The answer is quite a lot. First of all, the fact that ownership of a corporate jet requires enormous resources is obvious on its face. So in the theology of these prosperity gospel preachers, to own one is *prima facie* evidence of a great faith, since how much faith you have is directly related to how much wealth you have.

Neither Price nor Duplantis nor any of the televangelists with jets would disclose to me the total costs of owning these jets. The operating costs can vary widely. Used entry-level jets are less than two million dollars, while new top-end jets can sell for more than fifty million dollars. However, experts say that the fully loaded costs for these jets (including insurance and depreciation) can easily go over ten thousand dollars per hour. Even for the low-end jets, the operating cost is almost never less than two thousand dollars per hour. For most owners, that translates to a cost of several million dollars a year, even with minimal usage.

Are they worth it? Users of luxury aircraft are fond of calling their jets "time machines" that help them get to business destinations faster and fresher. But what about a return for the donors? Most of the organizations that have jets refuse to release financial information. "If the general public and especially the supporters of these ministries had any idea how much money is wasted to support the 'vanity airplanes' of these alleged men of God, they would be appalled," said Trinity Foundation's Ole Anthony. "Flying first class would be many, many times more economical." Anthony made one other point: these jets are not just donor concerns. "It is important to remember that every American citizen is paying for their outlandish lifestyles because their supporters can deduct their donations to the ministries, which makes our tax bill increase," Anthony said.

Legitimate Aircraft Uses

Of course, some Christian ministries, especially disaster relief and missionary organizations, have legitimate uses for airplanes, but the planes they're using are not luxury jets that can go literally around the world at nearly the speed of sound.

Dwight Jarboe has a long history in missionary aviation. He joined Wycliffe Bible Translators in 1972 to be an aircraft mechanic, serving in Brazil, among other places. He joined MMS Aviation in 1982. MMS Aviation is a Christian ministry that repairs and overhauls planes for the missionary aviation community. Jarboe was CEO from December 1983 through October 2016. He continues to serve there as president emeritus.

Jarboe estimates that there are about one hundred and twenty Christian ministries that use aircraft in their ministries. "The majority of these are small single-engine or twin-engine propeller planes," Jarboe said. These planes are used for disaster relief, transportation to remote locations around the world, or for special purposes in the United States.

"We work with a Maryland group who ministers specifically to the Chinese community in the United States," Jarboe said. They have a ten-passenger King Air they can use to move the entire team around at once, often traveling to locations that do not have commercial service. "But it's not a luxury plane," Jarboe added. "It's basic transportation."

MMS Aviation, which in 2018 received about $1.8 million in donations, does not charge Christian groups for its services. "If an airplane is used in Christian ministry, they don't pay for labor, only parts." Jarboe also said his organization doesn't work on the kind of jets that the prosperity gospel televangelists use.

Mission Aviation Fellowship and JAARS are perhaps the most well-known users of aircraft for ministry purposes. Their planes are generally outfitted to haul cargo, not people, and while both organizations have fleets operating in the United States, most of their planes are in remote areas around the world. Indeed, JAARS originally stood for Jungle Aviation and Radio Service and has an honorable and storied history supporting Bible translation efforts and missionaries in some of the most remote and hostile places on the globe.

The Evangelical Council for Financial Accountability

(ECFA) takes a pragmatic approach on the issue of aircraft. Dan Busby, the long-time president of the ECFA before his retirement in early 2020, told me, "It really comes down to whether a charity can justify business purpose for a jet, and many charities pass this test. If the business purpose test is met, then it is an issue of documenting any personal use and attributing the value of any personal use for compensation reporting purposes. So, in short, the proper use of jets for nonprofit purposes is a matter of documentation, documentation, documentation."

Any thinking Christian should, however, be concerned about this approach. Jesse Duplantis may be able to document that he used his jet to fly to Hawaii in order to hold a rally, the primary purpose of which is to ask people to give him money so he can then fly his jet to Tahiti and ask for more money. In Duplantis' world, these are ministry purposes. And so long as the documentation is complete, both the IRS and the ECFA are apparently satisfied. But should we be satisfied?

My answer to that question is no. And once again we see that any hope either the IRS or the ECFA will protect the interests of donors or theological integrity is badly misplaced.

What Would Wycliffe Fly?

It's easy to dismiss these prosperity gospel preachers as outliers in the evangelical world. It's easy to say, "Yes, we evangelicals have a few 'crazy uncles,' but this is not what we are about as a family. You're nut-picking, as the saying goes: you've found a few nuts to try and convince us that the entire evangelical world is corrupt."

It's a fair criticism. That's why I want to say again that the vast majority of Christian ministry leaders live modestly, even sacrificially. Such people as I have described so far in this chapter are indeed outliers.

But they are no longer unique. Their practices are creeping

into more mainstream organizations.

I cite as one example: Wycliffe Associates.[13]

Wycliffe Associates is a Bible-translation organization named after John Wycliffe. John Wycliffe famously translated the Bible into English, and was one of the seminal figures of the Reformation. But he was more than a translator. He was an outspoken critic of clergy opulence. He wrote tracts condemning the luxurious lifestyles of many church leaders.

One wonders what Wycliffe would say about the private airplane owned by Wycliffe Associates, an airplane apparently used by WA's President Bruce Smith and other Wycliffe senior executives to court wealthy donors.

Wycliffe Associates' plane is a high-performance turboprop called a TBM 700. The plane was introduced in 1990 and is no longer manufactured, but used models are typically $1 to $1.5 million. Its successor, the TBM 900, sells new for about four million dollars. During early 2020, when I looked into the WA airplane, the ministry kept it at Orlando Executive Airport.

Bible-translation organizations that operate in road-less parts of the world often use aircraft for basic transportation. We've already mentioned that Mission Aviation Fellowship and JAARS have used airplanes for decades to move personnel and material to remote parts of the world.

However, an examination by MinistryWatch of flight records obtained from FlightAware by the Dallas-based Trinity Foundation found that the Wycliffe Associates aircraft engaged in no such work. Flight records for the six months ending in early 2020 found that the most distant airport the plane landed in was in Reno, Nevada. Indeed, the vast majority of the destinations were not remote locations at all, but major US cities, including Atlanta, San Antonio, Nashville, and St. Louis. Almost all of the smaller destinations—including Wichita, Naples, and Tuscaloosa—had commercial airports.

The only destinations too small for commercial flights appear to have been refueling stops. For example, on the trip to Reno, the plane made a thirty-minute stop in Andrews, Texas, population thirteen thousand, thirty miles east of the New Mexico border.

In short, the plane went to destinations that could have been visited far more cheaply on commercial flights.

How much more cheaply? That's hard to determine without knowing information Wycliffe Associates will not disclose. Repeated requests for information went unanswered.

It's worth noting here that Wycliffe Associates has not released its Form 990 to the public for more than a decade, after having itself re-classified as a church by the IRS. It also withdrew from membership in the ECFA in early 2020 while it was under review for non-compliance with the ECFA's ethical standards.

Though Wycliffe would not disclose its costs for operating its plane, it is possible to estimate the costs from easily obtainable information. The fixed costs of owning a TBM, according to a TBM owners group, are about six thousand dollars per month. The operating costs are about two dollars per nautical mile. A September 2019 flight the Wycliffe Associates plane made to Atlanta and back to Orlando was about one thousand nautical miles, or about two thousand dollars—not including the fixed costs. A roundtrip ticket on a major airline ranged from just over one hundred dollars to about three hundred dollars, depending on the time of day. The TBM 700 seats five people plus a pilot. So even if the Wycliffe Associates plane was full, it would still have been far cheaper to fly commercial.

Wycliffe Associates President Bruce Smith is a pilot who has the ratings to fly himself. At least one other Wycliffe Associates executive, Brent Ropp, is also a pilot with sufficient ratings to fly the high-performance plane. Brent Ropp left Wycliffe Associates in 2020. After a series of articles in 2020 by MinistryWatch that highlighted Bruce Smith's aircraft usage and other issues, he too left the organization.

As I mentioned earlier, some aircraft owners talk about the time-saving value of their planes. But this argument is negated by a close look at the Wycliffe Associates' flight information. The plane often sat on the ground for days at a time at the final destination. It wasn't being used to make densely packed trips. Another irony of using the time-savings argument for the Wycliffe plane is this simple geographical fact: the offices of Wycliffe Associates are nearly adjacent to Orlando International Airport, the home of most of Orlando's commercial flights. The Orlando Executive Airport where WA's plane is hangered is a half hour from Wycliffe's offices—on a day when there's no traffic.

Also, if the executives are so pressed for time that they need a private aircraft, it's hard to explain why the only trip the plane took in January of 2020 was a one and a half hour trip that began in Orlando and ended in Orlando. Again, WA would not answer specific questions about individual trips, but experienced aviators told MinistryWatch that could have been a part of the plane's maintenance routine.

Most evangelicals do not think of Wycliffe as being similar to the ministries of Creflo Dollar, Fred Price, Jesse Duplantis, Mac Hammond, Joyce Meyer, Trinity Broadcasting Network, Daystar, Perry Stone, and Kenneth Copeland—all of whom own aircraft. Wycliffe Associates was, after all, originally a subsidiary of the highly respected Wycliffe Bible Translators. It was a charter member of the ECFA.

But Wycliffe's 2020 resignation from the ECFA tells us that perpetual vigilance by donors and ministry boards are the price of integrity and a good reputation. It is a reminder that even ministries that start off well can get off course.

The ownership of the plane did not play a factor in the review of Wycliffe Associates, according to ECFA President Emeritus Dan Busby, who said, "While we looked at various factors in relation to ECFA's standards, our concluding focus was strictly on the accuracy of WA's communications with donors and whether those communications established realistic expectations in donor's minds in terms of what the gifts would accomplish."

Where Do We Go from Here?

All six of the Grassley Six televangelists owned or leased luxury corporate jets. Kenneth Copeland owns at least two. Paula and Randy White's Without Walls International Church bought a Gulfstream II jet for about $1.5 million in 2006. Before then, the Whites frequently chartered planes.

Was it these jets that put them on Senator Grassley's radar screen? Jill Gerber, then a spokesman for Grassley, told me, "The jet ownership itself isn't necessarily a cause for concern. The questions are whether the ministers use the ministry-owned jets for personal use and whether they reimburse the ministries for any personal use."

However, both Gerber and Grassley said reports by media organizations and watchdog groups originally brought them to their attention. And the ownership of jets was often what brought these ministries into focus for media organizations, airplanes landing in exotic locations make great visuals for television news reports.

They should also provide powerful warning signs to donors that God's money is being wasted. A former employee of Paula White's Without Walls International Church told NBC News, "We blew a lot of money out the tail of that jet."

That is a fact of jet ownership that Warren Buffett, sometimes called the “Oracle of Omaha,” a regular passenger himself on “The Indefensible,” could have predicted.

High Style

Just as bird watchers develop life lists of birds they have seen, so plane spotters develop lists of planes and celebrity owners they have seen. A number of sites on the Web, including those managed by the Federal Aviation Administration (FAA), give hobbyists and journalists a way to track planes by their identifying tail number. Below is a sampling of Christian ministries and the luxury jets they own, compiled from some of these sites. For the truly intrepid, type the tail number into an Internet search engine, and you can learn even more about the planes and where they've been.

Organization	Type of Aircraft	Tail Number
Agape Church	Cessna 500 *	N700VC
Billye Brim/Glorious Church Fellowship	Cessna 550	N888HS
Creflo Dollar/World Changers Church	Learjet 25B	N65A
Fred Price/Crenshaw Christian Center	Grumman - G-1159 **	N132FP
Dave Roever/Roever Evangelistic Assn	Learjet 25D	N43DR
Jerry Savelle Ministries	Cessna - 500	N715JS
Jesse Duplantis Ministries	Dassault - Falcon 50	N770JD
John Hagee Ministries	Cessna - 650	N800GM
Joyce Meyer Ministries	Canadair - CL-600	N7JM
Kenneth Copeland Ministries	Cessna 750 *** Cessna500	N1962J N501KG
Kenneth Hagin, Jr.	Canadair CL-600-2B16	N91KH
Leroy Thompson, Sr./ Word Of Life Christian Center	Cessna 650	N818DE
Mark Cowart/Church for All Nations	Learjet 24D	N929MC

Organization	Type of Aircraft	Tail Number
Michael Freeman/ Spirit of Faith ChristianCenter	Hawker DH 125-3A Grumman G-1159	N685FFN685SF
Moore Life Ministries	Cessna 421C Cessna 560	N74KP N61KM
Nahum Rosario/ Maranatha World Revival	Cessna 550	N741T
New Light Christian Center	Grumman G-1159	N829NL
Randy Gilbert/Faith Landmarks Ministries	Lockheed 1329 731****	N58TS
Tony Brazelton/Victory Christian Ministries	Rockwell NA-265-60	N1GM
Paula White/Without Walls International Church	Grumman G-1159	N374PS
Word Of Faith Christian Center	Learjet 24D	N711PC
Word Of Faith Christian Center	Hawker HS125 Series 700A	N225BJ
Word Of GodFellowship	Cessna 550	N717DT

* The Cessna 500 series jets are often called Citatio jets.

** The Grumman G-1159 is often referred to as a Gulfstream jet.

*** The Cessna 750 is often called the Citation X and is the world's fastest civilian airplane available.

**** Often called a Jetstar.

SOURCE: Various online sources, including FAA sites. Information believed to be accurate at the time it was compiled. Subject to ownership changes.

Chapter 9

What Happened at Willow Creek?

The problem with the modern American church is that it is far too "modern American" and not nearly enough "church."

—Stanley Hauerwas

In the seventies and eighties, radio personality Casey Kasem would often punctuate his "American Top 40" program with the phrase, "And the hits just keep on coming." The expression became a catchphrase of the era.

It was the same era in which Chicago-area's Willow Creek Community Church rose to national prominence. But Casey Kasem's famous phrase could also describe the church's decline: "The hits just keep on coming."

The first hit came in 2018, when whistleblowers accused longtime pastor Bill Hybels of sexual misconduct. The church's leadership initially rallied around the pastor, who denied the accusations. And that may have been the church's second mistake: to uncritically accept Hybels' word against credible accusations rather than to investigate the accusations.[1]

But the early whistleblowers gave others courage, and the church's denials made them defiant. Soon, the allegations were so numerous—and so credible—that Hybels was forced to resign. So did others in Willow Creek senior leadership who had backed

Hybels so uncritically for many years.

As the church was recovering from these hits to its credibility, more troubles followed. In January 2020, a longtime church member shared in a public Facebook post that Gilbert Bilezikian —known widely as Dr. B—kissed, fondled, and pressured her to have sex with him between 1984 and 1988.[2] Bilezikian, a retired college professor who was for decades a mentor to Hybels, is considered one of the "founding fathers" of Willow Creek Church. Hybels himself once said, "There would be no Willow Creek without Gilbert Bilezikian."[3]

It appeared at first that Willow Creek leadership had learned its lesson. Rather than deny the accusations and stand behind Bilezikian, acting lead pastor Steve Gillen acknowledged the accusations against Dr. B immediately. "We believe that Dr. B engaged in inappropriate behavior, and the harm he caused was inexcusable," Gillen wrote in an email.

But it turns out the acknowledgement came ten years too late. Soon it came to light that credible accusations against Bilezikian had been made a decade earlier. At that time, the church's elders had quietly restricted Bilezikian from serving, but failed to inform the membership of Willow Creek of Bilezikian's problems. In fact, about that time, Willow Creek gave Bilezikian an award for his role in the development of the church.

These cover-ups were so pervasive that Gillen had to resign as acting lead pastor. Further, the search for a new lead pastor—a role which Gillen was a leading candidate—came to a halt.[4]

With all these problems, problems that have involved large numbers of senior leaders over decades, it is worth asking the question: What happened at Willow Creek? Are these problems anomalies, are they "baked in" to the kind of independent megachurch that Willow Creek became—and modeled for so many others?

To answer these questions, it is helpful to step back a few decades to look at the founding of what has become one of the most imitated churches in America.

Willow Creek's Headwaters

Willow Creek Community Church and its dynamic and then young pastor Bill Hybels were, in many ways, strategically located to have an impact on the entire nation.

For one thing, it is in the suburbs of Chicago, the third largest city in the United States. Perhaps more importantly, it is also near some of the most influential Christian ministries and colleges in the country, including Wheaton College, Trinity Evangelical Divinity School, Trinity International University, and the Moody Bible Institute.

The suburb of South Barrington, Willow Creek's home, is the kind of "edge city" or exurb that drove economic growth in the country in the last quarter of the twentieth century. In other words, it was one of the most affluent and fastest-growing towns in the US. In many ways, South Barrington in the 1980s was what America aspired to be.

And Willow Creek Community Church became what many churches aspired to be. It became the archetype of the modern evangelical megachurch. It grew from start-up to megachurch (more than two thousand in regular attendance) in a matter of a few years. By 2005, the church claimed 21,500 members, making it the sixth largest Protestant congregation in the United States. It eventually "topped out" at around twenty-five thousand in 2015.

What really distinguished Willow Creek, though, was not its size or the speed of its growth, but its influence on other churches. By creating the Willow Creek Association (now doing business as the Global Leadership Network), an organization that ultimately had thousands of churches as members, it has mentored others in its strategies and techniques for church growth.

Youth Group For Grown-Ups

Willow Creek, like so many megachurches and parachurch organizations, was born out of youth ministry—in this case, the youth ministry of another suburban Chicago church called South Park Church, in the nearby suburb of Park Ridge.

South Park Church itself was no mainline, old-school church. Though the "mother church" of Willow Creek Community Church, it was barely an adolescent itself. Founded in 1947, South Park was also a nondenominational, evangelical church. In 1972, Bill Hybels began leading a youth group there. The group called itself Son Life, and within a year, the group had nearly tripled in size on the strength of Hybels' personality and teaching and the style of the meetings themselves, which eschewed hymns in favor of the early seventies equivalent of praise and worship songs.

Those who studied under Hybels have likely heard him say that every group needs a mission. In May 1973, Son Life was intentionally re-engineered to give it a more explicit mission: to be an outreach to nonbelieving youth.

Hybels saw the move as a way both to attract new kids who were unchurched without losing the youth who were already there. The kids who had been there a while and who might have grown bored with the same evangelistic messages week after week tolerated them because growing the youth group became their mission too. They would have a reason to come after the novelty of the informal worship service wore off, or was duplicated elsewhere.

This decision may seem logical and well intentioned. Indeed, many youth groups today are considered outreaches of the church, groups primarily designed to attract, not necessarily for spiritual formation or discipleship. In fact, the approach even has a name: the attractional model. Organizations such as the Billy Graham

Evangelistic Association pioneered the approach in the forties and fifties, but Willow Creek was on the vanguard of bringing it to the local church and perfecting it. The seventies and eighties became the era of "pizza and paintball" for many youth groups. Heavy on fellowship, food, and fun, but light on faith formation.

This 1973 decision by Hybels, to reach out to unchurched people and not "go deep" with current members, was a turning point for Hybels, according to G. A. Pritchard, who wrote a critical history of the Willow Creek movement.[5]

It was also a turning point in evangelicalism. One of the unintended consequences of a church that is constantly focused more on outreach than spiritual formation is that this model all but ensures that every generation has to be re-evangelized, since adults raised in such a church do not have the spiritual training to raise its own children in the nurture and admonition of the Lord.

Pritchard is careful to say that none of these consequences were engineered out of malice or a desire for celebrity or empire. They were truly the unintended consequences of young men and women with limited training doing the best they could, the best they knew how.

And by some measurements, their best was pretty good. The reengineered Son Life grew rapidly. The young leaders of the group had numerical evidence to support the idea that God was blessing their efforts. By 1975, Son Life had grown to more than a thousand young people, far more people than South Park Church, its host church, had in attendance at that time. Indeed, the large group was no longer meeting at the church, having outgrown it. Some of the people attending had "aged out" of the original youth group, but they kept coming anyway and bringing their friends.

So in 1975, the leadership of Son Life decided to implement the same "principles on an adult level by starting a church," wrote Don Cousins, one of the organizers of the church.

A key figure during that period was a man we have already mentioned: Dr. B—Dr. Gilbert Bilezikian.

A Wheaton College professor, Gilbert Bilezikian is sometimes called the theologian of Willow Creek. He was on a two-year teaching assignment at Trinity Evangelical Divinity School in Deerfield, Illinois, when a young Bill Hybels came into his classroom in 1975. Hybels was deeply influenced by the Wheaton professor, and would ride his motorcycle to Wheaton to get advice from his former professor. In fact, it was on Bilezikian's lawn one afternoon that Hybels said, "Dr. B, you and I are going to start a church." That church, founded in a movie theater, became Willow Creek Community Church.

Most of the staff of the new church came from the staff of the youth group. Because they were creating a new kind of church, Hybels believed they had to grow their staff from within, as those coming in from traditional church structures outside of Willow Creek wouldn't "get it."

This decision was another vital and defining one. Because Hybels had little formal theological education and because the church recruited most of the leadership from the youth group, another unintended consequence was virtually guaranteed: the spiritual maturity of any new leaders would likely not rise above the level of the current leadership.

That would be fine if the church had somehow stumbled on a method or process for disciple making and spiritual formation heretofore unknown or lost somewhere in the history of the church. But it was a risky and presumptuous decision.

It's likely, though, that the young leadership of the church understood neither the risk nor the presumption of the decision. Don Cousins, for example, defended the decision. "It is extremely difficult to judge a person's character or spiritual authenticity in an interview. You have to see them at work for some time." For this reason, Pritchard said, "Willow Creek does not like to hire individuals who haven't demonstrated their character there." This statement, in retrospect, is ironic and eerily prophetic.

One positive consequence of this strategy has been that, over the years, Willow Creek has seen stability among its senior leadership team that is uncommon. Pritchard said that during the time he studied Willow Creek, Hybels supervised three individuals in a management team, who in turn managed the rest of the staff. Two of these three were students in the original thirty-member youth group.

But the other side of that coin leaves one man—Bill Hybels—in firm control, and the leadership tends to be insular.

Pritchard wrote, "Virtually all the church's work has remained firmly in the hands of people who shared the common experience of the youth group." A related consequence is that despite the fact that Willow Creek has gotten bigger and older, it remains essentially, in methodology and content, a youth group. Mike Breaux, who was a teaching pastor at Willow Creek, said Willow Creek was "youth ministry for big people."

"Non-Churched Harry"

Because Willow Creek is so intentionally youth ministry for big people, entertainment, or infotainment, is at the center of the church's methodology.

The founder of the youth ministry Young Life, Jim Rayburn, famously said, "It's a sin to bore a kid with the gospel." Willow Creek took this admonition seriously, filling its sermons with drama and music, all strongly supported by state-of-the-art audiovisual accoutrement. Something is always happening on stage. And that activity is designed specifically to help "non-churched Harry"—as Hybels often describes the generic seeker—see that church and Christianity are not boring.

Pritchard quoted Hybels from one of the many pastor's conferences that Willow Creek gives through its Willow Creek Association: "Variety, variety, variety, variety. You'll get sick of hearing that in the next couple days. But friends, in every other environment except church, non-churched Harry is exposed to variety."

That non-churched Harry might be coming to church to encounter something permanent and unchanging is a point lost here. That the church should be offering something permanent and unchanging, regardless of whether non-churched Harry wants it or not, was—for many years—doubly lost.

Ideas Have Consequences – Bad Ideas Have Victims

Cracks in the Willow Creek veneer began to show up nearly fifteen years ago, when Hybels himself admitted that the church's brand of ministry had been a "mistake."[6] The confession came in the wake of a book published by Willow Creek. *Reveal: Where Are You?* was co-written by Willow Creek Executive Pastor Greg Hawkins and Callie Parkinson, who led Willow Creek's Reveal ministry. *Reveal*—the book that bears the ministry's name—contained the results of a multi-year study on the state of the American church. The study suggested what many critics of the Willow Creek model have said for years: Most churches are not doing a good job of true disciple-building.

"We made a mistake," Hybels said at Willow Creek's annual Leadership Summit in 2007, where his team presented the results. "When people crossed the line of faith and become Christians, we should have started telling people and teaching people that they have to take responsibility to become 'self-feeders.' We should have gotten people, taught people, how to read their Bible between services, how to do the spiritual practices much more aggressively on their own."

Callie Parkinson told me then[7] that the Reveal study would result in a "broadening of the movement. There's been a breakthrough in our understanding." But she reiterated that Willow Creek remains not just "seeker-focused. We are seeker-obsessed."

Not everyone was impressed with Willow Creek's "confession." Michael Horton, a professor at Westminster Seminary California, told me then that American evangelicalism was likely to see "more of the same" from Willow Creek.

"In the 'seeker' view, evangelism and outreach are spiritual technologies that must be made more efficient," Horton said. "Having a survey tell you that you need to add 'discipleship' to the list of technologies that we're trying to make more efficient doesn't solve the fundamental problem."

Horton said surveys may have their place, but they are not a replacement for true church community, for mentorship between people who actually know each other, for true spiritual discernment that has been tested by the truth of Scripture.

Horton criticizes the idea of church, worship, or the gospel as "product," and lost sinners as "consumers." People, he said, "are not consumers who need to be satisfied. They're sinners who need to be justified. Preaching is not a technology. It is a means of grace."

Horton admitted, though, that though the "the state of the church in America today is poor, it's a condition you can't blame on Willow Creek alone. It's increasingly difficult to swim against the tide of materialism, consumerism, and narcissism in the culture."

Willow Creek had to weather another controversy in 2015, when one of its worship leaders—Darren Calhoun—spoke and helped lead music at a pro-gay conference in Atlanta called The Reformation Project.[8] The Reformation Project was led by Matthew Vines, author of *God and the Gay Christian*, a book that was widely criticized by those who uphold a biblical standard regarding human sexuality.

Willow Creek spokeswoman Heather Larson (who later became Willow Creek's Lead Pastor, and who later still resigned under pressure after the Hybels debacle) told me that having an openly gay man in leadership at the church did not signal a change in direction for Willow Creek. And that may have been true, since Willow Creek's position on homosexuality had been the subject of debate for years.[9]

"Darren is held to the same standard that we have for everyone in our church," Larson said. "He is able to serve in a worship role because he has committed to all of the characteristics outlined in our Leadership Covenant, which includes living a life of sexual purity. For Darren, this is a commitment to celibacy."

Once again, the passage of time turned the statements of both Calhoun and Larson on their heads. Darren Calhoun left the staff of Willow Creek Church and is now an openly gay activist calling for "more queer voices in the church."[10] When Bill Hybels was forced out as lead pastor in April 2018, Larson got that job, but her involvement in the church's leadership for many years had eroded her credibility. The church's lead teaching pastor, Steve Carter, also resigned, saying he could no longer continue at the church in "good conscience."[11]

For our purposes, the key issue here is not homosexuality, but the transparency and integrity of the senior leadership. Willow Creek's practice of growing its own leadership meant there were few people in senior leadership roles whose credibility was untainted. Eventually, virtually everyone in senior leadership and the church's entire elder board had to resign.

Or, as Bob Smeitana wrote in *Christianity Today*, "Church leaders had been blinded by their faith in their founding pastor and had failed to hold Hybels accountable."[12]

Willow Creek elder Missy Rasmussen put it this way: "We trusted Bill, and this clouded our judgment."

Picking Up The Pieces

A church the size of Willow Creek won't just disappear, of course, but the events of the past few years have taken a toll. Weekly attendance at all Willow Creek campuses has fallen below eighteen thousand by early 2020. That's down from twenty-five thousand in 2015. At its main campus in South Barington, attendance had fallen to six thousand. The COVID-19 outbreak caused the church to suspend services in late March.

With the departure of Hybels, Larson, Gillen, and so many others in senior leadership, and a "back to the drawing board" approach to finding a new pastor, it is not clear what the future holds for Willow Creek, though in April 2020, the church did announce a new pastor, David Dimmitt, who had attended Willow Creek while an undergraduate at Wheaton College.

But G.A Pritchard's 1996 book on Willow Creek also takes on an eerie resonance when read with the benefit of hindsight. He concluded:

Imagine Hybels and his team attempting to save someone being swept down a swiftly moving river. Hybels reaches out to try to catch the unfortunate soul before he or she is swept away. Hybels is using the tools of our culture to reach out to the unchurched Harrys being swept away to the judgment. Yet in attempting to reach out to others in the fast-flowing river of our culture, Hybels and his followers also sometimes fall in.

Chapter 10

Mark Driscoll Buys A Bestseller

Rather fail with honor than succeed with fraud.
—Sophocles

The news hit the evangelical world like a tornado going through a trailer park, damaging some of evangelicalism's most storied publishing houses, and—in the end—destroying one of its largest and most famous churches.

That news came in March of 2014, when *WORLD* published a story I had been working on for months, the story of Seattle's Mars Hill Church and its famous pastor Mark Driscoll.[1]

The church had paid a California-based marketing company called Result Source at least $210,000 in 2011 and 2012 to ensure that *Real Marriage*, a book by the church's pastor Mark Driscoll and his wife Grace, would make the *New York Times* Bestseller List. According to a document obtained by *WORLD*, Result Source, Inc. (RSI) contracted with Mars Hill Church to "conduct a bestseller campaign for your book, *Real Marriage* on the week of January 2, 2012. The bestseller campaign is intended to place *Real Marriage* on *The New York Times* bestseller list for the Advice How-To list. Additionally, RSI will work to put *Real Marriage* on *The Wall Street Journal* Business Bestseller list, and on the *USA Today* Money list, BN.com and Amazon.com bestseller list."

The letter of agreement, dated October 13, 2011, was signed by Mat Miller of Result Source and John Sutton Turner of Mars Hill Church. Sutton Turner was then executive pastor and executive elder of Mars Hill Church.

The campaign worked. *Real Marriage* ended up on the *New York Times* bestseller list. With that credential, both the book and Mark Driscoll moved up another level in the book publishing world. New printings carried the magic words "*New York Times* Bestseller." Driscoll was now and would be for the rest of his career a "*New York Times* Bestselling Author."

The book itself was now on a list published in newspapers and websites around the world. Bookstores—not just Christian bookstores, but the major national chains—carried *NYT* bestsellers on special racks near the checkout counter, a move that further accelerated sales.

It was the beginning of something big for Driscoll and Mars Hill Church.

It was also the beginning of the end.

How To Buy A Bestseller

The details of the arrangement between Mars Hill Church and Results Source are intricate, but the big picture is not all that complicated.

Each week, the *New York Times* compiles its bestseller list by surveying bookstores around the country. Making the bestseller list can be worth hundreds of thousands of dollars, if not millions, in sales to a book, so the *Times* keeps its process—including the list of stores it surveys—a secret. This secrecy keeps authors and publishers from "gaming the system," from buying a relatively few books at a few *NYT*-reporting bookstores and creating the illusion that the book is a big seller.

But the secret is a poorly guarded one. Insiders know, or

can guess with reasonable accuracy, which of the thousands of bookstores around the country are reporting bookstores. So an author or a publisher can still beat the system if he willing to buy thousands of books at hundreds of bookstores around the country.

This behavior—to make targeted buys at reporting bookstores—is considered unethical by both the *Times* and by most publishers. The largest and most respected publishers know this, and they don't want to risk damage to their reputation. This ethical barrier prevents most of them from even trying this scheme. Plus, buying lots of books at a lot of different locations is easy to say, but difficult to do without getting caught. It requires thousands of buyers in hundreds of cities all across the country, all acting in concert so that all the sales get reported in a single week. For Christian authors, there are additional hurdles. The ECFA specifically prohibits the behavior. Several of the ECFA's standards address the practice either directly or indirectly. One of these standards says that authors and ministries should purchase books at the lowest possible price if the ministry wants to use the book as a giveaway or gift to donors. And that means purchasing the books at the so called "author price" directly from the publisher, not at retail price, which is the only kind of sale that gets reported to the bestseller lists.

But Results Source—the company that pulled this scheme off for Driscoll and, as we'll see, for other authors—is a for-profit organization, not a ministry. It was willing to do this kind of work for Christian authors.

It worked like this.

Results Source (RSI) received a fee to manage the project. In the case of Mark Driscoll's book, that fee was twenty-five thousand dollars. That fee paid Results Source to coordinate a nationwide network of book buyers. These book buyers would purchase the books at locations that were likely reporters for various bestseller lists, including the *New York Times*.

Mars Hill Church also paid for the purchase of the books themselves. According to the terms of the contract between RSI and Mars Hill Church, "RSI will be purchasing at least 11,000 total orders in one week." The contract calls for the "author" to "provide a minimum of 6,000 names and addresses for the individual orders at least 90 names and address [sic] for the remaining 5,000 bulk orders. Please note that the make up of the 6,000 individual orders include at least 1,000 different addresses with no more than 350 per state."

The purpose of this instruction appears to be to outsmart systems in place by the *New York Times* and other list compilers to prevent authors from buying their way onto bestseller lists. RSI apparently uses other techniques to work around the safeguards of the bestseller lists. According to the contract, "RSI will use its own payment systems (ex. gift cards to ensure flawless reporting). Note: The largest obstacle to the reporting system is the tracking of credit cards. RSI uses over a thousand different payment types (credit cards, gift cards, etc)."

It is this stipulation of the contract that not only would most mainstream publishers consider unethical, but which is a direct violation of the ECFA's ethical standards as well. And the language in the contract makes it clear that RSI knew it was intentionally trying to subvert the reporting system.

In the end, these purchases would total approximately $123,600 for the individual sales and $93,100 for the bulk sales.

Unethical, but Illegal?

What Result Source does is not illegal, though it is possible that it is abetting an illegal activity. When a ministry purchases the book at the steeply discounted author price, the author does not receive a royalty. But when RSI purchases a book at the full retail price, the author of the book does get his royalty. So it is possible that this book-buying scheme created what is called "private inurement," or the use of ministry funds to provide financial benefits not approved by the ministry's board of directors. Private inurement is strictly illegal.

Further, even though buying a book onto a bestseller list is not illegal, every organization that publishes bestseller lists discourages such practices. Most bestseller lists get raw data from Nielsen BookScan, which tracks sales at thousands of bookstores and online retailers. Neither Nielsen, the *Wall Street Journal*, nor the *New York Times* responded to my request for interview, but in a 2013 *Wall Street Journal* article about Result Source, Jonathan Stolper, the general manager of Nielsen BookScan, said, "Stringent rules and controls exist to help validate consumer sales, and confirmed bulk sales are always flagged and pulled from BookScan's bestseller chart-making process."[2]

If you measure success by short-term results, Mars Hill Church and Results Source did achieve its end. In early 2012, *Real Marriage* spent one week on the *New York Times* Bestseller List. It immediately fell off the list. That fact alone strongly suggests the book-buying scheme, and not the public's acceptance of the book, put the book on the list.

Nonetheless, almost immediately Mark Driscoll's official biography began to read: "Pastor Mark is the author of over 15 books, including the #1 *New York Times* best-selling *Real Marriage: The Truth About Sex, Friendship, and Life Together*, coauthored with his wife, Grace."

When I was reporting this story for *WORLD*, I made repeated calls to Results Source, none of which were returned. When I asked Mars Hill Church about the church's relationship with RSI, spokesperson Justin Dean responded with an email statement. The statement read in part: "Mars Hill has made marketing investments for book releases and sermon series, along with album releases, events, and church plants, much like many other churches, authors, and publishers who want to reach a large audience. We will explore any opportunity that helps us to get that message out, while striving to remain above reproach in the process. Whether we're talking about technology, music, marketing, or whatever, we want to tell lots of people about Jesus by every means available. That's what we're all about and have been since 1996."

Dean also said Driscoll's books "have generated over $200,000 in income to the church. Pastor Mark's generosity has never been in question, and both our board and senior staff is [sic] convinced that the church benefits both spiritually and financially from this writing ministry." However, because neither the church nor Driscoll made available the details of their financial arrangements, it was impossible to verify Dean's claims.

But by now, many people in Driscoll's own church had lost confidence in him. Mars Hill signed the contract with RSI in 2011. His book *Real Marriage* ended up on the *New York Times* Bestseller List in 2012. I discovered and started reporting on Driscoll and Mars Hill's book-buying scheme in March of 2014. The revelation of his book-buying scheme brought Driscoll and Mars Hill under closer scrutiny, and other issues emerged, including issues with his leadership style.

By August, Driscoll, saying he needed to "take a break" from ministry, announced a leave of absence, but that leave turned into his resignation in October.

The next month, in November of 2014, Mars Hill Church—which just a year earlier had fourteen thousand people in regular Sunday morning attendance—suddenly announced it would be closing its doors for good.[3]

Driscoll Is Not Alone

The Driscoll case was the tip of an iceberg that the Christian book publishing industry ran into in the early 2000s. Here are a few recent incidents that cast a cloud over the credibility of the industry:

- In 2015, Tyndale House pulled the million-selling 2010 book *The Boy Who Came Back From Heaven* after Alex Malarkey, the boy in the title, recanted his story. Alex later claimed he was exploited and in 2018, he filed a lawsuit against Tyndale House, accusing them of charges including defamation and exploitation. He sought damages equivalent to the book's profits.[4]
- Tyndale also pulled David Barton's *The Jefferson Lies* in 2012 after credible claims of plagiarism surfaced. The book was later published (in 2015) by conservative publisher WND Books.[5]
- Speaking of plagiarism: Before Mark Driscoll's book-buying scheme became public in 2014, he had already been embroiled in a plagiarism scandal of his own. His 2013 book *A Call To Resurgence* was met with credible claims of plagiarism. Driscoll later apologized for "mistakes" in attribution.[6]
- Lifeway Christian Stores, the retail arm of the Southern Baptist Convention, pulls *The Boy Who Came Back From Heaven*, *Heaven Is For Real*, and all "heaven visitation" books from its 186 stores. But the damage to Lifeway's credibility, plus technological and other changes in the book publishing and retail industry, ultimately led to the closure of Lifeway's retail stores in 2019.[7]
- South Carolina megachurch pastor Perry Noble admitted in 2014 (after the Mark Driscoll story broke) that he too used the marketing company Result Source to purchase

copies of his 2012 book *Unleash*. He later apologized and said he would not resort to such efforts again. However, this incident was a factor in Noble's unraveling. On July 10, 2016, Perry Noble was removed as senior pastor. On November 1, 2017, Noble announced his divorce from Lucretia Noble after seventeen years of marriage. In 2018, he started a new church.[8]

- Family Christian Stores, the nation's largest Christian retail chain, with 290 stores in thirty-six states, declared bankruptcy in 2015, owing publishers tens of millions of dollars. It closed all its stores in 2017, but returned as a web retailer in 2019.[9]
- Pastor and ministry leader David Jeremiah has also used ministry funds to boost his books. Though he did not directly use Result Source, he credited Result Source President Kevin Small as the "genius behind the plan." (We'll have more about David Jeremiah in the next chapter.)

It's important to say that secular publishing has also undergone profound change. Many major chains have gone out of business or dramatically reduced their retail footprint in the past decade.

But the sheer number of scandals in the past couple of years is troubling, making it worth asking the question: Are these isolated incidents, or examples of systemic corruption—or at least profound pathologies—in Christian book publishing? It is hard to answer that question definitively one way or the other, and that itself should be troubling for those who think that Christian publishing (Christian *anything*) should be above reproach.

Some of the factors affecting secular publishing are also having a dramatic impact on Christian publishing. The industry is consolidating under the ownership of publicly traded companies, and that means blockbuster books become increasingly important to the bottom lines of these companies. A rapidly evolving electronic media landscape means that most publishers are not interested in authors without their own "platform," which is a robust radio, online, television, and social media presence.

And these platforms are almost always built by the ministries these authors lead, and they are built with donor funds. All of which is why MinistryWatch has taken the position that book royalties should go not to the individual author, but to the organization which made the book royalties possible. This was the position of Chuck Colson, whose book *Born Again* sold millions of copies. All the royalties went to Prison Fellowship Ministries. That position should be the "gold standard" for authors who also lead Christian ministries.

Because bestsellers have become so important, it's easy to see why manipulating bestseller lists has become such a significant temptation.

Every Christian book publisher I contacted says it discourages such manipulation. Justin Taylor at Crossway Books strongly condemned the practice, calling it "dishonoring to the Lord." Todd Starowitz, director of public relations at Tyndale House, said, "Tyndale House Publishers does not contract with anyone or any agency who attempts to manipulate bestseller lists." Perhaps, but Driscoll's *Real Marriage*, the book Result Source bought on to the bestseller list, was a Tyndale book. Perry Noble's books were also published by Tyndale.

Despite the denials of Tyndale and other publishers, do the publishers in fact empower the practice by giving their authors large advances? It takes about two hundred and fifty thousand dollars to put together a campaign that would buy a book onto the bestseller list. Such campaigns are therefore out of reach of most Christian authors. But not those who can direct their churches or ministries to use donor dollars for this purpose, or those who get large advances from the publishers. The large advances that publishers pay Christian celebrities provide the financial fuel for the process, while also allowing publishers to wash their hands of the deed itself.

Tyndale President Mark Taylor admitted, "There are a number of Christian authors getting advances in the range of five hundred thousand dollars to one million dollars. And a few would get advances in excess of that."

Taylor also confirmed that even Christian publishers "now depend on a big hit, a bestseller," so authors who bring multimedia platforms to the publishing deal—often platforms built with donor dollars—are the authors who command the biggest advances.

Both Zondervan and Thomas Nelson, the two largest Christian publishers, are now owned by the secular publisher Harper Collins, a part of Rupert Murdoch's News Corporation. And this consolidation of Christian publishers under secular ownership is not a new phenomenon. Zondervan, founded in 1931, became a part of Harper Collins in 1988.

The trend has accelerated. Harper Collins acquired Thomas Nelson in 2011 for about two hundred million dollars. Faith Words, which signed David Jeremiah to a multi-book deal in 2009 reportedly worth three million dollars (as we will discuss in the next chapter), is part of French publisher Hachette. Howard Books, another major evangelical publisher, is part of Simon and Schuster. In 2006, Joel Osteen signed a deal with another Simon and Schuster division, The Free Press, that the *New York Times* said paid him a guarantee of thirteen million dollars. [10]

Marvin Padgett, a Christian publishing industry veteran, said, "It's hard to blame the changes we've seen in Christian publishing solely on the consolidation." But he acknowledged that consolidation of the major publishers into the hands of publicly traded corporations has contributed to the need for blockbusters. After all, a book that sells only a few thousand copies has no material impact on the financial statement of a News Corporation, which rang up more than nine billion dollars in revenue in 2018.

Princes of the Power of the Air

The only publicly traded company whose primary business is the Christian market is Salem Media Group.

Salem is the largest Christian media company in the nation, with more than one hundred radio stations, most of them in the nation's largest markets. Founded by brothers-in-law Ed Atsinger and Stu Epperson Sr., it went public on the NASDAQ exchange in 1999 and by 2018, had reached a peak in revenue of more than two hundred and sixty million dollars a year, though by 2019, Salem's revenue had fallen to two hundred and fifty-four million dollars. In March 2020, Moody's had lowered the rating of the credit worthiness of Salem.[10]

Though Salem owns a variety of media properties, eighty percent of its revenue comes from radio and related activities. And much of that revenue comes from "block programming." In other words, revenue that comes from David Jeremiah's "Turning Point" and other donor-supported ministries. In short, though Salem is a for-profit company, in some years, a quarter or more of its revenue comes indirectly from donors to Christian ministries.

The sale of block programming time used to be the norm in radio and television, but now it is almost exclusively the province of Christian broadcasting. In essence, the ministries purchase time from the radio stations and use the time on-air both to preach and teach—and to raise money. Fundraising takes up at least a few minutes of virtually every Christian program on the air today, usually in the form of asking for money in exchange for a gift—often a book based on that day's teaching. Many teaching programs are infomercials for the book from which the teaching comes. This process forms a "three-legged stool" of author, publisher, and media outlet, with each leg dependent on the other for financial success. The power—and by that I mean the financial interdependency—of this three-way relationship may have been why Janet Mefferd's life took a dramatic turn for the worse when she confronted Mark Driscoll on her program, presenting evidence of plagiarism to him on her nationally syndicated Salem program, the 2013 episode we mentioned above. "Tyndale House was attacking me publicly. Salem forced me to apologize on the air," she said. "It was one of the most stressful times of my life. I now regret the apology. What I should have done then was resign in protest."

Mefferd's producer, Ingrid Schlueter, did resign. She wrote this, explaining her decision:

> I was a part-time, topic producer for Janet Mefferd until [December 3, 2013] when I resigned over this situation. All I can share is that there is an evangelical celebrity machine that is more powerful than anyone realizes. You may not go up against the machine. That is all. Mark Driscoll clearly plagiarized and those who could have underscored the seriousness of it and demanded accountability did not. That is the reality of the evangelical industrial complex.[11]

Mefferd chose to weather the storm, in part because her husband also worked for Salem. When he found a position elsewhere, she did resign.

This alliance between publishers, celebrity authors, and their broadcast platforms became even more intimate at Salem when the company purchased Eagle Publishing in 2014 for more than eight and a half million dollars. Eagle Publishing, which includes Regnery Books, also represents yet another turn away from the

Christian market for Salem, as it publishes many political, and not distinctively Christian, authors.[12]

Further evidence that politics and profitability are as important as Christian principles at Salem is their ownership of the conservative website Townhall.com. Townhall's political editor Guy Benson, who also hosted a radio program on one of Salem's Chicago stations as well as a Fox News contributor, sent a shockwave through the evangelical and conservative world by coming out as gay in 2015, and in 2019 marrying Adam Wise.[13] Salem indicated in 2015 it would stand behind Benson, allowing him to keep both his radio program and his job as political editor of Townhall.com. Jonathan Garthwaite, the vice president and general manager of Townhall Media, said, "Guy is a talented reporter and political analyst for Townhall. He has been since 2009 and will be in the future as he covers the 2016 presidential race." As of early 2020, Benson remains the political editor at Townhall.com.

Janet Mefferd said, "Salem is not the Christian organization I started working for years ago. It makes me and many of us terribly sad."

Not Beyond Repair

By many measures, Christian book publishing—and book publishing in general—has experienced something of a rebound in recent years (though the impact of the COVID-19 crisis is still not fully known as of the writing of this book).

Sales have rebounded since the 2008 Great Recession. Independent bookstores have been under tremendous pressure from both chains and from online retailers, but the closure of Borders and its nearly seven hundred stores in 2012 seemed to rationalize the market, and the number of independent brick-and-mortar bookstores has stabilized. Also, while online sales continue to grow, the sale of digital books appears to be leveling off at about fifteen percent of the market.

But the industry is not through with disruption and change. Cokesbury Stores, the retail arm of the United Methodist Church, closed in 2012. And we've already mentioned the closures of LifeWay and Family Christian Stores.

The industry has seen other casualties. The Christian Booksellers Association suspended operations in 2018, but before doing so, its International Christian Retail Show—the organization's largest annual event—was reflecting the spiritual chaos of the industry. The show included a booth featuring the Mormon Church's Brigham Young University. The book section of the trade show had shrunk and the gift section had grown relatively larger. In the gift section, you could buy a sandwich press that would toast your bread with the image of Jesus. The product was marketed as a "Grilled Cheesus Sandwich Press." Such "Jesus Junk" or "Christian Kitsch" has further eroded the credibility of the Christian retail industry.

Markets have a way of sorting out the financial issues, but what about the theological ones? And what happens when these financial and theological issues are not confined to the fringes of the Christian world, but begin to take hold among its most trusted voices?

Chapter 11

David Jeremiah and the Christian Industrial Complex

"Corruptio optimi pessima." ("Corruption of the best is the worst.")

—Latin Maxim

On the evening of February 28, 2020, on the final night of the annual meeting of the National Religious Broadcasters at Nashville's Opryland Hotel and Conference Center, one of religious broadcasting's best-known figures, David Jeremiah, took the stage as a conquering hero.

He was inducted into the NRB's Hall of Fame. This exclusive club has less than ninety members, and they include Billy Graham, Chuck Colson, and Jerry Falwell. It is easily the highest honor a Christian broadcaster can receive.[1]

In accepting the honor, he talked about his early days doing college radio at Cedarville University in Ohio, and he closed with an appeal to support NRB itself. After mentioning that he had been coming to NRB meetings for fifty years, he added: "It's important that we become ardent supporters of NRB. What we do is more important than it has ever been."

Much was unspoken—but well understood by this audience of religious broadcasting insiders—about David Jeremiah's appearance.

First, his words were an intentional show of support for an organization that has had its share of troubles the past few years. So much trouble, in fact, that Jeremiah made his appeal to a half-empty room, at the end of a conference that had barely half as many people in attendance as it did just three years prior.

Secondly, his appearance and induction marked the end of a season of exile for Jeremiah. For many years, the NRB required its members to also be members of the ECFA. But in 2010, David Jeremiah's Turning Point Ministries lost its ECFA membership.

ECFA President Dan Busby said the organization has a policy of not giving reasons for an organization's resignation, but a former chief financial officer, George Hale, said a book-buying scheme—the same practice that brought down Mark Driscoll and Mars Hill Church—was a key reason for the resignation from ECFA membership. The book-buying scheme engaged in by Driscoll was unethical and a violation of ECFA standards. Now David Jeremiah, one of the elder statesmen of the evangelical world, was doing the same thing. George Hale said the practice was "deceptive and unethical" and ultimately Hale resigned from the ministry, and Jeremiah's Turning Point Ministries left the ECFA.

Since, in 2010, if you weren't a member of the ECFA, you couldn't be a member of the NRB, Jeremiah couldn't be a member of the NRB either.

As we have already discussed, the ECFA began in the 1970s as a response by the federal government to regulate Christian ministries. We have also discussed the limitations of the ECFA in policing evangelical ministries, especially its limited ability to police member organizations in a meaningful way. If the scrutiny grew too intense, a ministry could simply, and quietly, resign.[2]

Despite these limitations of the ECFA, the NRB decided that membership in the ECFA was better than nothing at all, so the NRB started requiring members with more than one million dollars in revenue to be members. This rule was good for the ECFA. The NRB's recruitment efforts essentially became a marketing arm of the ECFA. For many years, both organizations grew together.

Then David Jeremiah, one of the lions of Christian broadcasting, resigned from the ECFA, creating an awkward situation for everyone involved. Something had to change.

Et tu, David Jeremiah?

As we discussed, no single event brought down Seattle's Mars Hill Church and its celebrity pastor Mark Driscoll. Driscoll and Mars Hill Church had leadership and governance problems that went well beyond the use of nearly a quarter million dollars in church funds to buy one of Driscoll's books onto the *New York Times* bestseller list.[3]

But his "gaming" of the *New York Times* bestseller list was certainly a key factor. Indeed, Driscoll had weathered accusations of plagiarism and other controversies going back to 2009 or before. But when my *WORLD* story broke on Driscoll's book-buying scandal, in March of 2014, a cascade of events quickly followed. Driscoll was gone by October, and the church—once one of the largest in America—dissolved just a few months after that.

We've mentioned that Perry Noble engaged in the practice too. It's not clear how many other Christian authors used Result Source, but they include, in addition to Noble and Driscoll, Les and Leslie Parrott, and Ken Blanchard.

So the practice was common among big-name Christian authors before the Driscoll scandal blew the cover off of it. It was common in part because Sealy Yates was the literary agent for David Jeremiah, the Parrotts, Perry Noble, Mark Driscoll, and others.

Sealy Yates also serves on the board of directors for David Jeremiah's Turning Point Ministries, so any payments he may have received in that capacity should have been disclosed on Turning Point Ministry's Form 990 as a so-called "related party transaction." No such fees are recorded on the Form 990. It is possible that these payments came from Jeremiah himself, since the royalties went to Jeremiah.

According to George Hale, Turning Point did what Driscoll did, but on a much larger scale, purchasing copies of at least three of Jeremiah's books to push them onto the *New York Times* bestseller list.

The practice, which BuzzFeed called "distasteful if not immoral," was so common, in fact, that Kevin Small and Result Source were often credited in the acknowledgements of the books on which they worked.

In the acknowledgments section of David Jeremiah's 2012 book *God Loves You*, he credits the president of Result Source, Kevin Small, as the "genius behind the plan." When *WORLD*'s Marvin Olasky asked Jeremiah about his marketing practices in an interview, he was vague on the specifics but did say, "You can't just write a book and say I'm not going to have anything to do with marketing. If you don't care enough about it to try and figure out how to get it in the hands of other people, nobody else is going to either."

The success of the books helped David Jeremiah turbo-charge his ministry. The ministry doubled in size from 2007 to 2012, a time when—because of the Great Recession—many Christian ministries struggled to maintain their donor bases and break even. In 2012, the ministry took in about forty million dollars. The growth continued. In 2019, David Jeremiah's ministry took in nearly sixty-four million dollars.[4]

Hale, who was chief financial officer of Turning Point Ministries from July 2007 to January 2010, says the growth was the result of many changes in the ministry, but it coincided with the beginning of the book-buying plan. Hale said each time Jeremiah released a book, Turning Point radio and television programs promoted it, promising a free copy for a donation.

This is standard fare for Christian radio. But, according to Hale, Jeremiah and Turning Point bought at least some of the books—not at wholesale prices direct from the publisher, but at full retail prices from bookstores. This is a direct violation of the ECFA's requirement that ministries purchase books at the lowest available price.

Hale says he became aware of the book-buying scheme "shortly after I got to Turning Point in July of 2007. David and his son [David Michael Jeremiah, now Turning Point's chief operating officer and a member of the board] told me we needed to buy a bunch of books. They asked me to use my personal American Express card. When I asked them how much, they said about a quarter of a million dollars' worth." Hale says he told them he would not put that much on his card without prepayment.

On October 4, 2007, Turning Point made two payments of $99,999.99 each to George Hale's credit card, both via wire transfer. (Hale provided MinistryWatch with copies of his American Express statement showing the payments.) Hale says after he was sure the money had cleared and American Express had credited his account, he okayed the ministry's two online purchases using his American Express card at BarnesAndNoble.com: one for $113,038.40 and another for $141,298.00. Hale's American Express statement also shows these purchases.[5]

On October 29, 2007, Turning Point made another payment to Hale's American Express account of fifty thousand dollars. Hale said that even though he cooperated with these transactions, he was uncomfortable with them; but does say one of the effects was to "cause secular stores to stock and sell the books."

I placed dozens of calls to David Jeremiah and other

members of the Turning Point staff to confirm Hale's version of events and to give Jeremiah the opportunity to explain his version of events. None of these calls was returned.[6]

According to George Hale, these were the activities that led to the January 31, 2010, resignation from the ECFA of Turning Point Ministries. Which in turn led to his resignation from the NRB.

Hale added, "I very much admire David Jeremiah and believe him to be one of the best Bible teachers in the world today … I believe that David is blessed and chosen by God for this purpose." But he too believes Turning Point's book-buying practice was "deceptive and unethical."

"When a book is bought at the full retail price," Hale said, "the author gets a royalty and the agent gets a percentage." This scheme not only made it look like the book was selling well at the retail level, and therefore causing the book to show up on bestseller lists, but it also raises the possibility that ministry donations went directly into the pockets of David Jeremiah and Sealy Yates.

How much money is involved? George Hale says millions of dollars. "I never saw a contract between David Jeremiah and a publisher," Hale said. "But I did see an advance check made out to David for three million dollars for a multi-book deal." Hale said the advance came from Faith Words, a Nashville publisher whose stable of authors includes Joel Osteen, Joyce Meyer, and T.D. Jakes, among others. The books covered by the advance were *The Coming Economic Armageddon* (2010), *I Never Thought I'd See The Day* (2011), and *God Loves You* (2012), the book in which he prominently mentioned his relationship with Result Source.

It is possible, of course, that these facts have an innocent explanation. Did David Jeremiah donate the three million dollars Faith Words advance to the ministry? If he kept the money, did he disclose this income to the boards of Turning Point Ministries, which is responsible for setting his salary? Again, I placed dozens of calls to David Jeremiah and other members of the Turning Point staff to confirm Hale's version of events and to give Jeremiah the opportunity to explain his version of events. None of these calls were returned.

However, in January of 2010, Jeremiah bought a two million-dollar condominium on Coronado Island, a resort community near San Diego.[7]

Jeremiah has used a variety of publishers over the years. He is currently listed on Tyndale House Publishers' site as one of its authors. Tyndale's reputation—as we have already discussed—has taken a number of hits recently. Tyndale is, for example, the publisher of Mark Driscoll's *Real Marriage*, the book that led to Driscoll's downfall. Tyndale recently had to pull *The Boy Who Came Back From Heaven* after the book's subject, Alex Malarkey, said the story wasn't true. Tyndale also published David Barton's *The Jefferson Lies*, which it subsequently pulled from circulation after credible threats of plagiarism. It also published Perry Noble's *Unleash*, which also used Result Source.

Tyndale House Publishers is not the only common thread. David Jeremiah's agent Sealy Yates, who is also on the board of directors of Turning Point Ministries, is the founder of the literary agency powerhouse Yates & Yates. He is also a long-time friend of Result Source founder Kevin Small. In an interview with me for stories I did on Mark Driscoll, Sealy Yates called Small "a man of high integrity."

The controversies related to Driscoll and Perry seem to have driven Result Source and Kevin Small underground, at least as far as Christian books are concerned. But Result Source has not avoided controversy and accusations of ethical compromise. In 2017, a young adult book called *Handbook for Mortals* debuted at number one on the *New York Times* Bestseller List. But industry insiders, suspicious that an unknown author with a small publisher could pull off such a feat, started investigating. They discovered Result Source behind the book's marketing plan. *The New York Times* revised its calculations to take the Result Source client off its list.[8] So why did it take George Hale so long to come forward with his information? He told me he had signed a non-disclosure agreement upon leaving Turning Point Ministries.[9] Hale said he's willing to talk now in part because he is retired and in no fear of damage to his career, and because of the fallout from the Driscoll scandal. "Mark Driscoll was exposed for attempting in a small way to do what David [Jeremiah] had successfully done for years," he said.

Hale, a CPA and former special forces soldier and bank president, also served as the chief financial officer of Jeremiah's Shadow Mountain Church and another Southern California megachurch, Mariners Church, before working for Turning Point Ministries. He spent a total of seven years working for David Jeremiah in various capacities. That relationship meant he did not become a "whistleblower" without a lot of soul searching and prayer. But, he said, "I became very concerned that this cancer was spreading. When David Jeremiah spoke openly with *WORLD* Magazine during June 2014 about his method of promoting his books, I felt that he had placed this subject into the public domain for discussion."

Hale concluded, "Is this practice okay as Sealy Yates and David Jeremiah proclaim or is it deceptive and unethical as I believe? I have taken my stand."

Hiding In Plain Sight

Since Jeremiah's resignation from the ECFA, the ECFA has implemented stronger guidelines to prevent ministries from purchasing books in order to manipulate bestseller lists or to enrich the authors. That may be why David Jeremiah has never re-joined the ECFA.

And the NRB has loosened its ties with the ECFA. In 2010, when ECFA membership was a requirement for all NRB members, Turning Point's resignation from the ECFA meant it had to resign its NRB membership as well. A few months later, Jeremiah— who was scheduled to speak at the 2011 conference—was removed from the agenda.

This is a key point. These twin resignations mean it is likely many leaders in the evangelical world knew of Jeremiah's activities. But it is in not in the interest of either Christian broadcasters or publishers to speak up. Book publishers are obvious beneficiaries of these retail book sales. Broadcasters receive large fees from Jeremiah in order to air his program. In 2016 alone, Turning Point Ministries spent more than $19.7 million on "broadcasting costs." That meant buying air time, mostly from NRB member stations and networks (including Salem, the Christian broadcasting giant). It spent another $9.3 million on "product fulfillment," which is the cost of books and other materials sent to donors.

So it would not be fair to call what happened with Mark Driscoll, David Jeremiah, Perry Noble, and others a massive cover-up. After all, most of the information I have shared in the last two chapters have been "hiding in plain sight," just waiting for someone to connect the dots.

But it is clear that unethical activities in the evangelical world had gone far beyond boundaries of the Prosperity Gospel world.

It is also clear that for David Jeremiah, one of the nation's largest Christian broadcasters, *not* to be a member of NRB was awkward for both the NRB and Jeremiah. So the NRB changed its rules. It made it much easier for organizations like Jeremiah's to be a member without being a member of the ECFA.

Here's the new rule, in full, from the NRB's website:

> Nonprofit members of NRB whose donated broadcast revenue equals or exceeds $1,000,000 annually must be certified as meeting the financial accountability standards of ***one of the current nationally recognized charity-assessment organizations, including ECFA, Better Business Bureau Wise Giving Alliance, or others as designated by the NRB Executive Committee.*** (Emphasis added.)
>
> Nonprofit members of NRB whose donated broadcast revenue is less than $1,000,000 annually will meet NRB's in-house standards established by the NRB's Ethics Committee.
>
> Denominational and church-sponsored broadcasts are exempt from the accountability requirements.
>
> ***For-profit members of NRB are exempt*** but are asked to comply with membership standards as set by the Ethics Committee.

For-profit members would include such organizations as Salem Media Group.

So while Turning Point Ministries is still not a member of the ECFA, it has nonetheless returned as a member in good standing of the NRB. And in 2020, Jeremiah was inducted into the NRB Hall of Fame.

Lilies That Fester

One of Shakespeare's best-known sonnets (Sonnet 94) bemoans the inconsistency, the unreliability, of the poet's young lover. The poet laments—or at least fears—the young lover's infidelity:

For sweetest things turn sourest by their deeds
lilies that fester smell far worse than weeds.

The words of this sonnet came to mind when I was reporting on David Jeremiah. As I said earlier, I made dozens of calls to his ministry in California. I was often placed on hold as people I was never able to talk with were informed I was on the line. They formulated a response for a long-suffering receptionist who Jeremiah's unwillingness to honestly answer a few questions was placing in an untenable spot.

I was sometimes on hold for as much as ten minutes. During those long waits, I listened to Turning Point Ministries' "hold music." However, the "hold music" was not music at all, but Jeremiah's sermons. Because I was on hold long enough to hear significant portions of them, I came away agreeing with George Hale's assessment: David Jeremiah is a gifted communicator. His sermons were clear, thoughtful, Biblical.

But I knew I was calling to ask tough questions, so I could not help but note the irony of the situation, the same irony that Shakespeare used to such powerful effect: "For sweetest things turn sourest by their deeds."

Rusty Leonard, the founder and current chairman of the board of MinistryWatch, summarized the situation perhaps less poetically, but with no less powerful effect: "This sort of behavior used to be the province of the prosperity gospel preachers, but when Driscoll and Jeremiah do it, we've crossed a divide."

Is there a way back to a Christian publishing and broadcasting industry that has theological integrity and financial health? Leonard believes it's got to come from the pews. "It would be great if pastors would stand up," he said. "But too many of the most influential pastors are part of the system, so I don't see that happening. The current system works too well for those at the top. They're making a fortune. It's got to come from the bottom up."

Chapter 12

What The Grassley Six Tell Us About Ourselves

I am not implying that all Christians are liars,
but we've forgotten how to speak the truth.
—Phil Cooke

On November 6, 2007, Senator Charles Grassley, the Senate Finance Committee's ranking Republican, asked for detailed financial information from six Christian ministries, and he gave them thirty days to comply.

This marked the beginning of the investigation into the so called Grassley Six.

Those ministries included Paula and Randy White's Without Walls International Church, based in Tampa, Florida. Also named in the Grassley Six were Benny Hinn Ministries, Joyce Meyer Ministries, Kenneth Copeland Ministries, Eddie Long's New Birth Missionary Baptist Church, and Creflo Dollar's World Changers Church International.

Why these ministries and not others? Once again, investigative journalism and watchdog groups such as MinistryWatch deserve most of the credit—or blame, depending upon your perspective—for that.

In 2006, MinistryWatch's investigations into Joyce Meyer

and other Prosperity Gospel preachers started making national news. MinistryWatch founder Rusty Leonard was featured in the *Wall Street Journal* and on ABC's *20/20*.[1] That coverage set off a new round of scrutiny of these ministries, scrutiny that featured the extravagant spending we've already mentioned earlier, including large homes and fast airplanes. Senator Grassley himself later acknowledged that it was media coverage that first brought these ministries to his attention.

Grassley's 2007 announcement put these ministries in the spotlight again, and started a countdown clock. Would the Grassley Six comply with his deadline?

The answer was "no." Or mostly "no."

Only Joyce Meyer fully complied with the original thirty-day deadline, delivering boxes of material to Senator Grassley's staff on December 6, 2007. Benny Hinn and Paula and Randy White made some attempts at compliance. The other three ministries were openly defiant.

Kenneth Copeland issued a report defending his ministry, and put up a website to tell his side of the story. Creflo Dollar said the Senate Finance Committee (SFC) had no right to ask for information, and that he would respond only if required to be the IRS.

Months went by with no follow-up from Grassley, and it began to look like the defiant stand of the ministries would work. Would the ministries that did not comply simply get a "free pass"?

That was a possibility, because right about the time that Grassley should have been following up and doling out consequences for non-compliance, the financial crisis of 2007-09 hit his office in full force, and suddenly the SFC had more pressing business—such as playing a significant role in keeping the entire US economy from melting down.

Finally, Grassley acted. In early March 2008, he sent another letter to the non-compliant. This letter included the signature of Senator Max Baucus, the chairman of the committee. That was a significant development because when the chair and the ranking minority member agree, the committee can issue subpoenas.

But when the March 31, 2008, deadline on the Grassley-Baucus letter passed, little had changed. Kenneth Copeland and Creflo Dollar remained defiant. Copeland's organization had already mounted a spirited counter offensive, issuing a statement on April 11 that took up Creflo Dollar's earlier ploy: to ask for an IRS audit—but in accordance with the Church Audit Procedures Act of 1984 (CAPA). If Grassley wanted information, they said, he can then ask the IRS for it. It was a clever (if disingenuous) strategy because under CAPA, IRS audits are confidential, take a long time to complete, and immunize an organization from additional scrutiny for at least five years.

Also playing a role in the delays were other evangelical organizations who came to the defense of the Grassley Six. In May of 2008, a group of evangelicals went public with their contention that Grassley was overreaching. They wrote a letter to Grassley, a letter signed by twenty conservative and evangelical leaders, including Mathew Staver, founder of Liberty Counsel and then the dean of Liberty University's School of Law. Conservative icon Paul Weyrich, former Cincinnati mayor, and Ohio Secretary of State Ken Blackwell, and the American Family Association's Don Wildmon also signed.[2]

The letter says Grassley ignored normal processes and targeted organizations that "share the same branch of evangelicalism." By that they meant the Grassley Six were all Prosperity Gospel preachers. Again, it was a clever, some might say cynical, strategy. It was an attempt to deflect the public's attention from the gross financial abuses of these ministries and to turn the controversy instead into one about religious liberty, a government attempt to suppress religion.

Grassley rejected that line of reasoning out of hand. "Doctrine is not a part of this committee's review," he said.

But Staver responded, "This investigation sets a dangerous precedent. How these ministries use money may be unsettling, but the precedent Grassley is setting is even more unsettling."

So on July 7, 2008, eight months after he had issued his first thirty-day deadline, Grassley finally announced that only two of the six televangelists from whom he had sought information had made good faith and substantive responses. The two who complied were Meyer and Benny Hinn (World Healing Center Church). The other four ministries—led by Randy and Paula White, Eddie Long, Kenneth and Gloria Copeland, and Creflo and Taffi Dollar—failed to engage in what Grassley called "open and honest dialogue" with his staff.

In fact, not only were the ministries non-compliant, they had rocked Grassley's team on its heels. Grassley or his staff found themselves defending even their right to conduct such an investigation, constantly responding to religious liberty objections. Grassley spokesperson Jill Kozeny said then that the committee did indeed have the right to investigate organizations that would help them in passing laws and regulations or "evaluating the adequacy of those laws."

In a written statement she provided for an article I wrote for *WORLD* at the time, she added, "The investigation isn't concerned with church doctrine. It is considering the adequacy of tax-exempt laws, which haven't been updated in any substantial way since 1968."[3]

In fact, such investigations by the Senate Finance Committee are not new. Between 2001 and the beginning of the televangelist investigation in 2007, the SFC had investigated the Smithsonian Institution, college endowment funds, nonprofit hospitals, and nonprofit foundations. The guilty pleas and, later, other criminal convictions of Jack Abramoff were the results, at least in part, of investigations into tax-exempt organizations Abramoff had created.[4]

Kozeny added that "subpoenas are certainly a tool of the committee." Grassley said at that time he hoped the organizations would voluntarily comply with requests for financial information. When subpoenas start flying, the stakes go up: the last time the committee issued subpoenas, during the Jack Abramoff investigation, more than twenty people ended up in jail.

But in the case of the Grassley Six, deadline after deadline passed. No subpoenas. No nothing.

Eddie Long and New Birth Church

We will not look at each ministry individually, but it would help to pause here and look at a couple of them, in part because their stories reiterate some of the key ideas of this book.

Take Atlanta-based Eddie Long, for example. In 2005, the *Atlanta Journal-Constitution* reported that between 1997 and 2000, Long received more than $3.07 million worth of compensation and benefits from his nonprofit charity, Bishop Eddie Long Ministries Inc.[5] Long defended himself with a common dodge: he said the charity did not solicit donations from members but instead gained its income from royalties and speaking fees.

But the *Journal-Constitution* helped put Long on Grassley's list. This incident is yet another example of investigative journalism being a key factor in holding ministries accountable.

Further, credible accusations of sexual impropriety were made against Long in 2010—during the middle of the Grassley investigation—by Maurice Robinson, Anthony Flagg, Jamal Parris, and Spencer LeGrande.[6]

They filed lawsuits that said Long used his pastoral

influence to seduce them into sexual relationships with him. Long never addressed the charges publicly. In 2011, with Grassley's investigation drawing to a close, the lawsuits were settled out of court. Once again, it was a non-disclosure agreement that prevented the public from knowing the extent of the wrongdoing or the terms of the settlement.[7] That said, before the lawsuit was settled, publicly available court documents alleged that Long used "monetary funds from the accounts of New Birth and other corporate and nonprofit corporate accounts to entice the young men with cars, clothes, jewelry, and electronics."

Senator Grassley had the power to subpoena records and testimony that could have gotten to the truth, but he did not use that authority. In the end, Long avoided criminal prosecution, but neither he nor his New Birth Church emerged unscathed. The negative publicity from his lifestyle and the lawsuits took their toll, and that publicity did what regulators could not. Donations to the church dropped significantly in the aftermath of the lawsuits and of the Grassley investigation itself.

Long died on January 15, 2017, at the age of sixty-three. The church issued a statement describing the cause of death as an "aggressive form of cancer."

Paula White's Rise and Fall and Rise

Paula and Randy White and their Without Walls International Church was another subject of Grassley's investigation.

Paula White's story began in Elvis Presley's hometown of Tupelo, Mississippi, where she had a hardscrabble childhood. Her father died by suicide and her mother was an alcoholic. But when Paula was nine years old, her mother re-married, to a two- star admiral, and her life changed dramatically.

The family moved to suburban Washington, into one of the

richest zip codes in the country, and she got active in church. She eventually married Randy White, an assistant pastor at a church she attended, and together they founded The South Tampa Christian Center, in Tampa, Florida, in 1991.

The church struggled initially—to the point that the Whites drew almost no income and lived on welfare in those early years. In the first half dozen years of the church's existence, it moved at least three times.

But by 1998, the Whites began to get traction. By then, Paula White was doing a lot of the preaching and teaching, using her difficult youth to connect with others who had rough backgrounds. She discovered she could draw a crowd. By 1999, the church was meeting in a huge outdoor tent, with five thousand or more attending weekly services.

The growth continued. In 2002, Without Walls International Church expanded to a second location in Lakeland and the church reported fourteen thousand members and two hundred ministries including job training, evangelism among public housing projects, and a teen club.

Two years later, in 2004, Without Walls International Church had twenty thousand in regular attendance on the weekend, making it the seventh largest church in the United States. It was also making Randy and Paula White wealthy. When they were at home, they lived in a mansion. When they traveled to speaking engagements, they flew in a recently purchased Gulfstream II jet. An audit later made public by a US Senate committee showed that Without Walls received one hundred and fifty million dollars from 2004-06.[8]

But it turned out that the Without Walls Church was also a church without much of a foundation. In 2007, Paula and Randy White divorced, and for a while, Paula was romantically linked to another prosperity preacher being investigated by Senator Grassley: Benny Hinn.

In August of 2011, services at the Lakeland location ceased when the power there was cut off because the church had failed to pay more than fifty thousand dollars in electricity bills. By then, though, the property was already up for sale due to the ongoing financial difficulties.

Paula White then made a clean break with Without Walls, joining New Destiny Christian Center, which was then led by Zachery Tims, a nationally-known figure in Pentecostal circles. But Tims was having troubles of his own. He died of a heroin overdose in 2011, and she became the senior pastor in 2012.

Meanwhile, with Paula White now completely departed, Without Walls International Church collapsed. It declared bankruptcy, with debt to the Evangelical Christian Credit Union alone totaling twenty-nine million dollars. Paula White washed her hands of the problems at Without Walls. She claimed in an interview with journalist Erin Burnett, "I've never filed bankruptcy. I had resigned Without Walls. I had absolutely no part."[9]

Much of this drama was unfolding while Paula and Randy White and the Without Walls International Church were being investigated by Senator Grassley. Throughout that period, the Whites put up a wall of non-compliance. When Grassley concluded his investigation in 2011, he acknowledged that the Whites and Without Walls Church had not cooperated in the investigation, but also admitted that there was nothing he planned to do about those who did not cooperate.

By then, Randy White had retired from ministry and, also in 2011, he was arrested for driving under the influence. He spent time in rehab, and in 2018 launched an unsuccessful bid for the US Senate from Florida.[10]

Paula White has had a more successful "second act." She became an advisor to President Donald Trump and, in 2019, was tapped to head the White House's Faith and Opportunity Initiative, a successor to previous administrations' faith-based office that coordinates outreach to religious communities. She is sometimes called "the Trump whisperer" for her closeness to the president. She is also someone who never misses an opportunity for self-promotion. Her appointment by Trump coincided with the release of her latest book, *Something Greater.*[11]

Sound And Fury, Signifying Nothing

In the end, the investigation by Senator Grassley and the Senate Finance Committee yielded little of consequence. A dozen years after Grassley began his investigation, and nine years after he closed it with no criminal or regulatory action, none of the ministries in the Grassley Six—with the exception of Joyce Meyer—have made significant reforms. Several of the ministries have slid further down the slope of scandal. Kenneth Copeland and Creflo Dollar may even have been emboldened by winning their showdown with the US government. For Paula White, the notoriety helped launch her new career as a political insider and the de facto spokesperson for evangelicals in this country.

So what really happened? And what can we learn?

It's important to remember that Grassley's investigation, beginning in March 2008, corresponded almost exactly with the worst part of the financial crisis. In fact, one of the signal events of the Great Recession was the collapse of investment banking giant Bear Stearns, also in March 2008.

As part of my research, I interviewed Senator Grassley in his office on Capitol Hill. By the time we spoke, the recession, the banking scandals, and the Bernie Madoff and Allen Stanford scandals had pushed the Grassley Six televangelist scandal out of the headlines. So much time had gone by since the beginning of the investigation that many of Grassley's staffers, especially the ones responsible for initiating the investigation, were gone.

So I asked, "Have the banking crisis and other events conspired to give Paula White, Eddie Long, Creflo Dollar, and the rest of them a 'get out of jail free' card?"

Senator Grassley answered, "No. Absolutely not. Our investigation continues."

But, in fact, the investigation ended with almost nothing to show for it. That reality is one of the lessons here: federal government regulation does not have the focus or the flexibility to regulate effectively the more than one million nonprofit organizations in this country. The government can ensure an environment of transparency, but beyond that its efforts are mostly counterproductive. Regulations hamper those with integrity with compliance burdens, and they end up not being much of an impediment for those with no integrity.

Also, politicians are also slaves to, well, politics. In fact, that reality has become mythologized in a saying that even young interns on Capitol Hill learn during their first weeks in Washington: "You can't take the politics out of politics."

To see this entire episode in microcosm, consider one of the few extended public statements Senator Grassley made about his investigation. That speech took place in March 2009, exactly one year after Bear Stearns collapsed, one year after his investigation began, and after several deadlines he had placed on the televangelists had come and gone. He spoke to a forum of nonprofit executives. Grassley said the televangelist investigations made it clear he was thinking about new regulations with a speech to a forum of nonprofit executives. While not specific about his plans for legislative reform, he made it clear reforms could come.[12]

He noted the fortieth anniversary of the enactment, in 1969, of the last major regulatory overhaul of private foundations. Grassley said, "In these forty years, we've seen explosive growth in charities and charitable giving. What we haven't seen, though, is the law, and the enforcement of the law, keep up with that growth."

He then broadly spelled out the improvements he's hoping to bring about, including greater transparency for both charities and foundations. "I believe that sunshine is the best disinfectant," Grassley said. "So, I will continue to...conduct hearings and I will continue to write to specific charities to better understand their activities. I also expect my staff to continue drafting legislative proposals. Finally, I will continue to press the Internal Revenue Service to improve reporting requirements for charities."

But again, none of that happened, confirming once again Albert Meyer's contention that we should not look to government regulation or intervention to solve these problems.

So what about the EFCA?

Just a couple of days after Grassley's speech, on March 12, 2009, Joyce Meyer Ministries was accepted for membership in the ECFA.

But the timing makes obvious that it was not the Grassley investigation that motivated Joyce Meyer. In fact, it was at least in part the work of MinistryWatch, which had been scrutinizing and making public information about her ministry for years before the Grassley investigation. It was likely that MinistryWatch's activism, along with subsequent media coverage from *Christianity Today*, *WORLD*, CBS News, and ABC News made the real difference with Joyce Meyer Ministries.

Meyer so much as admitted that when the ministry was accepted into the ECFA, saying that she had made "significant" changes in the way the ministry does business. The ECFA's welcome of Meyer into its membership still took some by surprise, but ECFA President Dan Busby told me, "I personally visited Joyce Meyer Ministries, and they were completely transparent with us."

Also accepted for membership in the ECFA that year (in fact, it was the very next day: March 13, 2009) was Oral Roberts University. ORU was not the object of a Grassley investigation. However, at least three of the Grassley Six had previously been on ORU's board of regents: Copeland, Hinn and Dollar. (Another former regent was Jesse DuPlantis, who we discussed earlier.) ORU's acceptance into the ECFA was also the result of getting a years-long housecleaning at the college as a condition for receiving a seventy million-dollar gift from the Green family, the family that owns Hobby Lobby. That housecleaning included ridding the college of these prosperity gospel board members.

So the ECFA did indeed play a role. It set standards to which these organizations could aspire, and their membership indicates that they had indeed made progress. But the ECFA could not and does not provide any real punitive or coercive power to ministries that simply decide not to comply. Again, in the case of Joyce Meyer Ministries, media attention played the primary role. In the case of Oral Roberts University, it was a shrewd and informed donor, Mart Green.[13]

Senator Grassley continued to place much hope in the ECFA. In fact, in the same report announcing the end of his investigation, he asked the ECFA to lead an effort to look further at standards and accountability related to Christian nonprofits. In response, the ECFA set up the Commission on Accountability and Policy for Religious Organizations. The ECFA issued its final report in 2013. The report dealt almost exclusively with the rights and responsibilities of churches regarding political speech. Issues of transparency, governance, and accountability were almost completely ignored.

All of which seems to confirm Albert Meyer's assertion that

"government oversight is not worthless, it is worse than worthless, because it gives people a false sense of security, a sense that someone is paying attention, when in fact most of the time they are not."

Epilogue

We Have Met The Enemy, And It Is Us

If you see fraud and do not say fraud, you are a fraud.
—Nassim Nicholas Taleb

Years ago, I watched a television show with the flamboyant weight loss guru Richard Simmons. On this program, Simmons tried to help a man who weighed almost a thousand pounds. He was completely bedridden. In fact, in order for Simmons to move him, he had to hire carpenters to remove an outside wall of the man's house. The man could no longer fit through the doors. They ended up moving him out of his home using a forklift.

Early in the program, Simmons described the man's diet. I now no longer remember the details, except to say that he consumed massive amounts of unhealthy food, every day. Indeed, much of his day was spent eating, and much of his caregivers' time was spent preparing meals.

Only later did I think, "Wait a minute. If the man is bedridden, who brings him the food?" The answer was that these "caregivers," however well-meaning they may have been, were in fact—there's no other way to say it—killing him.

It occurs to me that this reality TV program is a near-perfect metaphor for the problems with the evangelical church today. We know on some level that what we're doing is killing us. We can see that it is killing our witness to an unbelieving world. Yet we persist. We tolerate these evildoers in our midst. We rationalize our own behavior, saying that the televangelists we love are different. David Jeremiah is not Benny Hinn. Mark Driscoll is not Creflo Dollar.

But is that true? The Ravi Zacharias scandal, which is still playing out as I write this, should have disabused ourselves of this notion. Certainly they're different in style and—for the discerning—in theology. But we should face this hard reality of life in a media-saturated culture: Unless we make concentrated, sustained efforts to draw distinctions, and to put safeguards in place to protect even the "good guys" from temptations, we can expect the stories in this book to repeat themselves. And the general public will not able to discern between the televangelists we love and the ones others love. Between pastors who serve humbly and sacrificially, and the ones who are "living large."

Before long, the well that is evangelicalism is polluted altogether. A little leaven has made the whole loaf inedible for most non-Christians.

For the truth is: We all start out to be different, to be better, to be free of the corruption that came before us. But when we put our foot on the slippery slope that the Christian Industrial Complex has become, it is difficult not to slide all the way to the bottom.

We can prevent that slide to the bottom. But, as some of the heroes of this book have both said and demonstrated, it will not be up to the government, and it will not even be up to groups such as the ECFA.

It will be up to us.

It will be hard. It will take courage. But no one else can do this. It will have to be us.

Acknowledgments

This book depends on the goodwill and strong support of so many people that I despair of naming them all, or of properly thanking those I do name. But the effort must be made, if only to let you, the reader, know that this book is not fully my own.

First and foremost, I want to thank Rusty and Carol Leonard, the founders of MinistryWatch. As you saw as you read this book, they are among the few heroes of the sometimes sordid and sensational tales I recounted. My debt to Rusty is great on many levels. Rusty and I wrote a column together for *WORLD* for two years. I did most of the reporting and writing, but most of the ideas (certainly most of the good ideas) came from Rusty. Many of those ideas and expanded versions of those columns are in this book. Rusty's spiritual maturity and hard-nosed realism (which is itself a kind of spiritual maturity) taught me much.

Albert Meyer, the whistleblower in the New Era fraud, is another hero of this book. He was generous with his time, and he sent me a box of original documents that helped me reconstruct events.

I also want to thank Joel Belz, Marvin Olasky, and Mindy Belz at *WORLD*. Joel is truly a pioneer in Christian journalism, and I was honored when, in 1994, he took an interest in my work. His interest and encouragement were the difference between quitting and continuing on more than one occasion. As for Marvin and Mindy, they have been the kind of editors that all writers need: loving and tough. They steered me to sources and steered me away from fuzzy thinking and imprecise language and, in doing so, from much trouble. Their commitment to the truth has been unfailing, and their work has made me a better writer and a better person. As a practical matter, I am grateful to *WORLD* for allowing me to use material originally published there in this book. Over the two-year period that Rusty and I wrote our charity column for *WORLD*, I did more than two hundred interviews, many of which did not make it into the final manuscript of this book, but all of which contributed to my understanding of the charity landscape at this interesting time in the early twenty-first century. Naming all these folk would reduce this page to a list that would cause your eyes to glaze over. So to all of you who allowed me an interview—thank you. I'm sorry I couldn't name you all here.

I will mention one interview, however. I interviewed Senator Charles Grassley in his office on Capitol Hill, and it was only after I arrived in his office that I discovered, to my horror, that the battery in my digital recorder was dead. An embarrassing rookie mistake. Fortunately, I had a power cord, but the only available outlet was under Senator Grassley's desk. So the tall, distinguished senior senator from Iowa, age seventy-six and dressed in an elegant dark suit, immediately got down on his hands and knees, crawled under his desk, and plugged me in. I watched in horror while several of his staff just nodded their heads in amusement.

The investigation into televangelists that he started did not end as well as anyone involved might have wished. Still, I developed a great respect for Senator Grassley during the three years I spent reporting on him and his inquiry. I came to understand that Senator Grassley is both a great man and a humble man and that in him, as in too few others, these qualities nourish each other.

I also want to acknowledge other journalists working mostly for smaller newspapers around the country. The rap on journalists working for mainstream papers is that they are liberal, secular, and anti-Christian. There is plenty of evidence for this conclusion. However, one of the themes of this book is that the profession of journalism is essential to the process of rooting out fraud—faith-based or other kinds of fraud. Journalism remains the indispensable Fourth Estate in our culture. In my research for this book, I found many excellent journalists in smaller towns who were doing the hard work of investigative reporting, yet were not simply trying to "stick it to the Christians." Their work is cited throughout this book, but I wanted to pay tribute to them en masse here. I would like to offer special thanks to Steve Stecklow, formerly of the *Wall Street Journal*, who read and provided helpful feedback to the chapter on John Bennett and the Foundation for New Era Philanthropy.

Many people read early drafts of all or part of this book and made helpful suggestions: Rusty Leonard, Tim Burns, Jackie Arthur, Julie Smith, John Allen, Julie Malament, Jamie Dean, David Wills, Albert Meyer, Phil Cooke, and Ed Pease. During the writing of the book, I had four interns, all of whom read various drafts and made helpful suggestions: McKinley Cobb, Natalie Garnett, Jaclyn Martin, and Sydney Thomas.

My wife Missy and my four children all read the manuscript in various stages and gave me great suggestions and encouragement, and tolerated my absences. So to Missy and my children, Brittany, Cole, Walker, and Morgan, I offer the usual inadequate expressions of gratitude.

This book is yours too.

Glossary of Financial and Other Terms

Affinity Fraud: A scheme where a certain group of investors is targeted because of belonging to a particular group, such as religious affiliation. The perpetrator often is or pretends to be a member of the same group. The perpetrator exploits the investors' trust because of the group affiliation.

Arbitrage: The practice of taking advantage of a price difference between two or more markets. For example, a highly specialized book might find no buyers at a garage sale, so the price of that book there would be close to zero. However, if that book is posted online so that those looking for that book can find it easily, the book has much greater value. The book is the same, but the garage sale market and the online market gave that book a very different price. When used by academics, an arbitrage often refers to simultaneous or near-simultaneous transactions. To use our garage sale example: a transaction that was a pure arbitrage would be one in which I bought the book at the garage sale *only after* I knew I had a buyer for it at a higher price. Such transactions create the possibility of a risk-free profit.

Audited Financial Statements: Audited financial statements are the product of an independent audit of an organization's financial statements. Audits provide limited assurance, but not absolute assurance, that an organization's financial records represent the true and accurate financial position of a company. Auditors perform a variety of procedures and tests to make these assurances. These procedures and tests are defined by Generally Accepted Accounting Procedures, or GAAP. (See GAAP, below.)

Certificate of Deposit (CD): CDs are similar to savings accounts and are normally virtually risk-free. The difference between a CD and a savings account is that money may be withdrawn at any time from a savings account. Money must be left in a CD for a specified period of time. CDs therefore often have a slightly higher rate of return than do savings accounts. Stanford Financial Group produced a CD product that it represented as risk-free, but which in fact contained many risky and illiquid assets. (See Chapter 6.)

Coupon: The interest rate of a bond.

Bond: In its simplest terms, a bond is a promise to repay. More commonly, a bond is a debt investment in which a bondholder loans money to an issuer. The issuer borrows the funds for a defined period of time at a specified interest rate. A bond is, in other words, a form of debt. The most common bonds are those issued by governments. When you buy a bond, you are buying a promise that the seller of the bond will pay back to you your original investment, plus interest. That rate of interest is sometimes called the bond's "coupon."

Due Diligence: Those activities a person or organization should go through before consummating a transaction. When you purchase a house, your mortgage holder requires an inspection and a title search, among other things. These are due diligence activities.

Escrow Account: An account that allows an independent trusted third party to receive and disburse money for two or more transacting parties, with the timing of the disbursement being dependent on the performance by the parties involved in the transaction.

Evangelical Council for Financial Accountability: The ECFA was formed in 1979 to create standards for financial accountability among Christian nonprofits. These standards eventually became the "Seven Standards of Responsible Stewardship." All members must commit to adhere to these standards. Of the nearly one million Christian nonprofits in the country, about twenty-four hundred are members of the ECFA.

Generally Accepted Accounting Procedures (GAAP): Auditors do not ensure that a company's financial statements are accurate. Rather, auditors certify that the financial statements are compiled, reviewed, and tested according to Generally Accepted Accounting Procedures, or GAAP. These procedures vary, depending on the kind of company being audited, but CPAs, or Certified Public Accountants, are required to know which procedures are relevant for the company being audited.

Internal Controls: Accounting policies and procedures inside an organization that minimize both mistakes and the possibility of financial fraud. Examples of common internal controls include: segregation and distribution of duties of key accounting functions, so that one person is not responsible for an entire process; a monthly review of financial statements by management personnel outside the accounting department; clear and written policies. Effective internal controls often include whistle blower processes and protections.

Qualified Opinion: When an auditor audits a company, the final product of that audit is an "opinion." The opinion says whether the financial statements being audited are compiled in accordance with Generally Accepted Accounting Procedures or not. A qualified opinion means that the financial statements were not compiled according to GAAP.

Market Capitalization: Sometimes called "market cap," is the total value of a company. The market cap of a company is the total number of shares outstanding times the price of a share. So, if a company's share price is one dollar, and one million shares are outstanding (available for ownership in the market), then the market cap of that company is one million dollars.

Ponzi Scheme: A financial fraud that usually promises high rates of return to entice people to invest. Investors are paid not with returns on their investment, but with the funds of those who invest money later. Ponzi schemes are often described as "robbing Peter to pay Paul."

Private Inurement: The use of one's personal influence in a nonprofit organization for personal profit or gain.

Prospectus: A formal legal document that provides details about an investment. A prospectus should contain all facts that an investor needs to know in order to make an informed decision.

Prosperity Theology: The belief that God provides prosperity to those whom He favors. It therefore follows that material prosperity is a sign of God's favor. Related to both of these ideas is the notion that God's favor can be earned or "loosened" by certain behaviors, including the donation of money to ministry. This behavior is sometimes called "sowing a seed of faith." Prosperity theology is therefore sometimes called "seed-faith" theology.

Pyramid Scheme: An unsustainable business model that involves promising participants payment primarily for enrolling other people into the scheme, rather than from any real investment or sale of products or services to the public. Pyramid schemes are a form of fraud and are illegal in the United States and most countries of the world.

Notes

Introduction

1. The fifteen-year history of *The Charlotte World* is a story for another book, except to say that this little newsletter ultimately led to a small chain of newspapers in seven cities. I should also add that the abortion fund that originally motivated me to start *The Charlotte World* has been eliminated, though the role of the newspaper was negligible. Credit for that change goes to a number of pro-family organizations, including the North Carolina Family Policy Council.

2. I have written extensively elsewhere on this topic, especially in my 2009 book *A Lover's Quarrel With The Evangelical Church*. For readers who want more, I recommend Chapter 1 from that book, "The Evangelical Myth," and Chapter 4, "The Christian-Industrial Complex."

3. "Wounded By A Pastor's Fall, The Journey Megachurch Gets Back On Its Path," by Eric Berger, Religion News Service, Jan. 17, 2019

4. "Darren Patrick, Megachurch Pastor and Author, Died by Apparent "Self-Inflicted Gunshot," by Bob Smietana, Religion News Service, as published by MinistryWatch.com, May 8, 2020.

5. Interview with Steven Furtick in 2008. This was the last interview I ever did with Furtick, though I have made more than a dozen requests over the years, including one request face-to-face, when by happenstance—we were both on the same flight from Dallas to Charlotte. (Furtick was in first class. I was in coach.)

6. To read about a few controversies related to Steven Furtick, see: "The House That Steven Built: A Charlotte Megachurch Pastor's Megamansion Raises Eyebrows and Critical Questions," by Warren Cole Smith, *WORLD*, Nov. 29, 2013. See also: "Signs and Wonders: Manipulated Baptisms and Steven Furtick's Vision from God," by Warren Cole Smith, *WORLD*, Feb. 21, 2014.

7. "Pastor and Mental Health Advocate Jarrid Wilson Dies by Suicide," by Roxanne Stone, Emily McFarlan Miller, Alejandra Molina, Religion News Service, as published in *Christianity Today*, Sept. 10, 2019

8. "Texas Pastor and Ministry Leader Richard Logan Kills Family and Self," by Steve Rabey, MinistryWatch.com, Feb. 15, 2020.

9. "A Young Pastor Preached About Depression, Then Killed Himself. His Widow Wants To Help Others by Talking About It," by Hailey Branson-Potts, *The Los Angeles Times*, Dec. 23, 2018.

10. I had lunch with Mark Dever and a young pastoral intern he was mentoring, Garrett Kell, in 2010, shortly after the publication of *A Lover's Quarrel With The Evangelical Church*, which Dever was using in his internship program. I asked Dever if he was afraid he would lose members when Kell or others in his pastoral mentoring program graduated and planted nearby churches. He said, "I'm not *afraid* it will happen. I'm *praying* it will happen." Ten years later, Garrett Kell is lead pastor of Del Ray Baptist Church in Alexandria, Virginia, and a Council member of The Gospel Coalition.

11. "A Wave Came In: How An Introvert Like Tim Keller Became A Great Preacher," by Marvin Olasky, *WORLD*, April 23, 2010.

12. "Matt Chandler's Village Church Ends Multisite Era," by Kate Shellnutt, *Christianity Today*, Sept. 28, 2017.

13. A few definitions: *polity* is a fancy word for how a church is organized and governed. There are basically three kinds of church polity: episcopal, presbyterian, and congregational. Episcopal churches have bishops. (In Greek, the word *episcopoi* means "overseer." Examples of episcopal churches include the Roman Catholic, Anglican, Eastern Orthodox, Lutheran, and Methodist churches. Presbyterian churches do not have bishops, but they do have a clearly defined hierarchical structure whose cornerstone is the ordained elder, and their congregations are not autonomous, but are typically part of presbyteries, or regional bodies. Presbyterian churches include most of the branches of Presbyterianism around the world, as well as the Church of Scotland. Congregational churches believe in the autonomy of the local congregation. Southern Baptists, the nation's largest denomination, is a congregational church, as are virtually all independent and nondenominational churches, by definition.

14. For a variety of reasons, including timing and the fact that other examples provided better "on ramps" for describing the issues of this book, I do not devote much time to James MacDonald and Harvest Bible Chapel. However, he has been the subject of extensive coverage at MinistryWatch. To read more: https://ministrywatch. com/?s=macdonald

15. "Out of the Dark: Ted Haggard's Secret Cost Him his Ministry, but Exposure Could Grant Him New Life" by Mark Bergin, *WORLD*, Nov. 18, 2006

16. Matthew 18:15-18 says, "If your brother sins against you, go and show him his fault, just between the two of you. If he listens to you, you have won your brother over. But if he will not listen, take one or two others along, so that 'every matter may be established by the testimony of two or three witnesses.' If he refuses to listen to them, tell it to the church; and if he refuses to listen even to the church, treat him as you would a pagan or a tax collector."

17. For those who are sticklers for historical accuracy, I should say that I'm quoting the movie accurately, but the movie took liberties with history. It was actually astronaut Jack Swigert who said, "Okay Houston, we've had a problem here." Astronaut Jim Lovell then repeated, "Houston, we've had a problem." I find no record of Kranz ever saying, "Work the problem people. Let's not make it worse by guessing." However, NASA engineers of the era say that the phrase was a common one. ("Apollo 13, We Have a Solution," by Stephen Cass, *IEEE Spectrum*, April 2005).

18. "Americans' Trust in Mass Media Edges Down to 41 Percent" by Megan Brenan, The Gallup Organization, Sept. 26, 2019. As the headline suggests, since 2016 confidence in media has rebounded a bit.

19. See my essay "Calvin as Journalist" in *Calvin and Culture: Exploring a Worldview* (Phillipsburg, NJ: P&R Publishing, 2010). This book was the final volume in the excellent *Calvin 500* series published to commemorate the five hundredth birthday of John Calvin.

20. Marvin Olasky and Warren Cole Smith, *Prodigal Press: Confronting the Anti-Christian Bias of the American News Media*, P&R Publishing, 2013.

21. Hank Hanegraaff, *Christianity In Crisis: 21st Century*, Thomas Nelson, 2009, p. 212.

22. Patti Roberts, *Ashes To God*, Jove Publishing, 1987.

Chapter 1: What Is Faith-based Fraud?

1. Arthur Brooks, *Who Really Cares?* (New York: Basic Books, 2006). This book is, in my view, one of the most significant books to be written about philanthropy in the past twenty-five years. It debunks the argument that evangelical Christians do not put their money where their mouths are. But more than that, it strongly affirms that private-sector philanthropy is much more effective than government aid in helping people, in part because it can respond much more quickly to new information. This book and Marvin Olasky's *The Tragedy of American Compassion* should be required reading for every college student—and for every elected official—who truly cares about helping the poor.

2. Of course, this massive number causes us to wonder what we're

getting for our money. It is estimated, for example, that foreign aid and philanthropy were responsible for 80 percent of the legal economic activity in Haiti before the 2010 earthquake. (I should add, too, that Haiti has been the "beneficiary" of more short-term mission trips from America that any other country in the world.) All that aid and all our missions trips have not lifted that country out of poverty. In fact, a strong case could be made that our efforts have left Haiti worse off than ever—less equipped to care for itself when times were good or to recover when catastrophic events strike. So what's the solution? One of the solutions and one of the recurring themes of this book is that transparency provides information that donors and others need to efficiently redirect money from those engaged in waste, fraud, and abuse toward more effective operators. For more on this topic see the Acton Institute's 2014 documentary film "Poverty, Inc." See also "Short-Term Mission Trip, or Donor-Paid Vacation?" by Brittany Smith, Evangelical Press News Service, Oct. 19, 2006.

3. "Plugging Leaks," by Warren Cole Smith, *WORLD Magazine*, May 23, 2009.

4. Ibid.

5. Ibid.

6. DeMoss was the founder, president, and chairman of the board of the National Liberty Corporation, a life insurance company that is still remembered (by those of a certain age) for its television commercials featuring Art Linkletter. DeMoss died at age 53 of a heart attack while playing tennis.

7. Interview with Rusty Leonard in November 2010.

8. Full disclosure: Rusty Leonard remains the chairman of the board of WallWatchers, the official name of MinistryWatch. That means that he is my boss.

9. That said, beginning in early 2020, MinistryWatch has begun to publish, on a weekly basis, the names of organizations who are removed from ECFA membership, either voluntarily or otherwise.

10. "ECFA Charter Member, Wycliffe Associates, Resigns Membership While Under Review," by Warren Cole Smith, MinistryWatch.com, March 7, 2020.

11. Of course, many people believe that it is impossible for the government to "re-regulate" anything without increasing regulation.

I am sympathetic to that view. However, it is important that we not let adherence to an ideology obscure the facts. I would note, for example, that over the past 30 years a number of industries have been deregulated with little or no negative effect, and often a positive effect. Two notable examples: the airline industry and the telecommunications industry. Deregulation during the 1970s and 80s resulted in innovation, lower costs, higher quality, and—for the airline industry—greater safety.

12. To read more about MinistryWatch's 5-Star Financial Efficiency Rating System, see "Explaining The MinistryWatch 5-Star Ratings System," MinistryWatch.com

Chapter 2: The Amazing Story of Charles Ponzi

1. A commonly recurring theme in financial frauds is the effort to separate work from wealth. Recovering what I call a "theology of work" is important to keep us from being victims of faith-based fraud and to keep us from unwittingly perpetuating an evangelical culture that doesn't value work as God given. One of the best discussions of this topic I have ever read is in Darrow Miller's book *LifeWork* (YWAM Publishing: 2009).

2. A version of the International Reply Coupon is still in existence today. For more information about IRCS, see: "Mailing Standards of the United States Postal Service, International Mail Manual," issued by the United States Postal Service, April 6, 2020.

3. "He Came, He Saw, He Conned: The Immigrant Who Fleeced the Public," by Joellen Perry, *U.S. News and World Report*, August 2, 2002.

4. "Why Are So Many Indian Arranged Marriages Successful?" by Utpal Dholakia, *Psychology Today*, Nov. 24, 2015.

5. Let me say again, I am not advocating arranged marriages.

6. Thomas Streissguth, *Hoaxers and Hustlers* (Minneapolis, MN: Oliver Press, 1994), 39.

7. The idea of getting "something for nothing" was satirized in the Dire Straits song "Money for Nothing." The song includes this verse: "That ain't workin'/That's the way you do it/You play the guitar on the MTV/ That ain't workin'/That's the way you do it/You get your money for nothing and your chicks for free." I share this verse to say that one of the roots of the problems we are discussing throughout this book—the devaluing of work and idolization of celebrities—is a pathology that even secular culture-makers recognize and decry. Part of the tragedy of modern faith-based frauds is that they push evangelicals to live in ways that even secular culture now recognizes as banal. We are losing the opportunity to provide to secular culture a healing alternative.

8. Mitchell Zuckoff, "What Madoff Could Learn from Ponzi," *Fortune Magazine*, January 13, 2009. Zuckoff also wrote what is perhaps the most comprehensive biography of Ponzi and its impact on American financial

life: *Ponzi's Scheme: The True Story of a Financial Legend.* New York: Random House, 2005.

9. While writing this book, I simultaneously read Marvin Olasky's *The American Leadership Tradition*, which uses the biographies of iconic American leaders to highlight the importance of character in leaders. I ran across this quote, which has a poignant relevance here because it highlights how much we Americans are suckers for a certain kind of scoundrel. Olasky quotes liberal commentator Chris Matthews, who says of Bill Clinton: "We, 49 percent of us at least, bought this box of cereal called Bill Clinton. Inside some of us expected to find, perhaps, one of those little plastic toys slipped in between the box and the wax paper. Instead, we opened the box one winter day this year to find not a harmless novelty item but a spider, an eight-legged hairy bug crawling in what we expected to be a hearty January breakfast. We now have to live with it, including those of us who are so hungry for leadership in this aging century that we heard [the telltale scratching in the box] and discounted [it] back when we had the choice. (Marvin Olasky, *The American Leadership Tradition*, page xvi.).

10. Stanley Hauerwas interviewed by Warren Cole Smith. *Voices that Carry: Conversations with Some of the Evangelical Church's Most Interesting and Influential People*, Xulon Press, 2005. P. 74.

Chapter 3: Jim and Tammy Faye Bakker

1. "Televangelist Jim Bakker Warned by NY Attorney General" by Anne Stych, MinistryWatch.com, March 6, 2020

2. Neil Postman's classic book on the modern media, *Amusing Ourselves To Death*, devotes a chapter to Jim Bakker and other televangelists. One of Postman's insights about media is sometimes referred to as "Postman's Smoke Signals." He uses smoke signals to explain that all media have certain abilities to communicate, but they also have limitations. It raises an interesting question regarding whether television, even when used well, might have what Postman calls a "net negative" impact on the message you want to send, which in this case is the Gospel itself.

3. Frances Fitzgerald, "Jim and Tammy," New Yorker, 23 April 1990

4. James Dobson ultimately left Focus on the Family, in 2010, to form another radio program, Family Talk with Dr. James Dobson, but Focus on the Family continued under the leadership of Jim Daly, and it remains a Christian radio juggernaut, with 2018 revenue of nearly $100-million. Dobson's newer organization has grown to about $9-million.

5. Marijuana use got a lot of publicity in the 1960s, but it was mostly confined to the colleges and the so-called "hippie culture." But it boomed

in the 1970s. By 1978, according to Smithsonian Maga- zine, "rates of adolescent marijuana use had skyrocketed, with 1 in 9 high school seniors smoking pot every day and children as young as 13 reporting that the drug was 'easy to get.'" Also gaining in popularity was LSD, especially in the early 1970s, with cocaine becoming the glamor drug of the late 1970s, peaking in the 1980s, when the scourge of crack cocaine hit America's streets. "Why the 1970s Effort to Decriminalize Marijuana Failed," by Emily Dufton, *Smithsonian Magazine*, April 25, 2019.

6. Interestingly, the city that eclipsed them all, Atlanta, has a very different history. Atlanta was originally called Terminus when it was founded in 1837, nearly a full century after Charlotte and the other Piedmont cities were settled. Atlanta was not founded by religious pilgrims, but by economic opportunists, as Terminus was so named because it was originally just an abstract spot on a map, a surveyor's calculation, a place to link proposed railways.

7. On the matter of the doctrinal confusion of the Second Great Awakening, see a more complete discussion in my 2009 book *A Lover's Quarrel with the Evangelical Church*, pp. 48-55.

8. Reliable viewership numbers from this era are tough to sort out. Bakker claimed 13 million viewers on 180 television stations and 1,300 cable outlets across the nation. It seems unlikely that these numbers are accurate, though it is likely that weekly viewership was in the millions.

9. A case in point: In 1970 a young billboard company owner, Ted Turner, bought a UHF channel in Atlanta that eventually became the cornerstone of his media empire, an empire that made Turner a billionaire and now includes WTBS, CNN, and Turner Classic Movies (TCM). But at the time there was so little original programming not owned by the major networks that Turner created a program called *The Now Explosion*, which featured Top 40 songs being played while people danced to them—often solo amateur dancers on a bare sound stage. Today, TV historians call the program innovative, a precursor to MTV. But I lived in Atlanta in 1970 and saw the show regularly. It was cheesy, low-budget television, and everyone knew it, a placeholder till something better came along. But such was the dearth of programming that *Now Explosion* became something of a cultural phenomenon. Today it even has its own fan website: www.thenowexplosion.net.

10. Billy Graham's childhood home moved again when The Billy Graham Library was built in Charlotte in the mid-2000s. (It opened in 2007.) All of which shows how closely Bakker aligned himself with otherwise mainstream Christian ministries—or, what some might say, ministries that should have known better. A final historical footnote: When the childhood home became a part of the $27 million Billy Graham Library,

critics said the facility was turning into a shrine to Graham. The facility is called the Billy Graham Library and not the Billy Graham Museum in part to neutralize that criticism. However, most of Graham's papers are housed at the Billy Graham Center at Wheaton College. All of this led to a joke heard often in Charlotte: "The only books at the Billy Graham Library are the ones that are for sale."

11. "Power Glory—and Politics" by Richard Ostling, *TIME*, Feb. 17, 1986. In a poignant footnote to this footnote: "Uncle Henry" Harrison continued to live on the grounds of the old PTL complex until his death in February 1995, of a stroke, at age 67. He stood by the Bakkers during the good times and bad, and he was rewarded for his loyalty by living long enough to see Jim Bakker released from prison, just six weeks before he died. The first public speech Bakker made after his release was to speak at Uncle Henry's funeral.

12. "PTL Fundraising A Tangled Saga" by Michael Isikoff and Art Harris, *The Washington Post*, May 23, 1987. The FCC ultimately backed away from pursuing any criminal action, even though it found the Bakkers diverted at least $350,000 that was supposed to go to mission work overseas to support operations at home. This episode is another argument for transparency over government regulation.

13. That said, the May 25, 1987 issue of *WORLD* devoted its cover to the scandal in an article titled "PTL Down the Tubes."

14. Though they may have been. "Private inurement" is prohibited by the Internal Revenue Service. Private inurement is the use of one's personal influence in a nonprofit organization for personal profit or gain.

15. Phil Cooke, *The Last TV Evangelist* (Conversant Media Group, 2009). This book is helpful in diagnosing some of the problems of TV preachers, but it stops short of asserting what I believe is the truth of television, and that is that television inevitably leads to a corruption of the gospel message. Pouring the gospel into television does not shape the television to the gospel, it shapes the gospel to the television. What ultimately comes across is only what television is good at producing: entertainment. For more on this topic see my discussion of media Chapter 6, called "The Great Stereopticon," in my book *A Lover's Quarrel with the Evangelical Church* (Authentic Books, 2009). See also Chapter 10 in *Prodigal Press*, "The Devil in the Electrons." Both of these discussions depend heavily on Neil Postman's *Amusing Ourselves to Death*, the classic work on the corrosive effects of television and other visual media.

16. A personal story: In 1979, while a college student at the University of Georgia, I did an internship with Senator Sam Nunn, the junior senator from Georgia. Once a week, Senator Hatfield would come to Senator Nunn's office for a Bible study. It was my job to go to the cafeteria in

the basement of the Senate Office Building and fetch Senator Hatfield's lunch, which was invariably a small container of yogurt and a package of sunflower seeds. As he handed me money to pay for his food, he often asked me, "Do you want anything?" or "May I buy you a Coke?" That and the fact that in a town where almost everything is done for political gain neither Senator Nunn nor Senator Hatfield ever publicized their involvement in this Bible study made a lasting impression on me.

17.Gary Tidwell, *Anatomy of a Fraud.* New York: John Wiley & Sons, 1993. p. 123.

18.Ibid, p. 234.

19."Reinvented Jim Bakker Looks a Bit like the Old," by Todd C. Frankel, *St. Louis Post-Dispatch*, February 23, 2008. Here's a telling excerpt from that article: "Bakker still owes the IRS more than $6.1 million, accumulated income taxes and penalties after his PTL ministry was stripped of its tax-exempt status, according to court records. He completed his federal parole in 1997, so there are no restrictions on his activities. The financial details of his church, including how much he earns, are not public record. His staff declined to provide that information."

Chapter 4: Todd Bentley Takes the Money and Runs

1. "Same Old Scam," by Rusty Leonard and Warren Cole Smith, *WORLD Magazine*, June 28, 2008.

2. I have also made similar requests of Benny Hinn. So far, no response.

3. "Heal or Heel?" *WORLD Magazine*, May 23, 2009. Much of this chapter originally appeared, in a shorter form, in this article. All stories were based on interviews I did in 2008 and 2009 with those on Bentley's list.

4. John Bowker, "Toronto Blessing," *The Concise Oxford Dictionary of World Religions* (1997). Again, we see the same troubling signs that we've seen in other frauds and scandals: a lack of oversight, an unwillingness to submit to accountability.

5. "Strange Fire: A Decade in the Life of Todd Bentley" by Warren Cole Smith, MinistryWatch, Jan. 3, 2020.

Chapter 5: New Era Philanthropy

1. "William E. Simon and the Social Entrepreneurship Awards That Honor His Legacy" by Julyssa Lopez, *Philanthropy Magazine*, Winter 2011.

2. It's worth noting here that almost all reputable fundraisers and all major

fundraising associations—the Association of Fundraising Professionals, the National Association of Hospital Developers, and the Council for the Advancement and Support of Education, among others—consider commissions to fundraisers to be unethical. For more on this topic: Kim Klein, "Why Good Fundraisers Are Never Paid on Commission," *Grassroots Fundraising Journal* (1992).

3. Interview with Albert Meyer, November 2010. Albert Meyer ultimately gave me several telephone interviews, answered and fact-checked much of this chapter via email, and provided a box of documents related to his work uncovering New Era. Much of this chapter is based on those interviews, emails, and documents.

4. We first met "Sir John" in Chapter 1. He was the billionaire investor with whom Rusty Leonard worked. What we did not mention there was that Templeton's philanthropy included a great many religious—though not always distinctly Christian—causes. For more on Templeton's fascinating life and on his interesting relationship to Christianity, see the obituary I wrote for *WORLD* when he died in 2008: "Maximum Optimist" by Warren Cole Smith, *WORLD Magazine*, July 26, 2008.

5. According to Wendell R. Bird, an attorney who has examined the transactions, "Prudential [Securities] was the depository for a substantial part of New Era's funds. New Era told donors and charities that their funds would be in 'quasi-escrow' accounts.... In fact, Prudential did not manage the accounts as escrow accounts and allowed New Era free access to the funds." "Foundation for New Era Philanthropy Scandal Rocks the Boat for Charities in Need of Funds" by Wendell R. Bird, *Journal of Taxation of Exempt Organizations*, September/October 1996.

6. "Crumbling Pyramid: Owing $500 Million, New Era Charity Seeks Refuge From Creditors" by Steve Stecklow, *The Wall Street Journal*, May 15, 1995.

7. Hans Finzel, interviewed in the MSNBC television series *American Greed*. "When Greed and Giving Collide: Confessions of a Con Man." Original air date: Oct. 19, 2009.

8. "New Era Founder Is Charged in $135 Million Fraud Case" by Steve Stecklow, *The Wall Street Journal*, Sept. 30, 1996.

9. Thomas Stanley and William Danko, *The Millionaire Next Door* (NY, Pocket Books, 1996). This book has become a classic in shattering myths regarding the sources of wealth of the American millionaire.

10. Brooks actually wrote his book to refute the idea that conservatives are not compassionate. The conclusion of Brooks' book, supported with bullet-proof data and documentation, is that conservative Christians are the most generous givers on the planet. (NY: Basic Books, 2006).

11. "Ex New Era President Seeks Early Prison Release" by Chris Bernard, *The Non-Profit Times*, June 1, 2005.

12. Ibid.

13. Jerri Williams retired from the FBI and is now a "true crime" author and podcaster. She devoted an episode to the New Era scandal: www.JerriWilliams.com. Click on the podcast tab and scroll to Episode 122.

14. "After 2 Years, The Whistle's Heard" by Sharon Walsh, *The Washington Post*, May 18, 1995.

Chapter 6: Prayers, Ponzis and Profits

1. "Crazy for Cricket" by Duncan Greenberg, *Forbes*, Sept. 19, 2008.

2. "After the Fall: The Messy Cleanup of Stanford Financial" by Andy Meek, *The Memphis Daily News*, Sept. 28, 2009.

3. "Broke, Sick, and Lonely, Allen Stanford Heads to Court" by Anna Driver and Eileen O'Grady, *Reuters*, Jan. 21, 2012.

4. "Extreme Prejudice" by Warren Cole Smith, *WORLD Magazine*, April 11, 2009.

5. Criminal complaint filed against Allen Stanford, et alia, by the Securities and Exchange Commission in the U.S. District Court for the Northern District of Texas, Feb. 17, 2009. Much of the information in the rest of this chapter comes from this and subsequent court filings. This filing can be found here: https:// www.sec.gov/litigation/complaints/2009/comp20901.pdf

6. "FBI Finds Financier Suspected of Fraud" by Eric Lichtblau, *The New York Times*, Feb. 19, 2009.

7. "Allen Stanford: Descent from Billionaire to Inmate # 35017-183" by Jeanine Ibrahim, CNBC, Oct. 5, 2012.

8. "Victims of that other Ponzi scheme—Allen Stanford's—say they have been short-changed," by Scott Cohn, CNBC, Feb. 20, 2019.

9. Stock manipulation was specifically outlawed by the Securities and Exchange Act of 1934, the sweeping overhaul of the financial markets in the aftermath of the Great Depression. But price manipulation has continued over the years, and it has even developed its own vocabulary. Schemes for manipulating stock include: churning, pooling, stock bashing, pump and dump, ramping, lure and squeeze…the list goes on.

10. "Sen. Chuck Schumer among politicians giving up money from Bernie Madoff" by Glenn Blain and Richard Sisk, *New York Daily News*, Dec. 15, 2008.

11. "Trust in financial markets was biggest victim of Madoff case" by Susan Kelley, *Cornell Chronicle*, July 17, 2017.

12. "Mad About Madoff: Bernard Madoff scandal shuts down charities" by Warren Cole Smith and Rusty Leonard, *WORLD*, January 17,

2009.

13. "Madoff's eldest son hangs himself in NYC apartment" by Colleen Long and Tom Hays, The Associated Press, Dec. 10, 2010.

Chapter 7: Let a Thousand Toxic Weeds Bloom

1. "Man gets two years in Humble church pyramid scheme" by Zeke Minaya, *Houston Chronicle*, Feb. 23, 2006.

2. "Easy Marks: Pyramid scheme uses pastors to build trust and gain 'members'" by Rusty Leonard, *WORLD*, July 31, 2009.

3. A primitive website still existed for Elite Activity as late as June of 2020: http://eliteactivity.tripod.com/

4. "Pastors question what appears to be an online pyramid scheme aimed at Brazilians" by Liz Mineo, *The Marshfield Mariner*, June 3, 2009.

5. "Crime Spree Tests A More Secular Hildale and Colorado City" by Nate Carlile, *Salt Lake City Tribune*, Sept. 11, 2017.

6. "Though it was once banned by their prophet, multilevel marketing has caught on in Utah polygamous communities" by Stephen Dark, Salt Lake City Tribune, Jan. 8, 2018.

7. "'It Needs To Look Real': The Bitcoin Scam That Took Buyers for a

$722 Million Ride' by Kelly Weill, *The Daily Beast*, Dec. 16, 2019.

8. It's interesting to me that during the course of my reporting on faith-based frauds I heard the word *winsome* several times to describe the crooks who took advantage of other people. Perhaps I'm overly sensitive to that word since *winsome* became something of a buzzword for the evangelical church in the late 20th and early 21st century. Consider this editorial from the January 12, 2000 *Baptist Standard* called "Stay Winsome in Order to Win Some": "The best way to bridge or remove spiritual walls is by sharing good news-- the gospel--in ways that are positive, winsome and loving." One of the important subtexts of this book, which will become an explicit part of the text in the later chapters, is that it is precisely this sort of "winsome Christianity" that I believe is synonymous with what Dietrich Bonhoeffer called "cheap grace," that allows faith-based fraud—of both the financial and the spiritual kind—to flourish.

9. "2 former Vick advisers barred from pension work" by The Associated

Press, Dec. 24, 2009.

10. "Crazy Returns" by Warren Cole Smith and Rusty Leonard,

WORLD, Dec. 13, 2008.

11. "California Man Sentenced to Prison, Ordered to pay $1.5 Million

For Scheme That Swindled New Jersey Investors," Press Release from the Department of Justice, U.S. Attorney's Office, District of New Jersey, May 14, 2013.

12. I overstate the case to say the bank is usually "happy." For one thing, banks are not equipped to be property owners. As bankers are fond of saying, "We are in the money business, not the real estate business." Bankers buy and sell money, they do not want to buy or sell buildings, especially churches. Churches are hard to sell because there are so few buyers. It is tough for a church to be used for anything except a church. So it is never a good thing for the bank and certainly not for the borrower when the bank must take possession of a building.

13. The exact size of the church construction market depends on the year, of course. More than 4000 new churches were started each year, but more than 3000 churches close, or merge, each year. (From *The American Church in Crisis: Groundbreaking Research Based on a National Database of over 200,000 Churches*, by David T. Olson, Zondervan, 2008). Not all of them needed buildings, of course, but many of them did, or will. When you add this to the number of established churches that are building additional buildings, you end up with an industry that is in the billions of dollars annually.

14. "Indiana increases penalties for con artists who use religion to target victims" by Warren Cole Smith, WORLD, September 25, 2009.

15. "Gibson County Jury Convicts Church Financier," Associated Press, October 21, 2010.

16. "Guilty, Jury Says, on 9 of 10 Alanar Counts," by Arthur Foulkes,

The Tribune Star, October 21, 2010.

17. "Past repayments soon to be mailed to investors who sank savings into church-building scheme," Associated Press, Sept. 3, 2014.

Chapter 8: What Would Jesus Fly?

1. See my discussion of Joel Osteen in *A Lover's Quarrel with the Evangelical Church.* Osteen appeared on *Larry King Live*, in which he plainly espoused heretical views, only to later retract them when the public outcry would not die down (*A Lover's Quarrel with the Evangelical Church*, pp. 81-92.)

2. Journals of the American Congress from 1774-1788 (Washington: Way and Gideon, 1823), Vol. 1, pp. 286-287.

3. "Why Warren Buffett Owns A Private Jet" by Matthew Stibbe,

Forbes, Sept. 22, 2011.

4. "What Would Jesus Fly?" by Rusty Leonard and Warren Cole Smith, *WORLD*, July 12, 2008. Much of this chapter was originally published in this article.

5. "IRS Rarely Audits Nonprofits for Politicking." Report from the Center for Public Integrity, Jan. 22, 2015. The report says that for the five years from 2010 to the end of 2014 only 26 organizations had been audited for involvement in political activity (one of the activities that will trigger an audit.)

6. "Televangelist who said 'Jesus wouldn't be riding a donkey today' says he will donate old private jet if his followers buy him a new one" by Maya Oppenheim, *The Independent*, June 1, 2018.

7. "Televangelist Kenneth Copeland: Commercial jets are full of 'demons'." *Inside Edition*, June 4, 2019.

8. Fred Price, *Ever Increasing Faith Messenger*, June 1980, cited in Hank Hanegraaff, *Christianity in Crisis*, p. 347.

9. Fred Price, *Praise The Lord*, Trinity Broadcasting Network, Sept. 21, 1990, cited in Dr. John MacArthur, *Charismatic Chaos*, p. 349.

10. Fred Price, *Ever Increasing Faith*, Trinity Broadcasting Network, Dec.

19, 1990, cited in Hank Hanegraaff, *Christianity in Crisis*, p. 346.

11. Dr. Fred Price, *God Has a Financial Plan*, Monthly letter for June 2005.

12. https://www.faithdome.org/eifnewsletter/jan19/message.html
13."What Would Wycliffe Fly?" By Warren Cole Smith,

MinistryWatch, March 19, 2020.

Chapter 9: What Happened At Willow Creek?

1. "Willow Creek Elders and Pastor Heather Larson Resign over Bill Hybels" by Bob Smietana, *Christianity Today*, Aug. 8, 2018.

2. "Willow Creek Confirms New Sexual Harassment Claims" by Emily McFarlan Miller, Religion News Service, January 29, 2020.

3. Much of the history of Willow Creek is adapted from Chapter 3 of *A Lover's Quarrel With The Evangelical Church* by Warren Cole Smith, 2009.

4. "New Revelations Rock Willow Creek Leadership Team" by Emily McFarlan Miller, Religion News Service, January 31, 2020.

5. *Willow Creek Seeker Services: Evaluating A New Way of Doing Church* by G.A. Pritchard (Grand Rapids: Baker Books, 1996).

6. "Willow Creek Repents? Why the most influential church in America now says 'We made a mistake'," un-bylined article, *Christianity Today,* October 2007.

7. "Numbers Racket: Survey results on megachurch growth do not add up" by Warren Cole Smith, *WORLD*, Dec. 1, 2007.

8. "Jockeying For Position on Same-Sex Marriage" by Warren Cole Smith, *WORLD*, June 10, 2015.

9. See, for example, "Bill Hybels on 'Hope for the LGBT'" by Chelsen Vicari, Institute for Religion and Democracy, May 4, 2016.

10. Darren Calhoun's biography as a board member of the LGBTQ+ affirming community Q Christian: https://www.qchristian.org/ darren-calhoun

11. "Hybels Heir Quits Willow As New Accusations Arise" by Bob Smietana, *Christianity Today*, Aug. 5, 2018.

12. "Willow Creek Elders and Pastor Heather Larson Resign over Bill Hybels" by Bob Smietana, *Christianity Today*, Aug. 8, 2018.

Chapter 10: Mark Driscoll Buys A Bestseller

1. "Unreal Sales for Driscoll's Real Marriage" by Warren Cole Smith, *WORLD*, Mar. 5, 2014. Much of this chapter is based on reporting originally done for this article.

2. "The Mystery of the Book Sales Spike" by Jeffrey Trachtenberg, *The Wall Street Journal*, Feb. 22, 2013.

3. "Mars Hill Church to Dissolve" by Warren Cole Smith, *WORLD*, Nov. 3, 2013.

4. "Tyndale House Agrees to Pull The Boy Who Came Back From Heaven" by Leigh Jones, *WORLD*, Jan. 16, 2015.

5. "David Barton's Book on Jefferson Republished" by Mickey McLean,

WORLD, Dec. 23, 2015.

6. "'Mistakes Were Made': Mark Driscoll and Tyndale House Issue a Joint Statement Regarding Alleged Plagiarism" by Warren Cole Smith, *WORLD*, Dec. 19, 2013.

7. "LifeWay to Close All Stores" by Lynde Langdon, *WORLD*, March

20, 2019

8. "South Carolina Megachurch Pastor Fired" by Molly Hulsey,

WORLD, July 11, 2016.

9. "A Costly Closure: The Liquidation of Family Christian Stores Left Publishers and Lenders to Absorb Millions in Unpaid Debt" by Lynde Langdon, *WORLD*, May 23, 2017.

10. "COVID Concerns Hit Salem, Nation's Largest Christian Broadcaster" by Warren Cole Smith, MinistryWatch, May 4, 2020.

11. "Ingrid Schlueter Resigns From Janet Mefferd Show Over Mark Driscoll Plagiarism Controversy" by Warren Throckmorton,

WThrockmorton.com, Dec. 5, 2013.

12. https://www.sec.gov/Archives/edgar/data/1050606/000114420416087583/R12.htm

13. "Fox News contributor Guy Benson marries boyfriend, says Megyn Kelly brought them together" by Maeve McDermott, *USA Today*, Sept. 11, 2019.

Chapter 11: David Jeremiah and the Christian Industrial Complex

1. For a complete list of NRB Hall of Fame members: http://nrb.org/membership/media-awards/nrb_hall_of_fame/

2. Since early 2020, a little less quietly, since MinistryWatch publishes a weekly list of ministries whose ECFA membership status changes.

3. For example, months before Driscoll stepped down from leadership at Mars Hill, the church-planting network that Seattle megachurch pastor Mark Driscoll helped found has asked him to "step down from ministry for an extended time and seek help." The board of directors of Acts 29 sent Driscoll a letter expressing gratitude for the "leadership, courage, and generosity of both you and Mars Hill in not only founding the network but also sustaining it." But the letter went on to say the board could no longer support Driscoll because of what its members consider "ungodly and disqualifying behavior." "Acts 29 to Mark Driscoll: Resign and Seek Help" by Warren Cole Smith, *WORLD*, Aug. 8, 2014.

4. These numbers are from the Form 990 of Turning Point Ministries, which can be found at Charity Navigator or Guidestar. The financial statements are summarized at MinistryWatch.com

5. "Buying A Bestseller: Is David Jeremiah Another Gifted Pastor Who Has Used What Some Say Is An Ethically Dubious Method To Promote Books?" by Warren Cole Smith, *WORLD*, Feb. 6, 2015.

6. Soon after my Feb. 6, 2015, article "Buying A Bestseller" came out, David Jeremiah and I had an awkward face-to-face meeting in the hallway of the Opryland Hotel, site of the annual meeting of the National Religious Broadcasters in 2015. I told him then I would meet him at any time and place of his convenience so he could explain his side of the story. I invited him to record the session so if I misrepresented events he would have evidence of that misrepresentation. He has so far not accepted this invitation to meet.

7. To see the Grant Deed for this property, registered with the San Diego County Recorder's Office, go to www.MinistryWatch.com/ david-jeremiah-deed. In May of 2020, according to the real estate website Zillow, the condominium had appreciated in value to about $2.5-million and was still owned by the Jeremiah Living Trust, which listed David Jeremiah and his wife Donna M. Jeremiah as trustees.

8. "The Making (and Unmaking) of a 23-Hour New York Times Best Seller" by Lila Shapire, *New York Magazine*, September 2017.

9. "Thou Shalt Not Disclose: How Churches and Ministries Use Legal Agreements to Silence Victims and Conceal Sin" by Steve Rabey, MinistryWatch.com, Feb. 6, 2020.

Chapter 12: The Grassley Six

1. "How Rusty Leonard Watches Over Donors to TV Ministries" by Robert Guy Matthews, *The Wall Street Journal*, Oct. 30, 2006.

2. "The Tall Grass(ley): Taking cover from a Senate investigation could mean subpoenas for ministries" by Rusty Leonard and Warren Cole Smith, *WORLD*, May 31, 2008.

3. Ibid.

4. "House of Cards" by Jamie Dean, *WORLD*, Jan. 14, 2006.

5. "Bishop's Charity Generous to Bishop" by John Blake, *The Atlanta-Journal Constitution*, Aug. 28, 2005.

6. "Atlanta Pastor Cancels Interview, News Conference About Sex Scandal," CNN, Sept. 23, 2010.

7. "Thou Shalt Not Disclose: How Churches and Ministries Use Legal Agreements to Silence Victims and Conceal Sin" by Steve Rabey, MinistryWatch.com, Feb. 6, 2020.

8. "Trump's Spiritual Adviser, Paula White, Fires Back at Critics" by Daniel Burke, CNN, Jan. 7, 2017.

9. "Interview with Televangelist Paula White," Erin Burnett *Outfront*, CNN, Jan. 5, 2017.

10. "Randy White, former Without Walls pastor, faces DUI Charge," Associated Press, May 23, 2011.

11. "Paula White-Cain, One of the "Grassley Six," Named to Trump Administration" by Warren Cole Smith, MinistryWatch.com, Nov. 8, 2019.

12. "Let The Sunshine In" by Rusty Leonard, *WORLD*, April 25, 2009.

13. "Businessman Rescues Oral Roberts University," Associated Press, Feb. 5, 2008.

Index